light sleeper

a memoir by
laura jacob

Blue Forge Press

Port Orchard ✿ Washington

dedication

To my hilarious, dysfunctional family
who provided so much the content for this memoir.

acknowledgements

Thank you to my amazing and handsome husband, Micah, for teaching me that I am lovable exactly as I am, for convincing me that I should not be ashamed of my past and I should stop hiding behind the secrets, for helping me organize my stories into a cohesive memoir, and for being patient and understanding when writing this book took up all of my free time.

Thank you to Dr. V for giving me the tools to recover from my past and excel past all expectations, for giving me the confidence to tell my story while not reconnecting to any of the negative energy, and for calling me a hero when I did nothing more than use the knowledge you gave me to live life to the fullest.

Thank you to my oldest and dearest friend, Stacey, for listening and helping me stay positive since we were young children when life was incredibly unstable and for supporting me throughout the crazy writing process.

Thank you to my editor, David, for keeping my expectations realistic while still believing in my work and for encouraging me to keep moving forward with my goals.

Thank you to friends and acquaintances for listening to my story over the years and assuring me that it was a story worth telling, for helping me learn how to evaluate how much to share with others in any given situation, and for your love and support which taught me that not everyone is in it for themselves; there are warm, kind people in the world who want to lift you up and help you become the best version of yourself rather than tear you down.

Thank you to the children I worked with during the times in my career when I was the "one adult" who worked to teach them that abuse and abandonment are never a child's fault. Helping others helped me grow and thrive.

light sleeper

a memoir by
laura jacob

1
choking

I am thirty-eight, yet I still feel like that terrified, desperate, unworthy little girl whom I destroyed decades ago. I turn my head to glance at my dying father. Time slows so much it's as if I am scanning the room through a slow-motion film, one blurry fragment at a time. I barely recognize him, and I cannot look away. That fucker lied to me, broke my heart, and disgusted me once again after I foolishly gave him another chance. I squint my teary eyes in anger. Then, in a flash, my heart tightens with fear and sadness. My father looks so helpless. His scraggly, long, oily hair covers part of his face. His beard is wildly unshaven, and the rolls of his chin droop over his chest. I wish I could look into his beautiful eyes and see those tints of green, gray, and blue. I don't want to lose him.

I inhale deeply, and put my hand on my chest. I blink quickly to stop the tears and bury my emotions. "Never let anyone see you weak, Laura," I whisper to myself. It's

10 light sleeper

2016, and I quickly do the math. My father and I only reunited eight years ago. I begin to replay it all in my mind, searching for a moment when I should have figured out the truth. Did I miss a hint? How could I have been so naive, so stupid, so vulnerable?

I stand up and notice a mirror over a sink near the storage cabinets. I walk over to it and turn on the water so I can wash my hands. I look at myself for the first time in almost two days. In my eyes, I see exhaustion and I see strength—a strange combination. Deep down I know I can face him. I can confront him. I can do this. My jaw is strong—not because I was born that way, but because I spent decades forcing my lower jaw to protrude to try to match my upper jaw so much that I snapped all of the tendons on both sides of my face. This was all in response to years of being called stupid-looking by my mother because of my overbite. I hate my profile. The bloodshot corners of my eyes sharply contrast the blue-green-gray colors in my pupils. Each of my eyes is a different color, just like my father's. My left eye has a more blueish hue, and my right eye looks greener. Dark, blotchy bags droop over my cheeks. My make-up has melted away. I look terrible. *Who cares?* I think to myself.

I walk over to the window and peer out. From inside the filthy hospital room in Waterbury, Connecticut, I watch the barren trees sway against a purple-gray sky as a snowstorm approaches. A smell of urine, antiseptic, and bleach causes my eyes to burn and my stomach to turn sour. I swallow hard. I struggled to fit this visit in between business trips and mandatory training at my brand-new job in Seattle. I pulled it off, because I knew that if I didn't make the effort to see him one more time, I'd always regret it.

I plug in my laptop and sit in the chair next to the window to start working. Working remotely is both a perk and a curse of my new job; it means I can work anywhere, which means I'm expected to work everywhere. I feel the heat from my laptop on my thighs; it's soothing against the frigid air, yet I can't stop sweating. I'm trying to create a new medical course catalog for work, but I keep re-pasting the same text over and over again. I lose my train of thought. With the blizzard quickly approaching, I worry that I won't remember how to drive in the snow. Why is the damn hospital parking lot on a steep hill?

Vomit lurks in the back of my throat, and I cringe. The room darkens if I keep my eyes open for too long. I look toward the rolling cardiac monitor and imagine a large dark piece of stiff metallic paper slowly crinkling across the floor. The flickering fluorescent light causes each wrinkle to create a sharp edge of color reflecting light in a way that is hard to decipher. I have to keep blinking so that I don't lose focus. In my mind, I keep trying to iron it out and make it one muted color. I have visualized this all my life. As a child, I used to picture a piece of thick, metallic, black, wrinkled paper creeping into whatever room I was in, slowly taking over. It terrified me. I'd struggle to soften it, to make everything comfortable and warm; inevitably, I'd fail. I suddenly feel the urge to protect myself. "You're safe, Laura," I mumble to myself as my father struggles to breathe in the hospital chair next to me.

Since childhood, safety has been imaginary, like a facade or mirage. I feared emotional pain, physical injury, and even death. Unpredictable behavior surrounded me. Between the ages of seven and twelve, I visited my father, Ted, every other weekend. I comforted him over the loss of his wife after my parents divorced. I hugged him, cared for him, cooked for him, and cleaned his home. He did drugs and drank vodka and Coke until he passed out in his light brown recliner in the living room. "I can't sleep without it," he would say. While he slumbered in his chair, I either slept in a sleeping bag on the living room floor or in his bed. Some nights, he would spend the entire night in his recliner with his head slumped over his chest, just like it is now. I remember feeling his body heat radiating from that side of the room. I'd hop up off the floor and try to wake him up, but I hardly ever succeeded. "Wake up, Daddy. Wake up!!!" He wouldn't respond.

The few times I did wake him up, his eyes would open angrily, his face would turn red, and his raspy voice would yell, "What? What do you want? Where am I? What time is it?" Each question raised his voice louder and louder. So, I learned to stop trying. Some nights he would wake up himself, suddenly, with a snort of air booming from deep in his throat, and he'd stumble up the stairs to his bedroom. Sometimes he would get stuck in the kitchen, become confused, and yell. "Help. I need help! Where is my robe?" I learned to hide until he passed out. I'd hide between the couch and the wall, under the table in the kitchen, or in the hall closet. I couldn't help him, but I wanted to desperately. I learned to sleep lightly and to always be on guard.

His nightmares frightened me the most. Without warning, and with his eyes open, he would scream at the top of his lungs. Sometimes he'd make rambling, loud, screeching noises; sometimes I could make out my mother's name and various curse words. "Bitch! Fucking bitch! Cara, I hate you!" he'd yell.

On especially bad nights and if I slept too hard, he would find me on the floor in the living room before I could hide. He'd climb on top of me and put his hands around my throat. The flickering light from the television would make his face shine like a ghost's, and I would look into his blue-green-gray eyes in terror. His eyes looked darker and colder when he acted like this. I would grab his arms and push as hard as I could, yelling his name, begging him to wake up. I'd kick and squirm, but nothing worked. At seven years old, I was much smaller and weaker than him. He would shout and squeal while slamming my head against the pillow and the floor. Eventually, I'd either pass out or block out whatever happened next. As I faded, I would visualize myself as a muscular boxer with huge gloves, in a boxing stance, standing with my knees bent slightly, ready to strike at any moment. I'd close my eyes. I'd survive the night.

In the hospital room, I catch myself touching my throat

and rubbing my neck gently. *I wonder how long I've been doing this*, I think. I still can't stand to wear tight scarves or have my coat zipped all the way up to my collar. Then I think of my lips, and I remember that my father used to kiss me hard on the lips and slip his tongue into my mouth. I cringe. I close my eyes softly so no one in the hospital hallway notices my tears, and I picture my boxer stance. I perch on the balls of my feet, and I stand with my legs slightly bent for better balance. I twist my body *just so* to the left. I bend my arms and position my hands in front of my face for protection. I clench my fists and prepare to use my body's weight to strike strongly and quickly. My workouts and disciplined lifestyle have created my muscular body. I can hit back if I need to. I can fight.

I blink so the tears won't fall. *Never let them fall*, I learned as a young child. I stare at my father's gray face, and the folds of his cheeks and chin droop over his chest. His eyes are closed. He looks helpless. I can't help but feel sorry for him, and then I'm immediately furious with myself. I bang my hands against the windowsill. I hate weakness. I should be angry, sad, and furious. My body feels as light as a feather held by a barge, trying desperately to float away. I clench my fists. I'm too stuck, sick, and hardened to float away. I feel burning vomit slicing the back of my sore throat. I really don't want to puke in here. How could he have lied for so many years?

Just as my vision starts to blur again, my father's wife, Maria, arrives. *She's so young*, I think to myself. Her long, dark, wavy hair bounces as she walks. Her big, dark brown eyes, which I remember from two decades before, appear worried and strong. She looks frail, but beautiful. I stand up to reach for a hug. She holds me for much longer than I expect her to. I had always assumed that she hated me, so I'm quite surprised by the warmth of her embrace.

2
defeated

Twenty years earlier, I attended my father and Maria's wedding. I was eighteen. Prior to that, Maria lived Brazil. She was in her twenties and knew my father, who was almost fifty, for a few, short weeks before agreeing to marry him. My phone rang on the Tuesday evening before their wedding. "I won't be able to send you money for school anymore," my father said.

"Okay," I replied. I had no clue what else to say. This feeling of defeat equaled an ending, and it had nothing to do with the money.

"I'm marrying Maria next weekend. Her daughters are going to move in with us. I have to help them. Their father has been abusing them in Brazil, and I need to protect them," he explained.

He needed the money to cover the extra expenses of his new family, whom he didn't even know. I attended school full-time and worked full-time to cover rent and pay for food, medical bills, and utilities. My medical bills piled up every year. I struggled to get out of bed, to get dressed, to shower, to get to class, and to function. I'd lay in bed or sit on the couch and think of all the things I should do to take care of myself: take a shower, put on nice clothes, go for a walk, meet friends at a restaurant, wipe the kitchen counter, look for a better paying job— the list was endless. But my brain didn't allow it, and like steal, I remained solid and unmoved. My doctors diagnosed me with severe clinical depression, bipolar disorder, and severe anxiety earlier that year. I suffered from constant back and neck pain, and I slept with a heating pad on my back almost every night. This added to my sleeping problems.

"This MRI looks like that of an eighty-year-old's. Were you in a car accident?" the spine surgeon asked me after seeing my latest scan.

"No," I replied. I looked down at the floor and revealed nothing more.

Doctors prescribed pain pills for my back, neck, and migraines all the time. While I liked how numb they made me feel and they helped my pain, I did not like losing control or awareness of everything around me. Doctors prescribed antibiotics for my nearly constant bronchial and sinus infections. I puffed on an inhaler two to four times a day to keep breathing. For years I fell deeper and deeper into a hole, desperately searching for a way to connect with the strength that I knew hid underneath it all. I could feel a different person within me; she was hidden under a cloud of pain, but I knew she was there. I just had to dig deeper to connect with the intensely strong version of myself.

But that was impossible today. I started to shake and panic, and my eyes moistened. I had almost two years of school left before I graduated. Feeling dazed, I hung up the phone. He had nothing else to say to me either. I'd work harder and find a way.

When I called my mother and shared this news with her, her voice quivered when she firmly said, "We're just going to have to sue him!"

"That's ridiculous, Mom," I said.

"The judge will not tolerate this for a second!" she said. "We fought for this already. He owes you for half of all your college expenses. You need to get all of your receipts together to show all of your monthly expenses, immediately!" she barked. I instantly regretted telling her what my father had said, and I hung up the phone again.

My mother told me many times that both of my parents had signed an agreement written by their divorce lawyer in 1986. This document stated that each of them was required to pay for half of my college expenses including basic living expenses and books. When I asked to see it, she told me that she lost the contract. *Was it another lie? Another exaggeration? Another game?* I never figured out the answers to my questions.

While staring at the wall of the small apartment that I shared with my boyfriend, Matt, I tried to figure out how to get all of this documentation together. I could easily find canceled rent checks. I could search for old phone, cable, electric, and car insurance bills. I had collected all of my receipts for books. I could call my doctors and request records of my medical expenses. I had no way of recalling my grocery expenses, or gas for my car, but I could estimate. Detailing every penny that I spent for two years of living, only to fight for money that I didn't even care about, made no sense. What mattered at this moment was that I lost. My eyes sunk, and I felt my heart beat slower. I had failed at earning his love. My father's new family won. They won a safe place to sleep that I never had. They won his protection, while I constantly lived in danger. They won his support. They won his love. I began to resent these people whom I had never even met. Maria and her two daughters believed that they would be saved by my father. Yet he changed into a very dangerous man when he drank, and he became a volatile, impulsive person when he did drugs. He lied constantly and hid his demons well. I wanted to warn her.

I called my mother back. "Mom, I don't want to do this. I don't care about his money. I can get more student loans to cover my tuition. I can get more hours at the pharmacy. It's really not a big deal." I tapped a pen on the table as I sat unsteadily on the very edge of my dining room chair. I could picture the anger in my mother's face. When I was young, she had very long dark hair. As she got older, she permed her hair, and many people said she looked remarkably similar to the actress, Jennifer Grey. But when she was angry, she looked mean. Her childhood nickname of "Meanie" was fitting.

"It is a big deal! He owes you. He wasn't there for you when you were young. And when he was, he wasn't exactly a loving father. This is the least he can do. And he's going against the judge's orders by not helping you financially."

"I know, but I don't need the help. I'm almost covering everything now, anyway. Tuition isn't that expensive. I can talk to financial aid and get another loan. I don't want to fight him. I don't care," I replied.

"I care! The burden falls on me if he walks away from his financial obligations," she yelled.

My body's temperature rose and my face blushed. Hearing that word, "burden," as I had heard all my life, set my emotions on fire. It felt twenty degrees hotter in a few seconds, and I remembered all of my mother's sayings: "I filled out paperwork to divorce your father the day I found out I was pregnant with you!" "I stayed in this family for you!" "I stayed in Connecticut so you could be close to your father!" "I worked my ass of for you!" "Children are expensive!" "Help me with the groceries— it's the least you can do."

"I didn't say a word about asking you for more money, Mom. I said that I would work more hours and get another loan," I said, trying my best to sound stronger than I felt. I tossed the pen on the table and froze while I waited for her response.

"Don't make me feel guilty, Laura! Just get the damn paperwork." And she hung up the phone.

About a year into the process of gathering receipts, tracking expenses on a spreadsheet, and scheduling court dates, I learned that I would have to face my father in court. I refused. I told my mother that I didn't want to be put in the middle of their fight. I didn't want to see him. We hadn't talked in almost a year, and he probably hated me now. "It's all for you!" she shouted.

When I finished tallying my expenses and subtracted the money I had received from each of my parents, my father owed me just over $6,000, and my mother owed me about $11,000. "I need to see how you got to those numbers, Laura," my mother demanded.

I gathered the piles of organized printouts and receipts, brought them to my mother's house, and showed her how I calculated everything. She added the numbers using her calculator. I had used a new program that I recently learned, called Excel. I knew the numbers were right. After reviewing the records, my mother agreed to drop the lawsuit. I breathed a sigh of relief as I drove back up to UCONN, but this ordeal obliterated my last pulses of energy.

At work, my eyes would fill with tears at the slightest discomfort. And embarrassingly, they sometimes would fall. In class, I couldn't keep my eyes open. At home, I was no fun to be around anymore.

I worried that my father figured that I hadn't talked to him since his wedding because he stopped sending me money. I'm certain that's the picture my mother painted for him. But what I never found the courage to ask him was, "How can you stop helping the daughter you abused in order to help children you've never even met?" "What makes them worth saving?" "What makes them so special?" "Why wasn't I worth loving?" "What could they have possibly done to earn your love?" I couldn't stomach seeing him, hearing his voice, or smelling his sweet, musty cologne ever again.

For many years, when I couldn't sleep at night, I thought about Maria and her daughters while I stared at the popcorn ceiling in whatever apartment I lived in at the time. *Do they know, by now, how much my father changes when he drinks or does drugs? Has he gotten drunk and hurt anyone? Is he hurting them right now? Do they regret moving to America to be with him?*

I remembered how he acted on their wedding day. Ted drank Absolut vodka from a bottle that he hid in his coat pocket. His friends laughed and laughed. I cowered. I searched for a moment alone with Maria that day, to talk to her, to scream to her, "Don't bring your children into this home! They will not be safe!" But I did not have the courage. I did not have the strength. I did not take the opportunity. I walked away.

I always wondered if Maria hated me for not warning her. And now we were hugging each other in a hospital room a few feet from my father. We were two strangers with an unspeakable common link. While my father slowly died, Maria, my "stepmother" as people would call her, hugged me tightly. I looked into her eyes and immediately looked away in shame. She updated me on how much Ted had improved since he was admitted several weeks earlier. She spoke in broken English, and I needed to ask for clarification many times. She had a beautiful accent, but the facts about my father's condition were too important to miss any details. I probably annoyed her with my questions.

"Why is he in a chair and not in a bed? He keeps pointing at the bed," I ask Maria.

"His lungs have too much fluid, so he has to stay sitting up. He cannot lie down. He lie down and he cannot breathe," she explains.

"Is he eating food?"

"No, he has lots of needles in him. He eats Jell-O and can drink a little thick, goopy water. When he was on the machines, he looked so bad. The machines did everything to keep him alive. He was, ummm, sedated, sleeping, because he would wake up and get so angry and pull out his tubes," she says, while she flails her arms around her throat, as if she is pulling something away from her chest.

I rub my throat again.

"Why does he have bruises on his arms?" I ask, as I point at his arms that are in various stages of bruising from top to bottom.

My father opens his eyes slightly, and his wobbly head looks in my direction. "Hi, Dad. Maria is here. She is letting me know how well you've been doing," I tell him.

He nods in response.

Maria continues, "Because they had to restrain him, tie him to the bed, because he would pull at things and try to hit nurses and doctors." I knew the staff had restrained my father, but the awful bruises are surprising. They must hurt. I guess he had been pulling against the restraints a lot, like an angry caged animal, reminiscent of what he was like when I was young—nothing like the dad I thought I knew for the past eight years. I foolishly believed all of the bullshit.

3
the secret is out

About a month earlier, on the Tuesday after Christmas in 2015, my phone rang. My father rarely initiated contact with me, so I answered with a questioning tone.

"Hello?"

"Did you get my Christmas card?" he asked.

"I don't think so, but I just got back into town. Let me look around. Hold on one sec." I put the phone down, walked over to the desk in our living room, and thumbed through the pile of mail that had built up while we were away for the holidays. A good friend had been feeding our cats and checking on our new home each day. In this moment, I deeply appreciated that she had neatly stacked our mail in one pile. My father didn't sound right. His gruff voice sounded quiet and small. I picked up the phone and said, "It's not here, Dad. Are you okay?"

"Ah, it'll probably come today. I mailed it a little late this year. I'm doing okay. I'm in the hospital." He coughed several times, cleared his throat, and said, "congestive heart failure." He struggled to get out his words.

"You're in the hospital? Congestive heart failure?" I paused, inhaled deeply and quickly, and sat on my couch. I knew he was not an especially healthy person, and that his years of smoking and drinking would catch up with him one day. "I know a little about that from work, Dad. It's something that can be managed with medication pretty well. Do they know how advanced it is?"

In my new job in medical education, I learned how ultrasound can help doctors measure how hard the heart was working and how productive it was at moving blood through the system. But I didn't know much else.

"They're running more tests. I feel fine. I'm fine. I'm going home on Thursday," he announced.

"On Thursday? That's great, Dad. That's quick. They're running more tests?" I asked to confirm.

"Yes. Just to see what medications I need, I guess." My father took a lot of medications for high blood pressure. He had battled a blood disorder, causing his blood to be too thick, many years earlier. He smoked for decades, but he quit a few years earlier. And he hadn't had alcohol or done any drugs in thirteen years. While he didn't eat well, living mostly on red meat and fried foods, he seemed stable overall. He sounded a little nervous, but I knew he hated doctors and hospitals, so his nerves didn't surprise me.

"What hospital?" I asked.

"Waterbury. I hate this place. I wish I was at St. Joe's.

I told Maria I don't like it here. But that's where I am!"
He sounded irritated.

"It's okay, Dad. I'm sure they know what they're
doing. Just hang in there for a couple of days, and I'll talk
to you on Thursday when you get home, okay?"

"Okay, sounds good. Love you," he said.

"I love you, too, Dad." I hung up the phone and felt
wobbly and uncertain. I brushed it off and turned on the
television, thankful that the Christmas movies and
commercials were over for the year. I hate Christmas. I
picked up my iPhone and Googled "congestive heart
failure." The prognosis for living another several years
was actually quite good, depending on the stage of his
condition. I guessed that's what the tests were for. He did
not visit the doctor much, so I worried that his condition
might be quite severe.

The next day, I felt the need to call my father and
check on him. I sat at my desk, stared at my computer
monitor, and checked my phone constantly. I kept
looking at the time, wondering what was going on three
thousand miles away. Ted and I had become pretty close
over the past several years. He had cleaned himself up
and become safe. We talked weekly, and he no longer
sounded like the unpredictable and dangerous man I
remembered as a child. I felt a strong connection with
him, and I wondered if he was keeping vital information
from me about his health. I dialed his number. He did not
answer. This added to my concern, since he always
answered my calls or called my back immediately.

I stared out the window and pictured the backyard at

my new home. The relentless Seattle rain always created slabs and slabs of mud in our yard. Inside it's always cheerful and comforting, with lots of windows to let in the light, colors on every wall, and original oak wood floors throughout. After having lived in thirty-two apartments, buying my ninety-five-year old house exceeded all of my dreams. My dad never called me back that day, and I couldn't focus on anything else.

The following morning, my phone lit up indicating an incoming text message from a number with a Connecticut area code that I didn't recognize. It said, "Your daddy is not doing well. We are still at the hospital and they are taking him to ICU." I determined that the message must be from Maria. We had never spoken by phone. We had never texted. We had no relationship whatsoever.

I found a private room at work, away from the shared workspace, and called the unknown number. Maria's shaky, loud, and insistent voice explained that my father kept trying to hurt himself and hit other people and that he was drunk. She repeated, "He's drunk. He's drunk!" This did not make sense at all. He'd been sober for almost thirteen years, and how could he have access to alcohol in a hospital anyway? I felt my eyebrows furrow and my face turn red. I started to sweat and get the chills. I instantly remembered the smell of his cologne, as if someone sprayed it into the room, and my stomach turned. My mouth became dry, and I started shaking. I managed to sit in a chair without falling down.

My voice echoed in the small room as I kept

repeating, "Calm down. What do you mean, drunk? He doesn't drink anymore. Calm down—what do you mean?"

Suddenly it all came back, like a smack in my face. I put my head in my hands, leaned on the small round conference table, and the room blackened. I blinked to hold onto the light.

4
the cold porch

I remember very little from the years before my parents' divorce, and the memories I have for years after are scattered and untapped. I thought everyone forgot most of their childhood until I learned from my friends that I was not normal. I remember countless fights, a lot of drinking, and a decent amount of drug use that only fueled the tension. Slammed doors, cuts, bruises, bloody lips, and holes in walls were common. The smell of skunk and mold permeated the house. It came from the attic staircase. My mother warned me over and over that the stairs were too dangerous for me to play on whenever they were left open. "You'll fall and break your neck," she would say.

My father would stuff tiny white pieces of paper with "treats," as he called them, from the attic to make his cigarettes. He'd then place each one into a half-piped hole in a shiny, wooden box. Like a guillotine, he would press down hard on the top of the box, and it would slice the cigarette into two. The smoky house made it hard to breathe. I needed to use my inhaler several times a day.

One Easter morning, I woke up excited to see what the Easter bunny brought me. I ran out into the dining room and saw my Easter basket on the table. It overflowed with chocolate bunnies, marshmallow bunnies, and hard candy—it all sat on a pillow of plastic green and pink grass. I spotted my mother sleeping on the couch in the living room. She steadied herself as she stood, struggling to wake up.

"Mommy, why are you out here?" I asked her.

Her swollen face looked sad and broken. "I'm out here because the Easter bunny wanted me to tell you that there is a special Easter egg hidden in the backyard." She sounded awfully calm and quiet for such exciting news.

"Special, how? Is it gold?" I asked.

"Could be. I don't know." She acted strangely, like she hadn't slept much. She walked into the bathroom, and I heard her vomit.

She's sick. That's why she slept out here. She didn't want to wake up Daddy, I thought.

I searched the yard, peeking through the longer strands of grass, behind sharp bushes, and next to rocks on the small hill behind the little red house. I blocked out the noise of my parents yelling inside. While I did find the usual plastic Easter eggs with candies or small plastic toys inside each one, I couldn't find the special Easter egg. "I guess the Easter bunny lied," I said to my mom, and frowned.

"I guess so," my mother confirmed.

That day, my mother moved my bed and clothes to the screened-in porch. "I'm going to sleep in your room for a while," my mother explained. "I can't stay with your father anymore."

I slept on the porch for the next eighteen months. The cold, drafty, damp, insecure porch made my sleep problems worse. I hated going to my room; I couldn't get comfortable. When I complained, I was punished.

"I don't wanna go to bed! It's cold on the porch!" I cried.

"Go to bed!" my mother yelled.

"No!" I yelled back. That night my voice sounded more determined than ever. Sleeping on the cold porch scared me. My mother slapped me in the face so hard I fell to the ground, sobbing. I got up and hustled to my room. I could taste blood on my mouth, and I felt my lip start to swell. I tried to sleep, but not too deeply. I worried all night, every night. *What if someone tried to break in? What if my parents started to fight? What if?* I had so many concerns. I had to stay alert. I hugged my favorite stuffed animal and kept my eyes open for as long as possible every night.

A flimsy door existed between me and the cold outdoors. Three steps led down to the front yard, where a small tree stood in the center. I broke my ankle climbing that tree one day. That evening in the hospital room, the nurse asked me if my parents hit me. Of course, I said, "No, ma'am."

She asked, "Are you happy at home?"

"Yes, ma'am," I answered politely. I always protected my parents.

While sitting on the front steps outside my bedroom door one afternoon, my father sat down next to me. "I have a very important favor to ask you," he whispered.

"Okay, Daddy," I whispered back.

"This has to be a secret favor," he explained. "I need you to tell your mother that you told me that you caught her in bed with another man." At six years old, I didn't know what this meant.

"But Daddy, I don't understand. What do you mean, 'in bed'? I didn't see that. When did I say that to you? I didn't say that. I don't understand!" I cried, unsure of how to please my father.

"It's to protect me from your mother. You want to protect me, right?" he asked.

I nodded and asked, "What am I supposed to say?"

"That's enough," my mother said from inside the screened window. "Ted, leave her alone."

"Fuck," my dad cursed.

"Laura, go play with the neighbors," my mother commanded. I stood up and ran down the small hill on the side of the house to the neighbor's house as fast as I could.

"Is Zoe home? Can I come in?" I urgently asked after knocking on their door.

"Of course, Laura. Zoe is in her room," Mrs. Roberts said.

I hurried downstairs to find my friend.

My parents didn't speak to each other for several

days. And when they did, the anger in their voices terrified me. I wanted to please them, make them smile, and make them laugh.

I watched my father work on our car one day. He carried a heavy box into the garage and took the cover off of it.

"Mommy, what's Daddy doing?" I asked.

"He's taking the battery out of the car again, Laura."

"Oh yeah," I replied. I walked away, unaffected.

My mother would have to get permission to go grocery shopping, or take me to school. A few months after the conversation on the porch, my mother asked to take the car to run some errands.

"Where are you going?" my father demanded to know.

"To the grocery store and to buy some school clothes for Laura," she replied with an ice-cold voice.

"You better not go anywhere else," he said, and he slammed the door behind him.

My mother drove a few miles away from home and pulled over in a sandy patch on the side of the road. She pulled a newspaper out from under her seat and started looking through it. She scanned page after page with a serious look on her face.

"What are you doing, Mommy?" I asked.

"Looking through the classifieds," she responded.

"What are classifieds?" I asked.

"They're ads, for apartments. I just want to see what's available. Would you like to look with me?"

I had no idea why we would look at apartments, but I

thought it could be fun, so I said, "Okay."

That day we looked at one very small, one-room apartment across the street from Stew Leonard's grocery store in Danbury, Connecticut—the next town over. I didn't like it and neither did my mother. I never went with my mother to look at apartments again. But she asked me to start hiding my important things in my room. "Just put your favorite clothes and toys in this box and slide it under the bed," she whispered one evening after dinner.

"Okay, Mommy," I whispered back.

We began to sneak things out of the house and hide them at the neighbor's house. "Don't say anything to your father about this, Laura. He cannot know what we're doing. Do you understand?"

"I understand, Mommy," I replied. I felt closer to her; we shared a big secret.

While in my room one night, I picked up a photo of my father holding me as a baby of about nine months old. My mother had put it in a frame, and it sat on my dresser for years. In the picture, my father sat in a mustard yellow, burnt orange, olive green, and dirty white floral recliner, and I sat on his lap. He stared straight ahead at the television, and barely touched me. My mother told me that this was the first time he ever held me. "I just put you in his lap and told him to hold his daughter. He sat there. I took the picture and then picked you up." I couldn't lose this picture. I had to find a way to hide it, so I added it to my box under the bed.

Three days after Christmas in 1984, my mother and I

left my father. I was seven. We had been slowly moving our hidden clothes and other personal items from the neighbor's house to the one-room apartment behind Stew Leonard's in Danbury. We snuck around for a couple of weeks until my mother had the courage to tell my father the news.

We were all hanging out in the living room next to the Christmas tree that still had several presents underneath it, and the television blared. I colored in a coloring book on the floor. "Ted, Laura and I are moving out," my mother said, factually, firm, and strong.

I looked up at her and froze. I looked at my father, and my body melted into the floor. I started to cry, inaudibly. I watched as my father's face turned red, and he stood up from his recliner. My mother backed away, cautiously. My father started to play his usual "oh-poor-me games," as my mother used to say.

"But you did this to me. You made me this way. How can you do this to me? I can't live without you. I have no one!" He had been drinking, so he slurred his words and sprayed spit across the room. Everything smelled sweet like a mixture of alcohol, cigarettes, and cologne.

He creatively began to rewrite the past to paint himself as the victim of our family dynamic. "You made me insane! You're such a bitch! I love you! I love Laura! I can't be without you! I'm sorry!" He yelled and cried at the same time.

My stomach cramped as I lay as flat against the floor as I could.

I felt a jerk on my arm, and my mother pulled me

into a standing position. I couldn't stop myself from trembling, but I stayed silent. My mother's hand against my back guided me past the Formica dining room table and into the orange, black, and yellow kitchen. My mother handed me my coat and asked me to put it on quickly as she put on hers. "Hurry, Laura. It's okay," she said.

My father yelled louder, saying that if we left, he would kill himself. "I'll do it. This time I mean it!" he shouted. We had heard this many times before, but this time it felt different. I broke inside, but I didn't make a noise. I knew better than to make noise. Noise, I learned, led to punishment—just like hunger, fear, anger, being cold, or causing any inconvenience. My mother guided me toward the door and said, "Get in the car. I'll be right there." I took one more step, and like a statue, I froze on the steps outside the kitchen door in the cold, dark air. I listened to the commotion inside.

"You're going to kill yourself? Really? You mean it this time?" my mother asked, sounding strong and angry.

"You're damn right," my father yelled.

I heard one of the kitchen drawers slam shut. "Choose your weapon," my mother said. Within a couple of seconds, she joined me on the porch. She picked me up and before I knew it, we sat in the front bucket seat of the car.

My mother started the car, and a look of relief flashed over her face. I sensed that the sound of engine comforted her, since it confirmed he hadn't messed with the battery when we weren't looking. I yelled at my mother, "Why don't you just shut up, and then he won't get mad, and then we won't have to leave?"

She glared at me and said, "Don't make me feel worse, Laura."

As she drove, she looked stoic, blank. Her eyes had darkened, and her face was emotionless. I suppose she was scared, too. My father didn't react well when he wasn't in control of everyone. Tears fell down my face steadily as I spotted Christmas lights on houses all around. We used to drive around and look for Christmas lights on houses, just for fun. I couldn't remember the last time we did that.

After we arrived at the one-room apartment, my mother explained, "We had to leave, Laura. Your father is unsafe. We will be better off without him. Never trust a man." My mother repeated, "Never trust a man. Do you hear me?" I nodded, trying to understand. Then she pointed in the corner of the room and said, "Look what's over there." I tried to see through the sheets of hazy tears in my eyes. I saw my box—the box that was filled with all of my favorite clothes and toys that I had hid under my bed. I ran over to it and opened it. The picture of me and my dad sat on top. I cried as I looked at it.

My mother and I cuddled up in a few blankets on the floor each night until she bought a daybed and a sofa. She slept on the sofa bed, and I slept on the daybed with my stuffed animals. I missed my cat, Sneakers. He was a gray, tiger-striped kitty who used to sleep in my bed with me and my stuffed animals. He had a tough personality, his soft fur helped me get warm, and he made me laugh.

40 light sleeper

My Aunt Connie moved in with my mother and me for a while. When we pulled out the daybed and opened the sofa bed, half of the room turned into one large bed. We each had our section. It looked like a huge slumber party every night.

Since I suffered from asthma as a child, I used my inhaler before going to sleep. But inevitably, I'd wheeze and wake up Connie and my mother. "Shut up, Laura!" they'd yell in the middle of the night, waking me up. I'd open my eyes, look around for my medicine, and quickly puff on my inhaler to stop my noisy lungs. I silently felt horribly guilty until I heard them both fall back to sleep. I wouldn't allow myself to sleep deeply again. I kept my breaths shallow.

5
visitation rights

Eventually after several months, my father wanted his *visitation rights*.

"I'm not keeping you from your daughter, Ted. You haven't called." I heard my mother on the phone as I sat on the floor watching cartoons on our small black and white television that had a curl in the top corner of its picture. "I know I left. I had to leave. It's for the best. Yes, you're entitled to your visitation rights until we get everything else figured out. If you want to see Laura, you can come get her this weekend."

My heart raced, and I couldn't stop smiling while I waited for my father to knock on our apartment door. I sat on the floor and stared at the clock on the wall that hung over the small dining room table that my mother bought at a yard sale. I watched my mother do her usual Saturday routine of drinking coffee and doing her nails while I waited. I wondered how she felt about seeing him. "I can't wait to see Daddy," I announced.

"I'm sure he's excited to see you, too," she said distantly.

When he arrived, his red face and bloodshot eyes made him look tired and angry. His forehead glistened with sweat, and he smelled like alcohol. His hands shook as he gave me a brief hug. He tried to talk to my mother, but she didn't acknowledge him. She went into the bathroom and shut the door; it was the only door in the apartment. He looked down at me and said "let's go," and we walked out into the hallway together. He slammed the door behind me. *Visitation rights* had started.

My dad did not speak to me during the drive to his new apartment. The radio played quietly. A sweet love song by Sonny and Cher started to play, and I hummed along. My father quickly turned the radio off and said, "I don't like that song."

"Because it reminds you of mom?" I asked.

He scowled at me. "Don't you ever ask me about that again," he said, emphasizing the word "ever."

I nodded in fear.

I needed to change the subject. I asked if he had taken my cat, Sneakers, with him to his new home. He shook his head no, while he stared straight ahead. I worried about Sneakers, and I felt my heart ache. "Who is going to feed Sneakers?" I asked my dad.

He said the cat would be just fine, and he had run into the woods with another cat from the neighborhood. He said they magically became best friends, and they were living a great life together in the woods.

"But Sneakers doesn't go outside. How is he gonna find food?" My voice trembled with worry.

"He's an animal. He'll find food just fine. His new friend will teach him," he said, dismissing my concern.

I loved my cat. I missed Sneakers terribly, and my mother told me that my father would take care of him. But no one cared for Sneakers, and I would never see him again. I took deep breaths and tried to stop my tears from forming. I pressed the fingernail of my thumb into the soft tissue of my pointer finger to stop the emotion and distract myself. I made no noise. I made no tears. I wouldn't get in trouble.

We stopped at the grocery store on the way to his apartment. "Get whatever you want," he said.

"Really, Daddy?" I asked, while jumping up and down. He nodded.

I immediately grabbed two large bags of sour cream and onion potato chips and two bottles of Pepsi. I found M&Ms as well. My dad spent a lot of time in the cleaning supplies aisle. He bought some cleaners, various meats and some cheese from the deli, and vodka. We left the store and continued the drive to his new home. He lived in a one-bedroom apartment in a town near his work. The dark walls made the living room feel small, and the windows were decorated with plastic crisscross designs that looked like bars.

"Pretty," I said, as I pointed at the windows. My dad smiled. I could tell that he was in the middle of unpacking, as boxes, in various stages of disarray, littered the room. I tried to take in the new environment. As I looked around, I recognized some furniture from the little red house that we all lived in together just a few months earlier. They felt out of place, and they looked different.

My father stared at me as I looked around. "Laura, I need your help cleaning," he said.

"What, Daddy?" I asked.

He told me to start by emptying the boxes in the kitchen, as he emptied the bags of groceries he had just bought. He had new dishes and pots, but he didn't know where best to put them. I was happy to help my dad.

I shuffled into the kitchen and began my work. I dragged one of the dining room chairs, that I recognized from the little red house, over to the counter. I stood on it to reach the higher cabinets. I used the cleaners he bought and wiped the cabinets before putting his new dishes and glasses into their place. His new clear, plain dishes looked small inside the sparse cabinets, but I made sure they were located near the stove for when he cooked.

I'd never seen him cook, but he'd have to learn now. I cleaned the counters and opened the fridge. The bare fridge contained vodka, Coke, cheese, bread, salami, and bologna. I put my bottles of Pepsi on the shelf and closed the door. I should have put the Pepsi in the fridge before unpacking the dishes. Now it wouldn't be cold for hours. *That was stupid*, I thought to myself.

I heard the sounds of a car race on the television in the next room. I ran into the living room and waited for the cars to crash into each other. I loved it when they got into big piles. My father's Coke did not have bubbles, so I knew it contained booze. He looked at me, smiled, and said, "I'm glad you're here."

I asked him, "Does someone else live in our old house?"

"Don't ask about that dump. It's not your business," he said. He then asked me to unpack his records and put them in the cabinet next to the stereo that used to be in our old house.

Before I started, I asked, "Can I put them in alphabetical order? I need the practice." I smiled and looked at him with big eyes, seeking his approval.

He said that would be great.

I smiled bigger, because I was so excited to help my dad. He watched me organize his records.

After I finished, he asked me to dust all of his furniture. He got up out of his new, light brown recliner, which replaced the flowery one from my picture, walked into the kitchen, and returned with a bottle of Endust and paper towels. He showed me how to clean his stereo cabinet by mushing the wet paper towels in between the decorative wood etching. "Clean the rest of the wood in here. The tables, the windowsills, and the TV," my father commanded.

"I'm tired of cleaning. I don't want to do anymore," I complained.

"Don't whine, Laura. I have to teach you how to clean. It's your job now," he said. I did as I was told.

That night, I fell asleep on the couch. My father fell asleep in the recliner next to me. In the middle of the night, he carried me into his bedroom. I remember an uncomfortable, sick feeling while sleeping in the same bed as my father. I remember him saying, "It makes me feel better, since I miss your mother so much."

So, I did what I was told.

I spent every other weekend and every other holiday with my dad, and this pattern of cleaning, falling asleep on the couch, and waking up in his bed continued for years. My father would kiss me on the lips and sometimes use tongue. When I told him that I didn't like it when he used his tongue, he acted like a rejected little boy. I felt disgust in my stomach and pain in my lower back. Occasionally, he snuck his tongue in anyway, but most of the time he stopped himself. I did not enjoy kissing my father.

My parents argued about where I would spend each holiday or school break. They figured out ways to use me as a pawn to upset the other person. Neither of them wanted me around. So, when one of them hurt me to get to the other person, they achieved nothing, other than hurting me. I decided to stop letting my feelings show. I kept it all to myself, and this stopped them from playing their game. I found some strength. I found power. I was learning how to beat them at their own game. If I stay quiet, they can't denounce what I say. If I don't share the things that hurt me, they can't repeat them. If I tell myself I am lovable instead of relying on them to do it, I win.

Years after my mother found out that I slept in the same bed as my father, she asked me, "Has your father ever touched you?"

"What do you mean, Mommy?" I asked her.

"Well, there's good touching, like hugs. And there's bad touching, like touching you somewhere private or that makes you feel uncomfortable," she explained. "Has your dad ever badly touched you?"

"No, Mommy," I responded immediately.

"Are you sure, Laura?"

"Yes," I said, hoping she'd change the subject.

It used to comfort me if my mother or my father rubbed my back to help me fall asleep. My father's hand sometimes explored other parts of my body. I learned to pretend that I was asleep to make him stop.

I also remember waking up feeling unwell and very tired, too tired, with no pajama bottoms on early one morning. I searched the living room and found my pants in a ball under the coffee table. I quickly put them on before my father woke up. *Did he take them off? Did I take them off? Did I have an accident?* I thought of so many questions. I had problems with wetting the bed on and off for many years. My blurry memory from the night before did not give me any answers. When my father came into the living room, he changed the channel from cartoons to golf and didn't speak to me. He drove me to my mom's without mentioning anything out of the ordinary.

Another night, I woke suddenly from a deep sleep on the living room floor. The room felt as if it was vibrating, and the air turned sour and dark. I instantly felt terror and concern. I checked to see if all of my clothes were on and if my underpants were wet. I was clothed and dry, but I sensed danger. I looked toward my father, who was sitting in his chair and staring at the television. He didn't notice that I was awake and watching him. I looked at the television and saw a naked couple doing gross things next to a swimming pool. The man's face was on the woman's private area. They made strange noises, and it scared me. I rolled over, curled up into the smallest ball that I could, and tried to disappear.

My mother yelled at my father until he stopped making me sleep in his bed. "Ted, it's not appropriate," I overheard her yelling on the phone. "I don't care if you think it's okay. It's not okay. I'm her mother."

By this time, my father had bought a two-bedroom condo. He said that he found a place with two bedrooms so I could have my own room. "Can I pick out a bed?" I asked. "I don't like sleeping on the floor."

"You could have kept sleeping in my bed, but you had to go and tell your mother about it, didn't you?" he snarked.

"I'm sorry, Daddy."

My father never furnished or decorated the second bedroom. It remained empty, except for a few of his boxes. I sometimes hid in there to think and be alone until he'd yell for me to come back downstairs. At night, I slept in a sleeping bag on the living room floor. It was my punishment, he told me.

On Fridays at school, I dreaded the weekends. Either I stayed at home with my mother, who complained that she had a daughter or yelled that I didn't clean something correctly, or I had to go to my father's house, which felt worse.

In the car on the way to my father's house, I'd stare out the window. I'd focus on the painted line flying by the car along the highway. It flashed on and off when the line broke for exit and entrance ramps. When we traveled in the middle or left lane, I'd watch the dashed line flicker rapidly as we drove by. Sometimes I'd try to count the flashes, but they moved too fast. My father's hands shook while he drove, and he drifted all over his lane. I feared that he would crash into the wall or another car. His bloodshot eyes reminded me of a monster. I'd close my eyes, breathe deeply, and count to a hundred over and over again. I focused on the sharpness of my fingernail that I pressed hard into the soft flesh of my hand to distract myself from my emotions. The hours slowly ticked by each weekend.

to change schools," she stated.

We had never told my school that I no longer lived in the little red house with my dad, and we now lived in the wrong jurisdiction for me to attend that school. I hated lying, and I worried every day that they would figure it out. They found out after about six months, and they threatened to kick me out. I didn't want to leave my school and my friends. "You'll have your own room," my mother said.

"I don't care about that. I like sharing a room with you. I don't want to move in with Manny!" I cried. "Can I just move in with Barbara?" I asked, desperately.

Barbara, the babysitter, lived in the same town as my school. I loved being at Barbara's house. She called me "her helper," even though I was far from the oldest child in her care. I helped take care of the younger children, and I enjoyed helping her clean. I admired her for remaining so nice and calm, no matter how much noise we all made. I used to ask her, "How do you stand all of us kids?"

She would sit down and say, "I don't. I sit." She always made me smile.

At Barbara's house, two of the older boys liked to play house with me. They called me their shared wife, and touched me in funny places in front of the other children. When we got caught one time, Barbara told my mother. My mother yelled at me in the car and threatened to tell my father. I cried and begged her not to. I felt disgusting and worthless, and the strange back pain continued.

When my mother didn't pick me up from Barbara's

6
finally living her life

My mother began dating and was "finally living her life" as she said all the time. She went to happy hour after work and was late picking me up from the babysitter's house, where I would go after school, often. I missed my mother terribly when she went out on dates. She was beautiful, in shape, and exciting, so she got a lot of attention from men. Even when she was home, she stayed in her room and ignored me. At eight years old she told me that she met someone special. "You'll really like Manny, Laura. He has a lot of movies." She grinned. "And our lease is coming up soon."

"What's a lease, Mommy?" I asked.

"It's a piece of paper that allows us to live in the apartment for a period of time."

"And it's coming up? What does that mean?" I asked.

"It means we have to move. We are going to move in with Manny," she said. She seemed so proud. "You'll h on time, I would become more and more hyper by the minute. My mind would race, and I would bang my head against the wall or the floor to try to make my thoughts stop. Each strike caused a momentary pause in the torturous thoughts: *she forgot me, she doesn't want me, she hates me, I'm not important.* "It tickles," I would say as I giggled and banged my head over and over again. Barbara distracted me by asking me to help her cook dinner for her family.

Manny was very tall and thin. He had dark brown eyes, light brown hair that never looked messy, a perfectly manicured beard, and he always rolled up his sleeves so that his hairy forearms were exposed. He worked from home, so he would become my new babysitter after school. I had to say goodbye to Barbara.

When I first walked into Manny's immaculately clean home, he seemed a little jumpy because of my presence. His collection of over two thousand VHS movies was displayed on thirty shelves, in perfect alphabetical order, in the walk-in closet just off the kitchen. I smiled as I scanned the neatly written movie titles on the spines of the cases. "Laura, would you like to choose a movie for us all to watch tonight?" Manny asked.

"Really?" I asked. "Anything I want?"

"Yup," Manny responded. My mother smiled, and I immediately wanted to call Manny my new daddy.

Manny kept an eye on me, so my mother became more hands-off and distant. She hugged me less. She talked to me less. She didn't ask about my day. I would tell her anyway, forcing her to hear about my life. At times, I'd do the opposite, and go days without speaking to anyone. It went unnoticed.

I would run up to Manny's office to say hello when I got home from school each day. My mother would arrive a few hours later. She'd come home, make herself a cocktail, and sit on the couch to tell Manny about her day. Manny started to teach me how to "clean house correctly," as he would say. Apparently, my father wasn't teaching me good cleaning skills. I did my best to meet Manny's very particular requirements about how he wanted things done. I took these lessons with me to my father's house and showed him.

"This is how Manny taught me," I said as I showed my father. My cleaning impressed him. He stared at me, and then looked at what I cleaned; his eyes moved back and forth from me to my cleaning.

"Do you like Manny?" he asked.

"Yeah, he's nice, Daddy. I think you'd like him."

"Don't talk about another man in my house. I never want to hear his name again." My father walked into the bathroom and slammed the door. I heard him vomit.

Manny required me to complete a list of chores every Friday after school. This list grew to be eighteen tasks long: clean upstairs bathroom and tub, clean downstairs bathroom and shower, vacuum upstairs, vacuum downstairs, vacuum stairs, wash counters, clean windows, clean windowsills, clean the baseboards, sweep kitchen floor, mop kitchen floor, do my laundry, wash my sheets and blankets, clean out fridge, sweep outside deck, water plants (he had about forty plants), sweep the garage… It went on and on.

After I finished each week, Manny checked my work. "It's time for inspection," he'd bellow, as he stood up from his office desk chair. I struggled with vacuuming around all of his plants, and I always left a Comet soap film ring in the tub after scrubbing and rinsing it. I tried so hard, but I rarely passed his grueling inspection.

He would become very angry and yell that I wasn't trying hard enough. I wasn't good enough. After failing inspection for the third week in a row, something changed. As I stood behind him in the hallway near the downstairs bathroom, he noticed a soapy film on the counter and asked, "What the hell is this?"

"It's from the Comet. I'm sorry." I apologized for my screw-up.

"Comet is for the tub only. You use the all-purpose cleaner for the counters!" he bellowed. "How many times do I have to tell you? You have to use the right cleaner for each and every job."

I looked up at him and frowned. Before I could open my mouth to apologize again, I felt a violent jolt to the left side of my head. My neck jerked to the right, hard. My chin swung to the side, and my hair flew in front of my face as I fell to the floor. I stared at the clean, cream-colored carpet in shock. Time slowed to a crawl. *What just happened?* I thought. I raised my head and moved my hair away from my eyes. Manny's face was red and sweaty, and his eyes were dark and filled with hate. He had punched me hard. I could even feel where his huge ring had hit me in my temple. I had been hit by my parents before, but the hatred behind this blow was staggering. The room started to go dark. I desperately held on to consciousness. When I cried from the pain, he became enraged. He yelled, "Get off your ass and go to your room."

Too terrified to stand up in front of him, I stayed low to the floor and snuck around his legs. I ran up the stairs to my room. I crawled under my blankets on my daybed and gathered my many stuffed animals around me. They were my friends, and they kept me warm. I quietly cried until my mother came home. My head and neck throbbed from the pain. I felt my temple swell almost immediately. *Did he hurt my brain?* I thought.

I heard my mother and Manny talking downstairs. I didn't move. She came upstairs and asked me if I was okay. I did not peek out from under my covers, and I hid my swollen face. *Never let them see you sweat*, I remembered her teaching me. *Never let anyone see you weak.*

"Manny said you had trouble with chores today," she said with a serious tone. I nodded from under the covers. I couldn't let her see me.

After that day, I worked so hard to earn his love. I needed to make him love me so much that he couldn't bare hitting me. A few days later, I drew him a card and slid it under his office door. In the card, I asked, "Can I call you daddy?" And I told my mother what I had done.

"Go see him. Go see what his answer is," my mother advised. They had been talking about getting married, so I guess she was also curious about his response.

I nervously scurried up the stairs to his office and knocked on the door.

"Come in," he said.

I looked down at the carpet. The floor was bare, so I knew he had found my card. I saw it on his desk, opened. "Did you like my card?" I asked.

"Yes," he said.

"Well, can I?" I asked.

"Can you what?" he asked.

"Can I call you daddy?" I felt so small and humiliated as I asked this question. *This was a stupid idea*, I thought.

"We'll just have to see about that, won't we?" he replied. "I have to get back to work, Laura," he said, as he motioned toward the door.

My shoulders dropped, and I said "okay." I turned and walked back downstairs.

"Well, what did he say?" my mother asked.

"He said 'we'll see,'" I replied, regretting that I had ever asked the question.

At Christmas that year, I made a Santa Claus out of construction paper. It was quite intricate with slivers of white paper for a beard and bright blue paper eyes and bright pink paper lips. I wrote a sign for it that said, "To: Manny, Merry Christmas. Love: Laura." Manny worked late that night, so I left it by his coffee mug to find when he went downstairs to eat later that night. I went to bed with a smile on my face, hoping he would like my gift.

The next morning, my mother and I started our Saturday morning rituals. Since Manny had worked late the night before, he slept in late. I carefully shuffled through the townhouse in my pink fuzzy pajamas and did my best not to make any noise. I heard my mother in the kitchen, and I snuck downstairs to see her. "Good morning," she whispered.

"Hi, Mommy. Did Manny see my Santa?" I whispered, and I looked toward the kitchen table. There I saw a flattened pile of red and black construction paper. He must have crushed it with his fist. I pictured it so clearly. Bam, the impact through the paper onto the hard table must have made a loud noise.

"I'm sorry, sweetie. He was angry because you had left a glass on the counter." My mother tried to comfort me.

"What? But why did he? I made that for him." Tears formed in my eyes, but I turned away. She would never understand the battle I was facing. He punched or kicked me at least once a week, usually after inspection of my chores. But he also hit me for making noise, making a mess, or wetting my bed. And he never struck just once. He always managed to get in a few hits to the side of my head or my body before I could get away. Strangely, he never hit my face. I guess he knew the bruises would be too obvious. For him to hit me so hard and so often must have meant that he hated me. I had to try even harder to make him like me, love me, so much, that he'd never hurt me again. I'd clean faster and better. I'd smile more and be quieter.

At my father's house that weekend, I told him what had happened. "He crushed the Santa I made for him, Daddy. He is mean to me. He hits me sometimes."

"He hits you?" my father asked.

"Yes, but don't tell Mommy. I can do better."

"Where does he hit you?" my father asked.

"In my head and my back. But it's just because I don't clean right. I can do better next time. Never mind. I shouldn't have told you. I'll just get in more trouble. Don't say anything."

"Does your mother know?" my father asked, sounding a little concerned.

"I'm sure she does. She's home sometimes when it happens. It's okay, Daddy. I can handle it. I'll just do better."

"Okay. Are you sure you don't want me to say anything?" he asked.

"I'm sure. Thanks, Daddy." I just wanted him to forget what I had shared.

One morning before the bus came, I needed to look up some information for a school project. Manny stored a beautiful set of encyclopedias in the built-in bookshelf underneath the stairs. I turned the stereo on quietly and found the encyclopedia volume I needed. The song, "I Wanna Dance with Somebody," by Whitney Houston played softly as I flipped through the pages when movement out of the corner of my eye startled me. I gasped. "You scared me!"

Manny stood over me wearing his shorts and T-shirt that he slept in. His hair was a mess, and his face looked enraged.

"People are sleeping, Laura. It's early!" Manny scolded. His was voice quiet, but angry.

I was kneeling on the floor, and I tried to get up to defend myself. I dropped the book and shifted my weight, but I moved too slowly. He struck me on the left side of my head, and I fell to the right, into the bookshelf. One of his plants fell off the shelf and landed on the carpet, spilling dirt all over. He kicked me on my side, ribs, and back four or five times and said in the same calm, cold tone, "Clean up that mess, and go to school." Pain shot through my body like knives. My back twisted, and my stomach felt like it had been torn open.

I nodded. I didn't cry. There was no point. Manny quietly walked back upstairs, careful not to wake my mother. I looked at the pile of dirt and tried to think of a way to clean it up without making noise. The hand vacuum he taught me to use for messes like this would definitely be too loud. I went into the kitchen and grabbed a paper towel. I put the plant back on the shelf perfectly in its place, and I picked up as much dirt as I could with the paper towel. I then used my fingers to pick up each individual morsel of soil that I could see, and I put each one into the paper towel. I checked the clock. I couldn't miss the bus, because that would make them both angry. I rushed, but I was very careful to pick up every single piece until the carpet looked perfect. I left no evidence of my mess. I hoisted my heavy backpack onto my shoulder, and pain shot down my buttocks and legs. I walked as fast as I could to catch the bus, but my limp slowed me down. I could barely feel my feet touch the ground. My head and side hurt, but I couldn't think about that now. I had to get to school.

In first period, I asked to be excused to go to the nurse. "Again, Laura?" my teacher asked, sounding aggravated.

"Yes, please," I said, respectfully.

She handed me a hall pass, and I limped down to the nurse's office. "Good morning, Laura. Here for your daily visit?" the nurse joked.

"Yes, I'm sorry to bother you. I have another headache. Can I have some Tylenol?" I asked. I visited the nurse almost daily. I had almost constant headaches and backaches. I needed the Tylenol for pain. It didn't help much, and sometimes I didn't even take it; I'd put it in my pocket and save it for the weekend, just in case.

"You're never a bother," she said. That's another reason I visited the nurse; she was always nice to me. "Does your mother know you get so many headaches?"

"Oh yes. I see a lot of doctors; I just get headaches. That's all," I explained. I saw many doctors: a headache specialist, a pain specialist, a chiropractor, allergist, a psychologist, and my normal doctor. They all knew about my headaches and back problems.

A doctor had diagnosed me with migraines when I was a toddler. My mother told me I was the youngest person to be diagnosed with migraines on the East Coast. The beatings made even my good days bad. And the doctors prescribed so many medications that I was in a daze a lot of the time. But my mother told me I had to take them all. Her friends gave her a lot of attention and sympathy because she needed to care for her sickly daughter.

Occasionally, my migraines would come with vomiting in addition to the usual sensitivity to light and sound. When that happened at school, I'd need to go home to a dark room and put a heating pad or cold compress on my head and neck. The nurse would call my mother, and I'd wait patiently to hear the click-clocking of her high heels coming down the school hallway. Her feet always sounded so angry. She'd race home, drop me off, and go back to work. I'd only resort to this when I absolutely needed to be in bed, because I didn't like aggravating her.

The chores, inspections, beatings, and pain pattern repeated each week. I never got everything one hundred percent right on Manny's inspections. I would try to run away from him, and he would chase me. I'd try to get up the stairs to make it to my room. I'd be moving so fast that I'd bend down and use my arms to try to propel myself up the cleanly vacuumed stairs. If he caught up to me as I reached the bottom stair, he'd grab my head, hair, or shoulder and "kick my ass." I'd cringe, as pain would shoot through my lower back and down my legs. My room provided no safety. He would follow me in and punch and kick me. I spent many weekends with pain in my head, neck, back, buttocks, and down my legs. My mother would give me a heating pad to ease the pain.

I called my grandmother one day and asked if I could join her at church in the morning. "Of course, dear. But I go early in the morning on Sundays," she explained.

"That's great. Can you pick me up?" I asked. Church bored me, and I didn't agree with a lot that the priest said. But if I went to church, I'd get that morning off from beatings. Church provided safety, for one hour each week.

I listened to the priest. "God will grant what you ask for. But you must pray. You must not only pray in times of need. You must be grateful and acknowledge God in times of joy." I did not believe in prayer or God, because it didn't work. But I kept trying to get faith—to obtain this intangible thing that seemed to make other people happy. I was jealous of everyone in the room who so blindly believed in this character. *How could there be a wonderful powerful being, such as God, if a small child could be beaten on a regular basis? How was I supposed to honor thy mother and thy father when they hurt me so deeply? Why were my prayers for love, calmness, and safety never answered?*

None of the stories from those books made any logical sense to me. I couldn't follow them with my scientific way of thinking. While I couldn't relate to anyone in the room, I did feel safe. I ignored what the priest said, and looked around at all the families—envious of their love for one another. I would go to church every Sunday forever, as long as my mother would let me. I learned the prayers to make my grandmother happy. I memorized the words and recited them when asked. I followed along, like it was a play or a movie, and I was an actress. I'd count to a hundred over and over again. I'd keep my secrets.

Enuresis is the fancy word for bedwetting by children during sleep. It is caused by many things: genetics, difficulties waking from sleep, stress, abuse and molestation, slower than normal development of the central nervous system, hormones, urinary tract infections, abnormalities, or a small bladder. I struggled with it until age thirteen or so. When the abuse stopped, the bedwetting got better. If I didn't let myself sleep deeply, I stayed dry and in control. Liquids were not allowed after I got home from school. I worked even harder to stop my problem, and I didn't drink water at school much either. The dehydration certainly contributed to my constant headaches.

I used an alarm clock to wake myself up at 2 a.m. each night to try to use the bathroom, whether I had to or not. Some nights, when I did not hear the alarm, my mother would wake me up to tell me to use the bathroom. I slept too deeply on those nights, and that meant trouble. Other nights, Manny would sneak in to my bedroom and stand over me. He wouldn't jostle my arm lightly, like my mother did, to wake me up. He'd push against the side of my body with all his might. The sudden jolt frightened me awake. He'd stand there and stare. Then he'd lean into my face and whisper-yell, "Laura, this is your problem, not mine. I shouldn't have to wake up in the middle of the night to your fucking alarm clock. Get up and go to the bathroom so you don't piss yourself." His tone sent shivers through my body. I'd nervously run to the bathroom and desperately try to pee. He'd listen at the door.

"I didn't hear anything come out. Did you pee?" he'd ask, as I exited the bathroom and tried to get back to my room.

"I didn't have to go. I tried really hard," I'd reply, almost whimpering like a stray dog.

"You better not make a mess," he'd say, as he walked back to his bedroom where my mother slept.

I wouldn't let myself sleep too deeply, and I'd continually check to see if I felt like I had to pee all night long.

One of the nights that I had accidentally slept too well, too deeply, I felt a hard whack on the top of my head as I heard an alarm blaring in my ear. The sound swiftly shifted from being very close to my eardrum, to far away, and then close again, as another impact struck the side of my head. Then another one. It didn't feel like a fist. It felt harder, but it wasn't his rings. *Was it a book? A brick?* I couldn't imagine what he was hitting me with. The beeping of the alarm was louder and softer and moving quickly. I struggled to wake up and understand what was happening, all the while trying to protect my head. The impact hit my shoulder, and then I knew the object was the alarm clock. He was beating me with the alarm clock as my 2 a.m. wakeup call was going off. "I'm sorry, I'm sorry," I screamed. "I'll get up. I'll get up!"

"This is how you learn not to piss yourself, Laura. Get up and go to the bathroom, now!" he scolded, yelling and whispering at the same time.

I stood up and felt wobbly and disoriented from the multiple hits to the sides of my head. My shoulder hurt. I didn't cry. I stumbled, and quickly zigzagged my way to the hallway and past my mother, who stood outside my bedroom door. I ran into the bathroom, where I tried to force pee to come out. I stayed in the bathroom for a while as I heard Manny and my mother argue. I stared at the doorknob and wished I could lock it. I made sure I didn't have any pee inside me and cleaned my face. I looked in the mirror and imagined myself as a boxer. I looked deeply into my blue-gray-green eyes, and tried to look tough and mean. I hardened my posture and put my fists in front of my face. I twisted to the side and imagined what it would be like to hit back. I smirked at how silly this looked, since I was so small. I snuck back to my room, and tried not to sleep.

A few months later, we moved out of Manny's townhouse and into another apartment. My mother didn't speak much about this move. She said that she was heartbroken about another failed relationship. I felt tremendous guilt for breaking up her relationship. "I don't want to be alone," she said. "And why didn't you tell me?"

"I thought you knew," I mumbled. My mind filled with questions: *How could she not know? There were times when it happened while she was in the house. Didn't she hear my cries? The impacts? What else would explain why a nine-year-old had back problems all of a sudden?*

7
my strength underneath

My mother and I, the team, searched for a new life again.
"I guess we're on our own again," I joked.

"Laura. This has to stop. It can't always just be me and
you. I need my own life," my mother announced, yet
again.

Isn't a mother supposed to love being around their daughter?
I thought to myself. "But I like being with you. Don't you
like being with me?" I asked.

"You're just like your father," she barked. "You're
always whining and always the victim, right? I'm sick of
it."

"I don't think that. I'm sorry, Mom." Inside, I felt
myself cry.

"And why are you always hanging around me and my
friends? You need to make your own friends. Make your
own life," she commanded.

"But it's hard because I just changed schools, and now

I have to change again. I hate being the new girl. I love you the most, Mom."

She squawked and said, "That's fine, but I can't be your entire life."

My mother craved being the center of attention, by everyone. People described her as the host of every party, the loudest in every bar, and the center of every conversation. My health problems added to her relevance, and her friends went out of their way to support her; she had a sickly child that she needed to care for. She fooled everyone, showing her caring and funny side when other people were around. But behind closed doors, things changed.

I tracked my appointments with doctors and specialists on a calendar on the fridge. The doctors performed test after test to find the root cause of all of my health problems. "There has to be something to explain all of this," my mother said. "You're not well."

I was a sick kid.

Even at age eleven, I couldn't get through most nights without an accident. I tried so hard not to drink any liquids or sleep. My mother decided to bring me to the hospital for more testing. "They're just running a test on your bladder to make sure you can take a medication that will help you with your accidents. Wouldn't you like to be able to stay at your friend's house and not wet the bed?" she asked.

Of course, I agreed. I recently had an accident at a friend's house, and afterward I hid from her at school in embarrassment. My friend's dog had found the old-lady diaper that I had worn at night in the trash and tore it to shreds. Pieces of pee-soaked cotton were scattered throughout the bathroom, hallway, and living room. My friend's mom asked, while furiously cleaning it up, "What the hell is this?"

Her daughter and son said they didn't know. I shrugged my shoulders in agreement. I believe the mother understood my problem, but protected my secret and never said a word. I never went back to that friend's house, but I wish I could thank her for protecting my secret.

"Is it going to hurt?" I asked my mother about the bladder test.

"No, it's a simple test, and I'll be right there with you," she replied.

We entered the cold, sterile room, and the nurse asked me to undress. I wrapped myself in the extra-large hospital gown and opened the curtain. "I'm ready," I said.

"Dear, it's time for you to lay on the table," the nurse said.

I looked at the cold metal table that was about three feet tall. "That table?" I asked.

"Yes, dear."

I stepped on a stool and managed to get myself on the stainless-steel table.

"Sweetie, you have to open your legs, so we can begin the test," another lady commanded.

I stared at the ceiling, frozen, unsure if I had heard her correctly. "Why? What are you going to do to me?" I asked.

"It's okay, Laura," my mom said.

"We are going to put a tiny, little camera into your bladder to take a picture. Pictures don't hurt, right?" the first nurse said.

"What? What are you going to do to me?" Tears streamed down the sides of my cheeks onto the hospital pillow.

"Open your legs, sweetie. It will be really quick," a man said.

I held my breath to stop myself from crying, and I started to count to a hundred in my head. My mother held my hand. I opened my legs, and I felt surges of pain as they inserted the camera. "It hurts. You said it wouldn't hurt. It hurts," I sobbed.

"It'll stop hurting in just a moment. Take a deep breath, and relax your legs," the nurse said.

I tried to breathe, but I couldn't breathe deeply. I tried to relax my legs, but I failed. The pain subsided a bit, but I knew something was still inside me. After several minutes, I started to feel like I had to pee.

"I have to use the bathroom," I said, as I fought intense shivers.

"That's normal. We are filling your bladder with liquid. You can see it on the screen. See that? You can see fluid going into your bladder right there." The nurse pointed to a monitor. I looked and saw a bunch of gray shapes and a dark shape getting larger. "Your bladder looks nice and healthy, a good size."

"I have to pee really bad," I said, whimpering. I tried to move my legs and get up. But I felt a wire pull at my flesh. "Ouch," I sobbed.

"Don't move, Laura. You can't get up yet. You're almost done. You have to pee on the table, sweetie. That's what's supposed to happen. We need to watch your bladder empty," the nurse explained.

"What? Pee on the table? What?" *That can't possibly be true*, I thought.

"It's okay. You have to let it go, Laura. You have to pee on the table. Go ahead and pee. It's okay," one of the nurses said.

"Go ahead, Laura. You can pee on the table. It's okay," my mom said.

It made no sense. *Pee on the table? With my legs open? With a camera inside me? With everyone watching? What was I doing here? Why didn't anyone explain anything to me before I got here?* I had so many questions. I couldn't hold it anymore, and I started to pee. I peed for a long time.

"Your bladder was really full, Laura. You're doing good. Just keep peeing," the nurse said, as warm liquid spilled all over my body, the bed, and the floor. I felt humiliated, devastated, exposed.

The nurses cleaned me off and helped me stand up. My legs wobbled, and I worried I would slip and fall into my own urine. I wiped my face with my forearm. "Can I have a tissue?" I asked.

My mother handed me a tissue, and I walked toward my pile of clothes that sat on a chair in the corner. I closed the curtain and froze. I noticed a bathroom behind me. I snatched my clothes, ran into the bathroom, and shut the door.

"You should have warned her," I overheard one of the nurses say to my mother right before I closed the bathroom door.

"Then she wouldn't have come." My mother defended her decision not to tell me what to expect.

After I got dressed, I sat on the toilet seat for several minutes trying to calm myself. I shook violently. I wanted to hurt someone, scream, punch a wall. I desperately wanted to become a boxer in my mind, but I couldn't focus. I couldn't look myself in the eye in the bathroom mirror. I was nothing.

"Laura. Laura, honey, it's time to go. I have to get dinner started," my mother said outside the bathroom door, as she knocked lightly.

Dinner? Who gives a fuck about dinner? I thought to myself. *I never want to eat again.* I stood up, forced myself to stare into my blue-gray-green eyes in the mirror, and searched for that look—the look of toughness, of strength, of a fighter. I needed to know that I still had it, that this hadn't broken me, that nothing up to this point had destroyed my strength underneath. I could still see a glimmer of heat in my eyes. I opened the door, didn't say a word, and left the hospital with my mother.

The doctors had convinced my mother that I needed the test in order to determine if pee was backtracking into my bladder after urination. The test was used to make sure I didn't have a constant mild urinary tract infection, which would have explained the bedwetting. I passed the test. My bladder was healthy.

That also meant that another medication could be

added to my list. They started me on a beta blocker to help with all of my "problems."

A few months later, as my mother was driving me home from an appointment with the chiropractor, she brought up the topic again. "We have to figure out what's wrong with your sleeping."

"I just don't like to sleep, Mom."

"There's another test the doctors want to do. It's an overnight sleep test."

"You mean, spend the night?" I panicked. I didn't want any more things inside me. I didn't want to spend any more time at a hospital or doctor's office. "Mom, no more tests. I'm not going. I'm fine."

"You're going, Laura. This isn't normal," she said.

"No, Mom. I'm not going. I don't need any more medicine or tests or doctors." I was adamant.

"I made an appointment for tomorrow night," she announced.

"Tomorrow? But what about my test on Wednesday?" I shouted.

"You'll be able to go to school the next day," she insisted.

"No, Mom. I'm fine! I'm not going to do bad on my test because some doctor says I don't sleep enough. Screw that," I yelled.

She grabbed my arm hard enough to leave bruises with her right hand while her left hand was on the steering wheel, and firmly said, "You're going!"

From her tone, I knew that I had no choice.

The next day, I got ready for school and tried not to

think about the sleep test I was scheduled for later that night at the hospital. *What were the doctors going to do to me now?* I didn't know anything about a sleep test.

When we arrived at the hospital, I was asked to undress again. "Put on this robe. It's nice and soft, and it will keep you warm," the nurse instructed. I shivered and put on the enormous gown. I wrapped the fuzzy light blue belt around my waste twice and tied it as tightly as possible.

A young man walked toward me and introduced himself. "Hi, I'm Steve. I'm the tech who will be getting you all set for your sleep test."

A man! I panicked again. What was this man going to do to me? "Never trust a man. Never trust a man." My mother's words surged through my mind.

My mom said to Steve, "This is Laura. She's a little nervous."

"Ah. Laura, there's nothing to be nervous about. All you have to do is sleep. Sleep doesn't hurt, right?"

"Right." I saw no reason to trust any of the adults who stood over me. I stared at the white, speckled floor and tried to speed up time. I counted to a hundred in my mind as fast as possible.

"Okay, I'm going to have you sit in here, and then we'll get you all hooked up. Cara, you can wait over here," Steve instructed.

My mother walked into a different room. I sat down on a cold plastic chair and waited alone.

"We're going to put these electrodes on you to monitor you while you sleep. They do not hurt at all,"

Steve said, as he rolled in a large machine with about a million wires attached to it.

"Where…where are you going to put them on me?" I asked, as I started to sweat.

Steve looked at me with concern in his eyes. "Nowhere that hurts. I promise," he said. "Mostly on your head, some on your legs and shoulders, and a few on your back. That's all." Steve tried to assure me.

"You mean, in my hair?" I asked.

"Yes, we use this light glue. It will wash out in the morning."

"And I'll be attached to that thing?" I asked, as I pointed to the large machine.

"Yes, and if you need to use the bathroom, you can just roll this machine with you. We will be here to help you," Steve explained.

Steve and another nurse or tech started to glue the electrodes to my scalp, neck, and shoulders. Then they bent down to attach them to my legs. I hadn't shaved in a week. "Sorry, I didn't shave my legs."

"That's okay," Steve said. "Neither did I!"

I laughed a little, appreciating his effort. Once all of the electrodes were in place, I maneuvered myself down the hall as Steve rolled the large machine next to me. We walked toward a dark room that had a single bed inside. A small lamp and alarm clock sat on a nightstand next to the bed. I could tell they had tried to make the room look cozy.

"Where did my mom go?" I asked.

"Your mom has gone home, but she will be back in

the morning," Steve explained.

I have to be here alone. I wanted to seem strong, so I didn't say another word. *Never let them see you weak. Never let them see you sweat,* I thought to myself.

I slowly got into the bed and tried to avoid the wires and not pull anything out. When I snagged a wire on the bedspread, I could feel it pull against my hair. "Ouch," I said.

Steve immediately unwrapped the wire from the blanket to relieve the pressure from my hair.

"Thank you," I whispered.

After I lay in the hard, lumpy bed, I closed my eyes. I could feel the wires circling my body, face, and head. Each time I moved even a few inches, I could feel at least one wire snag on something or pull on my hair or skin. I tried to stay very still and keep my eyes closed. *Just try to sleep, but don't sleep too hard,* I inaudibly told myself over and over. *Try to sleep, but don't sleep too hard.*

The next morning, I opened my eyes as a nurse turned on the light. The bright, flickering, fluorescent light above me burned my eyes and made my stomach feel sick. I knew where I was immediately. I had spent the night in the hospital, to have an overnight sleep test, alone. "Is my mom here?" I asked.

"Not yet, sweetie. She should be here soon. Let's get those wires off of you."

I assessed myself quickly. I didn't have an accident, thankfully. I must not have slept too hard.

The nurse introduced herself as Brenda, and she slowly peeled away each electrode. She started with the ones on my legs. "I'm sorry, I didn't have time to shave yesterday."

"That's okay, sweetie. You're so young. You don't have to worry about that yet anyway," she said.

I had just turned twelve. I learned how to shave by watching older girls shave their legs by the river two years earlier. I went home and tried it using my mother's razor. I felt grown up, so I continued.

It hurt when Brenda took the electrodes off my head and out of my hair. She used a smelly liquid to dissolve the glue to make it easier. It made my hair and the room stink. As she put the machine away, my mother walked into the room.

"Are you all set, Laura?" She sounded like she'd had a great night's sleep. The bitch.

"Not yet, Mom. I need to get dressed. I need to take a shower," I said.

"We'll have to hurry to get you to school, because I have an early meeting," she announced, like her meeting was so fucking important.

"I'm going as fast as I can, Mom." I rushed, but glue stuck to me everywhere. I overheard my mother ask when the doctor would receive the results of my test.

"A few days," I thought I heard Steve's voice respond.

We rushed out of the hospital and got in the car. "Was it okay?" my mother asked.

"It was fine," I replied, as coldly as I could.

"Did you have an accident?"

"No, I didn't," I said, and I rolled my eyes.

"Don't you roll your eyes at me," she scolded.

"Sorry," I mumbled.

My mother drove us home and rushed me into the apartment. "Hurry up and get ready. I have to get to work."

"But I have glue in my hair, Mom. It might take me a while," I explained.

"Just wear a hat. You always wear a hat anyway," she demanded.

"I don't always wear a hat, and I don't want to today. And I stink like that glue stuff."

"Move fast, Laura." I heard impatience, irritation, and anger in her voice.

She's mad at me? That's insane, I thought. We left the apartment quickly, but I still missed my first class.

"You've made me late for my meeting," my mother complained, as she drove quickly to my school. I jumped out of the car, and she walked into the main office with me. She signed me in, and I went to class. I picked flakes of glue out of my hair all day, and I knew that I smelled. I didn't speak to anyone. I wanted to disappear.

Over the next year, I had an MRI and CT scan of my brain to determine the cause of my migraines. I had bloodwork done routinely to check my CBC count, and to look for any sign of abnormality to explain why I was so screwed up. I took several psychological tests to determine why I wasn't "socially normal" and why I was "feeling sorry for myself all the time." I scored in the 99th percentile for psychological functioning "given my circumstances," the doctor said. My bladder test, sleep test, and scan results were all normal.

My mother displayed my medications in a tan wicker basket on the round kitchen table. I'd have to pass the table before I left for the school bus and immediately after walking in the door at the end of each day. I'd count out thirteen medications, three times a day. I used inhalers, steroids, beta blockers, anti-seizure/mood stabilizers, antidepressants, anti-anxiety medications, allergy medications, and pain medications.

As I started to take my evening doses one night, I sat down on the kitchen floor and leaned forward. I put my head in my hands and cried. The drugs made me feel weak and confused, as if I was out of my own body. Without telling anyone, I stopped taking all of the medications except for one of the inhalers that I knew helped me breathe. "Yeah, breathing is important," I said to myself and smirked. After a few days, I felt less dizzy. After three weeks, I had more energy and less trouble finding the right words when I wrote or spoke.

My mother walked in with a white plastic bag from the pharmacy, stuffed with refilled prescriptions for the month. The red logo bent and folded around the bottles, and I knew I'd be in trouble for not taking my drugs. She sorted through the bottles, quickly assessed the number of pills, and slammed her fist on the table. "Why haven't you been taking your meds?" she hollered.

"But I feel better, Mom. Isn't that good? I feel better!" I stood tall and shouted.

"That was very dangerous, Laura. You shouldn't have done that. You need your medication. You need to be on medication because you are not healthy!" she insisted.

"Mom, I don't want to take pills anymore," I argued.

"I think you're being very stupid."

"I'm not taking them anymore. I don't care what you say." I walked into my bedroom and slammed the door. Grateful to have my own room and privacy, I sat on my bed and shivered. I was twelve.

8
nomads

After leaving my father, my mother and I lived in many apartments in various neighborhoods and towns around Connecticut. It was difficult to understand why we had to move sometimes. Twice, we moved to live with one of her boyfriends. A few times we moved because the rent increase was too high to stay. Many times, there was no explanation at all—just an announcement. We met a few neighbors here and there, but we kept our distance from everyone, like temporary guests. "It's like we're nomads," my mother used to say, and then she'd laugh. I didn't laugh. Moving around so often, and with very little warning, kept me on edge. I changed schools in third grade, sixth grade, and eighth grade. But even changing neighborhoods meant starting over, packing, and throwing away stuff I "didn't actually need," unpacking and finding a place for my things, learning a new bus or walk to school, and meeting new kids that lived nearby.

82 light sleeper

In school one day, I shared a story about my weekend of apartment hunting with my mother. I began, "My mother and I spent the weekend searching for a place to live...," and loud laughter from several kids interrupted me. I looked around and felt confused. I hadn't said anything funny. Some of the laughter changed to awkward giggles, and their faces changed from big smiles to sympathetic eyes.

"I don't get it. What's funny?" I asked my friend who sat at the desk next to me.

"It sounds like you and your mom are homeless," she said.

"Oh, ha! No, I meant we were searching for a *new* place to live," I said, emphasizing the word "new." I smiled, looked around, and joined in on the giggling.

Their faces changed back to smiles, and their laughs returned to normal before fading out.

"My mother was indecisive," I'd say when asked why I had sixteen addresses by the time I had turned fourteen. We left my dad when I was seven. When my mother and I shared a bedroom in several of the apartments, we would go to sleep while watching a very small, black and white television that had a wrinkled section of screen in the corner behind the glass. My mother turned the volume far too high on the old TV for our small bedroom. From the outside, the noise of the television made it sound like we lived with a man. My mother said that would keep us safe from intruders.

We also lived with her father—my grandfather, Ed— for six months in the middle of it all. I was nine, and my mother had to drive me to school, since we lived out of the district again. This apartment was part of a small house about six blocks from the beach. I loved to ride my scooter around the neighborhood. One day the gang turf-fights reached our block, and I no longer could leave the house. I had to stay inside with Grandpa Ed. Since he had abused my mother as a child, and I knew the stories all too well, I hated being alone with him. The loud television couldn't protect me from this unspoken danger.

At the time, my grandmother lived in Florida and my grandfather had just moved back to Connecticut to start over again. Grandma would be joining him soon, and we'd have to move again. My grandparents started over often; my grandfather had lost all of his money by gambling. He'd sometimes take me to OTB with him. When I told my mother about our trips together, her face became grim.

"What's OTB, Mom?" I asked her one night when we both lay in our beds in our shared bedroom.

"It's off-track betting. He's gambling on horse races. Damn it!" My mother was very upset about her father's addiction.

My grandfather missed my grandmother terribly; she was an excellent cook, and she took very good care of him. He didn't have to cook, clean, or pick up after himself. Here, he slept on a bed that was shoved in a corner of the living room, and no one cleaned up his messes.

"Grandpa, what do you want for dinner?" I asked him

one evening.

"Why? You cooking?" he griped.

"No, Mom's going to pick something up on the way home."

"Pork chops!" he yelled back.

"Pork chops," I repeated on the phone to my mother.

"Okay, I'll be home in a few minutes. You doing okay, Laura?" my mother inquired.

"Yeah, I'm fine. Just doing homework and hanging out with Grandpa's cat."

"Stay in your room, and leave Grandpa alone, okay?"

"Okay, Mom."

She asked me to stay in my room whenever I was home alone with Grandpa. I did what I was told. No one spoke much.

When I was ten, my mother met another man named David. I decided before I met him that I would not like him. He had big brown eyes and gray speckles in his hair. He seemed shy and quiet, but this only added to my suspicions about him. He played guitar, clarinet, and keyboard. He sang well too. David loved the outdoors, cars, and motorcycles. The three of us hiked together, and we once planned a seven-day backpacking trip to Minnesota. I couldn't wait to camp in the woods and carry my own backpack. David drove us from Connecticut to Minnesota, while I followed along using the maps. I learned how to figure out the best routes between the states. We traveled through New York, Pennsylvania, Illinois, and Wisconsin. I thought Chicago was beautiful.

"Mom, I can go anywhere now," I announced, while we all rode in David's black Ford Mustang. He sped down the highway and slammed on the brakes anytime his radar detector beeped.

"What do you mean?" she asked.

"With a map, I can find my way anywhere, to any town, to any state. It's cool!" I was excited. Until that moment, the world seemed so limited to my current room, in our current apartment, and in my current school. Everything else was unattainable: traveling, buying nice things, or even going to a concert. I never imagined myself leaving what little comfort I could find. The thought overwhelmed me, so I closed the map.

On the way back to Connecticut, we drove through Canada. We stopped at Niagara Falls to take some pictures. I would remember this trip for the rest of my life.

For my eleventh birthday, David and my mother bought me a full-sized, eighty-eight-key keyboard. "If you can learn how to play the keyboard, you can learn how to play any instrument," David announced. He taught me the chords to the Foreigner song "Head Games," and I learned them quickly. I could play with him while he strummed the guitar and sang. We smiled and laughed together a lot. I learned to listen closely to music, and to mimic the notes of what I heard on the keyboard. David said I had a natural talent for quickly finding the right key. I loved living with David.

While holding my favorite stuffed bear and fighting sleep one night, I heard yelling downstairs. I could barely make out the words.

"I know you cheated on me. I can smell it!" David yelled.

"You can smell it?" my mother yelled back.

"I smelled your underwear. You bitch!"

"You're insane!" she shouted. I heard several bangs as I hid in my room. I didn't say a word. I heard the front door slam, and I stayed silent. I could hear my mother grumbling to herself and throwing things around in the living room. Then I heard the doorbell. I got up and walked toward my closed bedroom door.

I overheard a conversation begin between my mother and two or three other people. I opened my bedroom door and peeked out. I could see red and blue police lights flickering through the windows. A spotlight lit up the front of the building, which made it look like daytime. I walked toward the stairs and called for my mother.

"Go back to your room," she yelled to me. I quickly turned around, frightened.

"No, officer, I don't want to press charges against him. My daughter is fine, too. Please just leave us alone," I heard my mother say to the police officers.

I wanted the officers to leave too. I didn't want to move out of the apartment with David. I had my own room again, and David treated me better than any man ever had. I didn't want to be the new girl in school again.

"He never liked you, you know," my mother said to me, as she drove the U-Haul away from the apartment we shared with David.

"That's not true," I said.

"It is. I protected you from him. He never wanted kids. And he certainly never wanted to date a woman with kids."

I didn't believe her.

Sensing my disbelief, she continued, "Remember when we went to Minnesota?"

"Yes," I said.

"Do you remember the argument we had when we were driving through Chicago?"

"Yes," I said, getting angrier with her. "Why?"

"He wanted to leave you in the car and go to a bar for a few hours, and I said no. I wouldn't leave you. I protected you. He didn't like having you around," she explained.

I tried to think back. I remembered their argument, but I didn't remember what it was about. I didn't know if she was lying or telling me the truth. I stared at the plastic floor of the truck and thought about meeting new people again at another new school. I'd be the new girl yet again.

9
safety

While kicking a soccer ball against a wall outside our next apartment one afternoon, a neighbor startled me. "Shut the fuck up, little girl!" he yelled, and he gazed at me deeply. I grabbed my soccer ball and quickly ran inside our apartment. I later learned that the man had been reported to police for taking pictures of children in the neighborhood many times. A year earlier, he had hung another neighbor's dog from a large tree branch that hung over the parking lot. A small cross marked the spot where the dog was found by his owner. I convinced myself that I could see a blood stain on the pavement.

My mother and I shared a bedroom again. "It's all I can afford," she said as we moved in. But I didn't mind. I liked sharing a room with her.

We lived on the first floor, which felt less safe and more exposed. One night, over the sounds of the television, I heard movement outside our bedroom window. Someone was pushing against the sliding window to try to force the lock to break, over and over again. I immediately imagined the scary neighbor, who yelled at me earlier that week, pushing on the other side of the flimsy glass.

"Mom, Mom! Someone's trying to break in," I whispered, trying to wake her up while not being too loud.

"Don't be ridiculous, Laura!" she mumbled. She was clearly angry that I had woken her up.

I tried to go back to sleep, but I could definitely hear someone outside our window and on our front steps. I listened intently to their movement.

My mother sat up abruptly. "Shhh," she whispered. My body froze with fear, and my bed filled with sweat.

She picked up the baseball bat that she hid behind the bedroom door and quietly walked out into the living room. I gathered my stiff, sweaty body and followed her. I could still hear them outside the window of our bedroom. She silently crept up to the door, and the doorknob moved slightly. My eyes widened, but I didn't make a sound. I could hear my heartbeat in my ears. I stood solidly in fear, trying to picture my fighter stance. But I couldn't move a muscle, and the boxer in me could not be found. My mother stood between me and the door. I heard a loud bang against the metal railing on our porch...and then silence. My mother's body relaxed, and she said we could go back to bed.

"Aren't you going to call the police?" I asked, while trembling and sweating.

"Nothing happened, Laura. It's over," she said.

"But what if we hadn't locked the door? What if they had kicked the door in?" I asked. My mind raced.

As if I my concerns meant nothing, my mother said, "Let's go back to bed. I have to get up soon for work."

For the rest of the night, I lay in bed with the blankets up to my chin. I kept my eyes open and alternated between shaking lightly and convulsing violently. I listened for more noise and waited for them to come back.

As I walked out the door to go to the bus stop the next morning, I noticed a bike lock hanging from the railing outside our front door. In an instant, I remembered that my best friend, whose name was also Laura, had left her bike on our porch the day before. The loud bang I had heard the night before was the stranger stealing her bike. I dropped my shoulders, and my heart pounded. *Laura will never forgive me,* I thought.

I ran back inside and told my mother what had happened. She called Laura's mother, who then called the police to report the theft. If I had remembered the bike the night before, I could have insisted that my mother call the police. Maybe they could have found the bike. I could have done something. It was my fault. I was eleven.

About six months later, my mother and I lived in another first-floor, one-bedroom apartment near the woods. My cousin visited us on weekends once in a while in the summer. Monica and I enjoyed hanging out at the recreation center in the complex. We swam, listened to music, played ping-pong, and played pool. It was a ten-minute walk through the complex back to the small apartment in the back corner. One day, the phone rang as we walked into the apartment.

"Hello?" I answered.

"Laura. It's Jen. You have to get out of your house." Her voice shook. Jen was my closest friend, and I had never heard fear in her voice before.

"What are you talking about?" I asked, almost laughing.

"I'm not joking. There is someone in your house. I just called and a man answered. I hung up and hit redial and you answered. There is someone there." She sounded genuinely concerned.

I then noticed the open sliding glass door that led to our little courtyard, and I saw large sneaker footprints in the recently vacuumed carpet. I heard movement in the closet next to the front door that Monica and I had just walked through. The slotted wooden closet door allowed me to see inside slightly and hear movement easily. In a flash, I realized that we were both in danger. A stranger hid in the closet a few feet away, and he could probably see us. I breathed in and couldn't force the air out of my lungs. My frozen body started to soak with sweat. Inside I panicked, but I noticed Monica looking at me with a questioning expression. I didn't want to scare her, but I had to do something to get us to safety. Time changed from very rapidly passing by to slowing down to a crawl.

I calmly said to my friend on the phone, "Okay, we'll be there in a second." I hung up the phone.

"Hey, Mon. We have to go back to the rec center. I

forgot something," I said with the steadiest voice I could muster.

"Oh, okay," she said.

I rushed us both past the closet door behind which the man hid. Once we walked a short distance away from the courtyard, I asked my cousin, "Hey. You wanna race there? I bet I can beat you!"

Monica smirked and bolted. I took off as well. We ran the rest of the way, and I stayed a few feet behind my younger cousin. I imagined the stranger chasing us, and I wanted to scream at the top of my lungs. But I held in my fear.

We entered the rec center, out of breath from running so fast. I asked for the manager. I quickly told him about the man in my closet and asked to use his phone to call the police. We waited at the rec center for over thirty minutes, and the police never arrived. Terrified to go back to my apartment alone with my baby cousin, I asked the manager to walk back with us. He entered the apartment and searched it for me. The intruder must have escaped after we left, because the door to the closet was now open. The sliding glass door remained open as well. I looked into the woods, terrified that I'd see someone standing among the trees staring at me. I shivered.

"It looks okay, Laura. Do you want me to stay with you until your mom gets home?" he asked.

"No, we should be okay. She should be home any minute," I responded. I wanted to keep my cousin calm.

I walked over to the sliding glass door, closed it

gently, and locked it. "Monica, let's see what's on TV, okay?"

"Yep!" Monica said, sounding confident that everything was okay.

When my mother arrived, I told her the story.

"You must be mistaken," she said.

I pointed to the footprints in the carpet and said, "See, those are the guy's footprints. That's how he got in!" I exclaimed. "And he hid in that closet!" I pointed to the open door. All of the fear I had suppressed flooded my words. My insides shook with intense emotions.

"You should have locked that door, Laura." She walked into our bedroom and shut the door. I sat on the floor in front of the television.

I obsessed about the man returning every night. While my mother slept, I'd creep out into the living room over and over again, to make sure the sliding glass door was locked. I'd battle with images in my mind. I pictured someone in the closet, someone breaking down the door, or someone opening the window and climbing into our bedroom. I'd try to focus on school, friends, skateboarding, dance, the show on the television, the sounds of my mother snoring…anything to keep my mind from wandering to dangerous visions. If I thought about the closet in the living room near the front door, I simply wouldn't sleep.

10
the end of visitation rights

Twelve was the legal age for children to decide to stop visiting their non-custodial parent in the state of Connecticut. I counted down the months, the weeks, and the days. When my twelfth birthday arrived, my mother said I could invite a few friends over, and she would invite some of her friends over for a party. While grocery shopping that day, she complained about so many things that I couldn't keep track, as she furiously fumbled through the store. She said, "I don't know what to cook. We need paper plates, and forks, and there is no time!"

I picked up some paper plates and put them in the cart, trying to help.

"Not that kind! Those are horrible. Get the other ones!" she commanded.

I picked up another package and looked at her hesitantly. I didn't want to fuck up again.

"No. The blue ones, Laura!"

"Okay," I said, and I grabbed the blue plastic plates and put them in the cart. I pushed the cart behind my mother and accidentally ran into one of her heels with the bottom of the cart.

"What the fuck? Laura, be careful! Watch where you're going!"

"Sorry." *That certainly didn't help the situation*, I thought.

I did not have the courage to tell my father that I didn't want to see him anymore. I didn't want to reject him. I didn't want to hurt him. I knew he'd cry, and I'd feel gross.

Months went by before I asked my mother if I could stop visitation rights. I hated the way I felt around my father. I hated cleaning his house, kissing him, hugging him, being touched by him, hearing his voice, and smelling his cologne. I wanted it all to be over. She called him and said, "It's what she told me, Ted. She doesn't want to see you." I waited for her to talk again after a long pause. "I'll figure out something to do with her." I could hear so much irritation in her voice. "Ted, the courts are on my side, and she is old enough now." I stared at my mother, envying her strength, trying to absorb it. "Don't you yell at me! I don't need this!" And my mother hung up the phone.

"Is he mad?" I asked.

"Yes, Laura. He is upset," she replied.

"I'm sorry, Mom."

I saw my father's car everywhere after that. And I second-guessed myself. *Was my mind playing tricks on me?*

Was it him? What did he want with me? He had lost another partner, and he didn't like it. I was sure that I saw his car parked in the driveway next to my bus stop; I know I saw it following the bus to school; and I definitely saw it parked outside our apartment. I could see an outline of the person in the driver's seat, but I could never get a good look at his face through the tinted windows.

"Mom, I think I keep seeing Dad's car everywhere," I admitted one day.

"You can't be serious. He's not stalking you, Laura. Don't be silly," she said as she rolled her eyes. "You're just trying to get attention, and I'm sick of it." She walked into her bedroom, and I followed her.

"But I just saw it this morning in that church parking lot, next to my bus stop!" I explained. "It makes me nervous, Mom."

"Okay, well, let me know if you see it again."

"But I've seen it many times. I really think it's Dad. I think he's mad at me because I'm not visiting him anymore." I tried to get her to understand how scared I felt.

"Did you get the license plate number?" she asked, flatly, unconcerned.

"No, I didn't," I said.

"Well, if it happens again, write down the license plate."

"Fine," I said. My worries continued. *What if he grabbed me the next time? I had to protect myself by never walking around alone. And I needed to figure out ways to stay hidden.*

The next day, my mother told me that she talked to the local police about my concerns. She explained that if I got scared or saw his car again, I needed to call 911 and hide the phone; they would link my phone number to a report and come right away.

I learned from my friend's father, a cop, that police officers never agreed to setups like that. He told my friend to tell me to never be alone, always watch over my shoulder, and constantly stay aware of my surroundings at all times. He also told me to write down the license plate number and call the police immediately if I ever saw his car again.

"I can't believe you told your dad," I yelled at my friend after she shared this information. "I don't want anyone to know about this shit! I can't trust you!"

"I was worried, and I thought my dad could help," my friend explained with an unsteady voice. She reached out to touch my arm. I pulled away, gave her the meanest look I could muster, and walked away without saying another word.

She followed me in between classes every day after that, apologizing over and over again. Impatient and annoyed by the attention she brought toward me, I knew of only one way to stop her. Suddenly, I got in her face. She looked at me with fear and sadness in her eyes. "I just want to help. You shouldn't be alone so much. I didn't mean to make things worse," she said.

"It's okay. I just don't want anyone to know this stuff. It's embarrassing," I said, as I looked around to make sure no one could hear us.

"You have nothing to be embarrassed about. It's not your fault," she said.

I felt puke burn the back of my throat.

I smirked, sighed, and swallowed the puke before I said, "When your parents, the two people who are supposed to love you no matter what, don't even like you, then why the hell would anyone else? It's humiliating." I turned around and walked away before she could reply. I felt tears burn the corners of my eyes, and I needed to hide. *Never let them see you weak. Never let the tears fall.*

"I'm sorry, Laura," she yelled down the hall.

"It's okay. I'll talk to you later," I yelled back.

11
keeping the secrets

My mother drove me to her mother's house on most weekends. "I don't know else what to do with you, Laura. You're so unhappy and miserable to be around. And now you even refuse to go to your dad's."

"But why can't I just stay home?" I asked.

"You're too young to be home by yourself at night, and I want to go out. I want to have a life!" she exclaimed.

Grandma Ellen called me, "Pippi" in response my third-grade class photo. Because of my buck teeth, I refused to show my teeth when I smiled. Between my goofy grin and my long reddish-blonde braids down the sides of my face, I was told I looked just like Pippi Longstocking.

At my Grandma Ellen's house, "shut the lights" meant to turn off the lights; and "tall person" referred to me, even though I was under five feet tall. She would call out for a tall person when she needed something on the top shelf in the kitchen. "Lou, Car, Con, Lor." She'd call out the first syllable of many names before finally getting to mine. She had nine children and fifteen grandchildren, and all of their names came to mind when she needed to speak to someone. My grandfather stayed in his recliner watching TV, oblivious to it all.

My grandmother didn't use potholders. "It takes too long," she'd say. She'd grab a hot pot right off the stove and then whistle a funny tune while she carried it to where it needed to go. It was as if whistling made the burning hurt less.

"Hey, Grandma!" I'd call out.

"Whatcha want, Laura?" she'd ask as she rubbed her burnt hands together.

"Is that a hot pot?" The answer was obvious, but asking anyway always made her laugh.

"Yeah, Laura. Yeah it is." She'd giggle and nod.

My grandmother showed me how to make various crafts and art projects. She knew how to make beautiful, three-dimensional designs out of small slivers of paper and sell them at church fairs. She could siphon out all of the liquid from the inside of eggs, and then paint intricate designs on the eggshells. She'd turn them into Christmas ornaments. She taught me how to crochet and work with various mediums. She set up a miniature art studio in the basement of their home. I once doodled the words *Never Never Never Give Up!* in a fancy font on a piece of notebook paper. My grandmother taped it to the refrigerator.

"Grandma, why are you throwing out all of that food?" I asked her, as she dumped out a pot of mashed potatoes after dinner one evening.

"Grandpa doesn't eat leftovers," she replied.

"Oh, I'll eat them. Please don't throw away food." I couldn't believe it. How could she waste all of that delicious food?

"I'll keep it then. But if you don't eat it tomorrow, he'll get upset and throw it out," she warned me.

"Okay, I'll eat it tomorrow. Don't worry," I reassured her.

They both expressed disappointment in me for ending my visits with my father. "Well, he doesn't beat you, so what's the problem?" my grandfather asked. I looked into his eyes, and I wanted to say so much. I knew the family secrets, and he was one to talk about abusing children. My grandmother would say, "He is your father. He deserves respect and unconditional love. It's what God wants."

I stayed silent. I couldn't tell them my secrets. I loved feeling safe at their house. I also knew I couldn't share with them how my father treated me. They would use their religion as an excuse to be angry with me for not honoring my father, unconditionally. "All he wants is love" is what I imagined them saying, and it made me sick.

My grandparents rented the first floor of a three-story house. I slept on the couch in the living room, but I did my best to stay awake so I wouldn't have any accidents. My grandmother always watched *The Golden*

Girls in the living room before she went to bed. A light blue curtain separated their bedroom from the living room.

My cousin, Donna, moved into my grandparents' house around this time. She had run away from her mom's home in Texas, and she had nowhere to go. She was seventeen, and I was twelve. We quickly became close friends. We shared the pull-out sofa bed in the living room, and we talked and laughed until way past my bedtime each night.

One night, I slept too hard. I woke up on the sofa bed in the middle of urinating. Sweat soaked my forehead and upper lip, and I trembled in fear. I desperately planned a way to hide my mess. I quietly picked up my overnight bag and scurried to the bathroom to clean myself. I changed my clothes quickly, and I searched the bathroom for anything that could help me cover up what I had done. I needed to keep my secret. I couldn't bare having anyone else think of me as a failure.

I grabbed some toilet paper, baby powder, and my cousin's hair dryer. Donna slept like a rock. If I kept the dryer on low, she probably wouldn't hear it. If I could get the bedding a little bit dry and put powder on it to cover the smell, I could get through the night. I would just have to get up before everyone else and wash the sheets first thing in the morning. I couldn't do anything about the cushions. I just hoped no one ever noticed the smell.

I snuck back out to the living room. The television blared, so I had some noise to cover up what I was about to do. I dabbed toilet paper onto the wet sheets to absorb as much moisture as I could. I found an electrical outlet behind the end table next to my pillow. I plugged in the hair dryer and coughed to cover up any of my noise.

I turned the dryer on low. Donna moved a little, but she stayed asleep. I kept the dryer on one spot for several minutes and held my breath. *If I took a breath, she'd wake up*, I thought to myself. It felt like an eternity. I dried the wet spot on the sheets a little bit and turned off the dryer. I reached behind the table and unplugged the dryer, being careful not to make any noise. I gently placed the dryer behind the couch. *I'll deal with that tomorrow*, I thought. I shook some baby powder into my hands and spread it onto the sheets.

"What's that noise?" Donna asked, sounding alarmed. She must have heard me shaking the baby powder canister.

"I can't find the remote. Is it on your side?" I asked.

"Oh. Yeah, yeah, it's right here. Here." She handed me the remote, and rolled over.

I turned off the television and sighed. I climbed back into bed, and tried not to think about what I was laying on.

I did not allow myself to sleep again that night. When I started to see the sunrise, I got up before anyone else and returned the hair dryer to the bathroom. I took a quick shower, hoping to get back to the living room before my cousin woke up.

"I'll take care of that, Donna," I said, as I gathered the bedding. Donna was just about to take everything off the pull-out bed, but I beat her to it. "I'm going to wash it if that's okay, Grandma," I asked for permission.

"Of course, dear," she said. My secret stayed safe.

12
in and out

When I was thirteen, my mother decided I was old enough to be home alone overnight. The apartment we lived in was on the second floor of an old house in a nice neighborhood, and I had my own room. The town was much safer, and most people who lived there had a lot of money. Knowing that we lived there, the outside of this house made it look like we had a lot of money as well. But we only rented out a few rooms.

My mother stopped making the trip to my grandmother's house to drop me off. "I don't have time to drive you all the way to your grandmother's house. Are you okay here alone?"

I didn't want to be called a burden anymore, so of course I said, "Yeah, that's fine, Mom. When will you be home?"

"You're not my mother. I'll be home when I get home," she said, and she left. I'd count the days and sometimes weeks that would go by before I saw even a hint of my mother's presence at home. I'd look around for moved objects, used shampoo, dirty clothes in her hamper, eaten food, or extra food in the fridge. I know she took trips with her boyfriends and girlfriends. She'd sometimes offer to invite me if I did something grand for her, but I was never allowed to go, no matter what I did. It felt as though she enjoyed holding things like vacations, or even braces to fix my buck teeth, over my head to get me to do tricks just like a dog. I heard her once say that she was taking a three-week trip on a motorcycle up to the top of a mountain. Sometimes I'd get worried about her and call the local bars to try to track her down. "Is there anyone there named Cara?" I'd ask the bartender.

"Cara? Is there a Cara here?" I'd hear him yell out, away from the phone. "No, miss, no Cara here. Is that your mom?"

I'd hang up quickly, feeling completely embarrassed.

One time she was home, and I asked to try on one of her dresses. She asked me which one, and I described the black dress with the rhinestones on the straps. She brought it out of her bedroom and said, "sure!"

I ran to the bathroom and put on her tight, black dress. It fit me perfectly. I felt like I was becoming a woman, and I wanted to be sexy and exciting like my mother. I walked out into the living room. My mother was sitting on the couch, and she looked up at me. Her mouth opened, and she exclaimed, "Laura, oh my god. You look…. I hate you! You can't wear that dress out in public."

My smile changed to a frown. I couldn't tell if she was impressed by how I looked or horrified. "What do you mean?" I asked her.

"With that body, you have to keep yourself covered up. You're only fourteen! No man will respect you if you wear clothes like that," she explained.

"Sorry, mom. I thought it would be fun."

"Take off that dress," she demanded.

I did as I was told, and I put my jeans and baggy gray sweatshirt back on.

I always feared she'd come home unexpectedly and scream and yell at me for not cleaning the kitchen or doing my laundry correctly. I didn't cook properly, either. When she had asked for help with dinner, I'd try so hard. I'd chop vegetables just the way she liked them, but I always made her angry. They weren't the same shape. They weren't the right shape. Or, I wasn't fast enough. I hated being in the kitchen with my mother.

One day she surprised me after she hadn't been home in a few weeks. She walked into the kitchen and found dirty dishes soaking in the sink from some baked beans and creamed corn I had eaten for dinner the night before. Canned food had become my comfort.

"You left dishes in the sink. I hate it when you leave dishes in the sink. Clean those!" she snapped.

I ran into the kitchen, turned on the water, and waited for it to get hot. "They were soaking, that's all," I said.

"How long do you possibly need them to soak for. Days, weeks? You better use the dish bucket!"

"Ma, it's faster this way. I'll be done in a second." I scrubbed quickly, and kept my head down to hide my red face.

I heard her open the fridge, and then she slammed the door so hard that it partially came off the hinges. Several things fell out of fridge door shelves and crashed onto the white and green tile floor. I turned around and caught her staring at the mess in shock. "Clean that up!" she yelled, and she went into her room to pack more clothes.

I picked up the larger pieces of glass and threw them in the garbage. I used paper towels to pick up glass shards and wipe up some maple syrup. I looked up at the broken door, unsure of how to fix it. I breathed in and out hard, heavy. *How dare she come into my home, get angry about how I cooked my food, and then make a mess in my kitchen?* I thought. I couldn't catch my breath. I didn't want to. I wanted to breathe as hard as I could, as fast as I could, in and out, for as long as possible.

"Why are you using paper towels? That's so wasteful, Laura!" she hollered, as she walked out of her bedroom and into the bathroom. I continued to breathe intensely, unwilling to calm myself.

"I didn't want to ruin the kitchen towels!" I yelled back.

"The towels can be washed! You're just wasting everything!" she screamed and slammed the bathroom door.

"There's glass everywhere, too!" I yelled back, louder.

"Don't talk back to me!" she shouted from inside the bathroom.

I used paper towels to finish cleaning the glass, maple syrup, and relish that had spilled. I dried my clean dishes with a towel and put everything away. I moved quickly, and my breath weighed a ton. I swayed, saw white spots, and the room started to go black. I had to sit down and calm myself, but I needed to finish cleaning up before she came back into the kitchen. I risked it, knowing that if she caught me sitting when the mess wasn't completely cleaned up that I'd be in serious trouble. I tried to sit down at the kitchen table to catch my breath. But I didn't make it that far, and I collapsed onto the floor in a sluggish pile of limbs. I lay still for a moment and then worked to get myself in a sitting position leaning against the cabinet. I heard my mother moving around in the bathroom. I didn't have much time to sit here safely. I took long breaths and started counting slowly to a hundred. I focused on the numbers and my breathing. The room stopped spinning, and my vision slowly returned to normal. My heart raced as I stared at the broken refrigerator door. I spotted the screw that must have dislodged lying several feet away near the pantry door.

I heard her turn off the bathroom water. "Laura, it's just dishes. She'll be gone in a few minutes. Slow your breathing," I whispered to myself, and I counted to a hundred silently again. I stood up before my mother entered the kitchen. I reached into the hall closet to find a screwdriver to fix the fridge door. I held the door up with the side of my foot and screwed in the broken hinge. It held.

My mother left as I walked back into the living room to continue my homework. I had recently missed a couple of days of school due to migraines, and I had to teach myself some math problems for a test the next day. I vaguely noticed that my mother was carrying another suitcase with her when she left. My chest and head hurt. I stared at the math problem, looked up the answer in the back of my textbook, and worked to connect the two.

I found out the next day at school that my closest friend, Chrissy, had seen my mother's car in town before our argument about the dishes.

"I tried to find you. Are you okay?" Chrissy said to me as we waited in the hall between classes.

"What do you mean?" I asked her.

"I saw your mom's car on Main Street, and I knew she hadn't been around in a while. I know you guys don't get along, so I wanted to tell you I saw her. When I spotted her car in her parking space, I knew I was too late to warn you. I'm sorry," she explained.

"It's okay, Chrissy. Thank you for trying," I said to reassure her.

"Did you guys argue?" she asked.

"A little, not really, no big deal." I brushed it off. Whatever.

13
betrayal

My seventh grade English teacher gave our class an inspiring assignment one day. She asked us to choose an adjective that described our life, and then write for twenty minutes explaining why. Mrs. Golden did not give us any time to plan our composition. She called it a "free writing" session and described it as a way to strengthen our creative writing skills without overthinking.

Without considering the consequences of sharing my thoughts with my teacher, I chose the adjective "stressed." I then wrote faster than I had ever written before, describing how scary, tense, sad, dangerous, and lonely my life outside of school had become. I wrote about how unloved, unimportant, and unwanted I was by my parents no matter how hard I tried to earn their love. I felt alone at school, because I didn't have many friends. I stayed quiet and kept my secrets to myself. As the timer went off, I realized that my neat handwriting had transformed into scribbles. I had written six pages. I suddenly did not want to turn in my paper, but I wanted credit for my work. I wouldn't do anything to jeopardize my "A" average in English. I hid my assignment in the middle of the pile of papers on Mrs. Golden's desk, and I tried my best to forget about what I revealed to my teacher. I predicted that she would corner me after class one day to make sure I was okay. I prepared my response and tucked it away in the back of my mind.

Three days later, I woke up with a horrible migraine. My mother was home for some strange reason, so I yelled, "Mom, I have to stay home from school. I have another migraine." I sat on the bathroom floor, leaned over the toilet, and waited to vomit.

"Okay," she yelled back to me from her bedroom.

"Will you call the school, please?" I reminded my mother. "I don't want my grades to go down."

Many of my teachers deducted a percentage point from our grades for every unexcused absence. And my mother forgot to call the school to excuse my absence several times that year. Add that to the mornings when she was nowhere to be found to call, and some of my grades were being affected.

"Yes," she yelled back, sounding annoyed.

I stayed in bed that day alternating a heating pad and an ice pack on my head, neck, and face. I attempted to find relief from the sharp, throbbing pain and nausea. A battle played out in my mind about how to calm my stomach. Would food make it better, or would it make me vomit? I tasted metal, and my belly gurgled. My migraines lasted anywhere from a few hours to a few weeks at a time. I focused on breathing in and out until the pain subsided or I fell asleep.

The next morning, I woke up without a migraine, and I sighed in relief. Then I smiled, feeling energetic and lighter than air. I always felt the urge to celebrate when one of my migraines dissipated. I went to school, paced myself to not trigger a relapse, and cycled through my classes. I noticed several classmates who had never acknowledged my existence say "hi" to me as I walked the halls.

"Hi, Laura," the beautiful, popular girl said to me as she smiled and walked by my locker.

I shyly waved in response.

"Hi," a cute boy, named Billy, said as he looked in my direction. I looked around to be sure he was talking to me, and smiled in return. He smiled.

Something felt different; people noticed me. I didn't feel invisible anymore. I never thought anyone would pay attention to my baggy clothes, worn-out shoes, and hunched back. Suddenly, it felt as if I was under a spotlight.

After English class, Mrs. Golden asked to speak with me. She stared at me. She was a short, brunette woman who wore different stylish glasses almost every day. Then I remembered my writing assignment. *Shit*, I thought. She must have read it, and she wanted to check on me. I deeply regretted sharing some of my secrets.

I looked her in the eye and snarled, "What?"

"Laura, I read your paper. And I wanted to talk to you for a few minutes," she began. My insides vibrated with unease, and I started to feel sweat on my forehead, upper lip, and back. I dropped my heavy backpack on the floor and waited for her to continue. "It sounds like you are very stressed out about your home life and some things at school. And I wanted to help." She paused. My heart pounded so hard that I felt my shirt moving. "I did something, and I really hope you don't get angry with me. I did it with the best of intentions, to help you feel a little less stress, and a little less alone."

"What did you do?" I stiffened my stance into my boxer pose, ready to strike.

"You wrote about not having many friends in addition to all of the stress that you are dealing with at home. You are handling your stress very maturely, and, well, I thought if people knew more about you, maybe they could help you, and be there for you." I heard regret in her rambling, and I sensed that she was worried about my reaction.

"What do you mean? What did you do?" My voice was stronger and harsher.

"I read your paper to the class," she blurted out.

My jaw dropped, my legs went numb, and the room spun. "You did what?" I raised my voice. Tears of fury filled my eyes. People in school now knew some of my secrets. Those who had said hello to me all day did so because they felt sorry for me, not because they liked me. I never wanted this. I did not want pity. I wanted to be treated like I didn't exist. I buried it all every single day and protected my parents. The strength inside me always masked my pain, sadness, and anger. And I worked hard to keep it that way. As soon as I shared a glimpse of my life with Mrs. Golden, she ruined everything.

"I'm sorry. I should have asked you first." Mrs. Golden's voice sounded incredibly small for an adult. She knew that invading my privacy was unforgivable. I knew I could destroy her in this moment.

I thought for several seconds, and took a deep breath before I said, "Thank you for telling me. You should have asked me. I would have said 'no.' I know you were trying to help. Please don't talk about it anymore—hopefully everyone will forget." I walked out of the room silently. That day, I decided to never talk about any of it to anyone.

I could handle it all myself.

14
uphill battle

Roseanne Smart, a social worker with an office in the town hall about a mile from my apartment, had her work cut out for her now. I visited her weekly, and she was determined to get me to talk about my feelings. I resisted and refused with all my might.

My mother forced me to see Roseanne because I depressed her. She described my bad attitude as abnormal and no fun to be around. "All you do is feel sorry for yourself all the time," she'd say constantly. "You're just like your father. You need help, or your life will be just as miserable and lonely as his."

I knew that what I really needed was room to tap into my strength without being beaten down with every step. I felt this core of resilience and determination deep within myself. I just didn't know how to access it.

But I knew I was changing. I stopped hunching my back when I walked. I started wearing make-up and styling my hair based on what the teen magazines advised. I also knew that I was nothing like my father. Fuck him.

"It's close enough that you can walk there. You have to go there once or twice a week. Do you hear me?" My mother persisted.

I acknowledged her words, but I did not speak.

Roseanne had short curly brown hair, and she was a few inches taller than my mother. She was a little heavier than my mother, and she exuded confidence and warmth. She continued to ask me how it felt to have a jerk for a father. "Your dad is the king of jerkdomhood," she announced one day. I looked into her eyes for the first time and felt the corners of my mouth turn into a small smile.

"That's not even a word!" I responded, laughing slightly.

"I know, but it makes sense. It's his official title. How about that?" she decided.

"Okay," I agreed.

"So, how does it feel?" Roseanne would never quit.

All I could ever say in reply to any questions about feelings was, "I'm pissed off." Any other *feeling* word made me nauseous, and I would sometimes vomit in her garbage can. "I'm so sorry," I'd say after getting sick. Usually, not much food would come out, just air. I couldn't handle talking about feelings or needs.

During our visits, Roseanne would push and then ease off in getting me to talk about my emotions, dreams, or opinions. Then she'd wait a while and push again in a different way. I figured out her game, and I had no interest in playing. After a few months of a lot of silence and the occasional small talk, Roseanne tried a different tactic. She pulled out a deck of cards and asked if I knew how to play.

"Yeah, my dad and I used to play," I answered.

"What games do you know?" she asked.

"Poker, Setback, Gin, Gin Rummy…that's about it," I replied.

"How about we play some Gin?" she asked.

"Sounds good," I said with excitement, because I knew it would take the pressure off from talking.

"So, what was it like playing cards with your dad?" she asked.

"Well, he cheated a lot," I said.

"He cheated! How?" she asked. Her voice stayed passive.

"Oh, he would cover up the suit of the card so it looked like they were all the same, like this." I covered up one card with another, revealing only the number in the corner, so that the suit of the bottom card was unseen. "It was stupid, though; I could tell," I said.

"What did you say when you noticed this?" she asked, hardly sounding interested.

"I'd say, 'You're cheating, Dad!' And I would move the card."

"Then what would happen?" she asked.

"He'd yell and throw the cards across the room. Another time, he started to cry because he was embarrassed. I had to comfort him with a long hug."

"So, you caught him twice?"

"No, I caught him all the time. I just only mentioned it twice. After he cried about it, I stopped saying anything. I didn't like it when he cried. It made my stomach hurt. Disgusting, you know?"

"Disgusting. Why was it disgusting? That's an unusual word."

"I don't know. It just was," I said. I suddenly felt wide open, like she knew everything. I always had a strange sensation in my stomach whenever I thought about my father crying. He cried a lot, usually because he missed my mom. And then I would have to comfort him.

"Can we talk about something else?" I asked.

"Of course! Did you play other games when you were younger?" she asked.

"No. Well, sometimes I did at the babysitter's house. One of the babysitter's houses was really nice. Her name was Barbara. I only played once in a while, because I liked helping her with cleaning and cooking. The other babysitter's house wasn't as nice. She didn't like me," I said.

"What do you mean?"

"She said I was too hyper and that I distracted the other kids from doing their homework. She kicked me out of her house and told my mom I had to stop going there." I frowned, recalling what it felt like to be hated by another adult.

"What happened then?" Roseanne asked. It hadn't dawned on me that she had tricked me into talking while we played cards.

"Nothing," I replied.

"Nothing? Where did you go after school after the second babysitter stopped letting you go to her house?" she asked. She delicately dug for more information.

"She hated me. My mother was mad at me. I just went home after school."

"Alone?" She stopped dealing the cards for just a second. I pretended not to notice.

"Yes, it was no big deal. I was a mature kid, you know. And on weekends, I would go to my grandmother's house, so I wouldn't be alone at night," I explained, defending my mother, as usual.

"I know. I can see that you are very mature for your age. You are more mature than a lot of adults."

"Thanks," I said.

"It's not your fault, Laura," Roseanne said.

"Whatever," I said with the typical teenager tone. I tasted vomit and my back tightened.

"Do you trust me?" Roseanne asked.

"No," I said, as I placed my cards down. "Gin!" I yelled.

"Well, maybe someday you will. Let's keep playing cards." She retreated.

"Okay," I said.

From that day on, we played cards every week. Roseanne would sneak in her questions. She would repeat the phrase "it's not your fault" often. And it always annoyed me and made me feel sick. She'd quickly change the subject each time. But she wouldn't give up.

After seeing her for a couple of years, she started to

notice that I talked more and more negatively about my mother. I hated being alone all the time, especially at night. I missed my mother.

"How often does your mom go out?" Roseanne asked.

"Almost every night. Sometimes I don't see her for a week or two," I responded. At this point, I trusted Roseanne more.

"Have you told her that you miss her?" Roseanne asked.

"Yes, well kinda. I told her that I don't like being alone. She gets upset, like I'm holding her back. She says that since I'm finally old enough, she can do what she wants."

"But you're only fourteen."

"Yeah, I know. It's fine, though. I've gotten pretty used to it. Except for at night. I don't sleep well, and every noise scares me. And then I really can't sleep. So, I put bottles and cans in front of the door so that I'd hear someone come in if they opened the door," I explained.

"Do you know where she stays at night?"

"I used to not know. But now I think she's staying with her boyfriend, Pete. She's moved most of her clothes there."

"Does she come home to see you after work, or before school—anytime—just to check on you?"

"No, she hardly ever comes home at all. And I never know when she will."

"What happens when she does come home?"

"We usually argue."

"About what?"

"Everything. Stupid things. She says that teenagers are just hard to live with. But that just pisses me off, because she doesn't really live with one anymore."

"I can imagine that hearing her say that would make you feel both angry and hurt," she said.

"Well, yeah. I guess."The nausea returned.

"Do you have enough food?" Roseanne asked me on another day.

"Yes, I have enough money from my job to eat Subway sandwiches after school," I replied. I had started working at the pharmacy in town a few weeks before my fifteenth birthday. It felt great to have some money to buy the things I needed, especially food. I continued, "And there's always plenty of vodka in the freezer." I laughed.

"You don't drink that stuff, do you?" she asked. I expected a more serious tone from her about the subject.

"Nah. It's pretty awful," I lied.

"And what do you eat for dinner?"

"I eat at work—usually just something in the pharmacy, like chips or crackers. They're cheap, and we get a discount!" I bragged. I learned how to make my money last. I found a thrift store a few miles away, where I could buy used clothes for very little money. I was proud of myself.

"What do you eat for breakfast, or at school for lunch?" Her questions started to get under my skin.

I shifted in my seat and grumbled, "No breakfast. I eat tater tots for lunch. They're only a dollar."

"Do you have food in your fridge or your cupboard at

home?" she asked.

"Nah, not really. But I'm fine," I said, getting nervous. I didn't want my mother to get in trouble, and I had already said too much.

I often thought of my friends' kitchen cupboards. I remembered seeing my friend Brenda's kitchen. The kitchen was about the size of my apartment, but that wasn't impressive to me. There were three huge cabinets full of food. We were hanging out after school one day, and her mother asked us what we wanted for an afterschool snack. I remember telling her that I wasn't hungry. Then she opened cabinet after cabinet, full of food, and my eyes lit up. Brenda's mom noticed my reaction and asked, "Don't you have food at home?"

I replied, "Of course I do—just not this much." Brenda's mom insisted on giving me a box of cereal and some crackers to take home. I was so embarrassed that I never returned to Brenda's house. I knew her mother could see through my lie.

"Come with me," Roseanne said, as she stood up abruptly.

"Where are we going?" My voice shook noticeably, and my body stiffened in the chair.

"Not far," she replied.

"In this building? Do we have to go outside?" I asked.

"Nope, we're just going down the hall and down the stairs," she explained. I had never been in the hallway, since she had a separate entrance to her office within the building.

I stood up and followed her to the basement level of

the town hall. We continued down a long, dark hallway.

I looked around in fear. *What happens in the rooms down here?* I thought to myself.

We entered a small room that was full of food. Jam-packed bags of canned and boxed food filled the shelves and littered the floor. It looked like a disorganized grocery store storage room.

"Take anything you want," Roseanne said. She took two steps away from me, relaxed her arms to her sides, and stopped moving.

"What? What do you mean? What is all this?" So many questions popped into my mind at once.

"This is donated food, for anyone who needs it. You are welcome to take as much as you want."

"But I don't need anything. I told you, I'm fine." My insides shook with embarrassment and fear. I had made her believe I needed food, when I didn't need help from anyone. What had I done?

"I know you're doing very well for yourself, Laura. You are very resourceful. You've found your own ways to take care of yourself. And you're doing an excellent job. But wouldn't it be easier if you had some food at home?" She sounded very convincing.

"Well, yeah. But my mother would be pissed if she knew I took food." I looked around and spotted some of my favorite foods, and the temptation began.

"Just tell her it's to help her out, too. Tell her you know that her bills are really high in this town, and that I just wanted to help her and you in any way I could. Do you see any food that you like?"

I hesitated, unsure if I believed her story. I worried that my mother wouldn't believe her story. Then I spotted my favorite cereal. The more I looked around, the more I wanted. This room was full of comfort food. My eyes must have lit up a little, because Roseanne said again, "Take as much as you want."

"Really? Are you sure it's okay?" I asked.

"Laura, this is a very rich town. There are not a lot of people around here who need free food, but there are a lot of people who can afford to donate. You can have first choice, and we can come down here every week if you want. How does that sound?" She was right. The people living in this town had a lot of money, and I didn't fit in at all. After living in a lot of poor neighborhoods, I called living in this town "culture shock."

"I'll just take some today. I don't want to get in trouble," I said.

I filled five bags of groceries that day. It weighed too much to carry on the five-block walk home. Roseanne offered to drive me to my apartment. We loaded the groceries into the back of her compact car, and she took me home. I carried the groceries upstairs and unloaded them quickly. Maybe my mother wouldn't be home for a couple of weeks and she would never know, I hoped.

I got away with getting free food for several months before my mother found out. When she asked, I told her the line that I had rehearsed with Roseanne several times: "Roseanne said she knows it's expensive to live here, and she wanted to help us in any way she could," I said, confidently. Practicing this response with Roseanne helped me stay strong.

"Oh. Okay. I just feel like I'm abandoning you or something," my mother said.

I didn't respond. She had used the right words, but she never changed her behavior.

I continued to bring home free food every week until I finished high school. It helped me tremendously, just like Roseanne said it would. I always had something to eat when I got home from school, before work, and after work before I went to bed. My life began to change for the better, slightly. I noticed that I slept a little bit better, and I woke up with headaches less often.

I mastered techniques for staying safe in every situation. I still needed to hide from my father. While I hadn't seen his car in a few months, it would appear on and off for almost two years. I never knew when or if he would be back.

I learned to time it so I got to the bus stop as close to when the bus arrived as possible, in order to avoid being alone outside for very long each morning. I sat near the front of the bus on the way to school, so I'd be hidden from any cars that followed us. Also, this made it easier to blend in with the other kids when we got off the bus and entered school together. In between classes, I always walked with friends, especially if I needed to change buildings.

Everything scared me. Being away from an adult for too long scared me the most. I ate lunch with a teacher, so I could be near an adult in case anything dangerous happened. I made sure that I never followed the same routine, at the same time, for too many days in a row. The more unpredictable and unseen that I was, the safer I felt.

After school every day, I ran to the bus. While on the bus ride home, my strategy changed from the morning ride, since I had to get off the bus alone. I chose to sit a few rows from the back, so I could survey the cars that followed us. I talked and laughed with my friends and acted like a normal teenager.

When I exited the bus, I would run inside my apartment. Or, I would take the bus to Chrissy's house so that I'd have company for a few hours. However, this meant that I'd then have to brave the walk home alone later. I left her house at different times, to not set a pattern, which confused my friend.

After I entered my apartment, I'd lock the door and then pile bottles and cans in front of it. If someone managed to open the door, the bottles would fall, and the noise would alert me to the intruder. To prevent getting into trouble with my mother for my mess, I'd move everything before the time she'd normally come home from work. I'd wait an hour or two. If she didn't show up, I'd restack the bottles and cans in front of the door.

I carried the phone with me everywhere even if it meant stretching out the cord, in case I needed to call 911. All of my plans and experience created a sense of safety and security. But if something out of the ordinary occurred, I panicked.

"Is everything okay, Laura?" Mr. Keller asked me during lunch one day, while he graded papers. I ate my food quietly and helped him with his work when permitted.

"What do you mean?" I asked, while eating my dollar tater tots.

"Is everything okay at home?"

"Sure, of course!" I said.

"You can talk to a school counselor if you ever want to, you know," he offered.

"I know." I shared nothing. The thought of saying anything caused my stomach to turn and my body to sweat all over. I barely trusted Roseanne. Confiding in another adult mortified me.

One day, after entering my apartment and setting up the bottles, my mother unpredictably came home. I hadn't seen her in a while, so I had stopped putting everything away.

"Laura, what the hell is this?" my mother yelled after she opened the door quickly and knocked over the bottles.

I ran into the kitchen. "I left bottles there in case anyone broke in," I explained.

"You're ridiculous, Laura. No one is going to break in. Stop being so paranoid. It's stupid," she said, as she slammed the door. "You're always trying to get attention," she yelled.

I cleaned up my mess and didn't say another word.

I looked out the window and watched her car leave again. I reset the bottles.

I peered out the window often to see if anyone lurked outside. I checked doors and windows several times a day to make sure they were locked. I looked over my shoulder everywhere I went. I secretly wished I had a mirror that I could hold up over my shoulder to see people who may be approaching me from behind.

I hated being alone, which became more and more common. I searched for my father's car, but I stopped seeing it. *Was I mistaken? Was it all in my head? Was I just trying to get attention?*

Second guessing is dangerous, I thought. *No one needs to know what you're doing. No one would understand.*

15
uncovered tracks

Throughout college at the University of Connecticut, I was terrified to be alone. I moved in with my boyfriend, Matt, immediately after graduating high school. If he was out too late at night, I'd panic and lash out in anger. I studied Graphic Design, which meant spending a lot of hours in the various art studios on campus. Sometimes I'd be stuck in a studio until after dark, desperately trying to finish my work as quickly as possible. Working in the photography dark-room scared me the most—especially when I was alone. Every noise made my heart jump.

As an adult, safety stayed a priority and a constant obsession. When Matt graduated, we moved as far away from Connecticut as possible. I never told my father that I moved to Washington. However, I found out that he knew the date and town in Connecticut where Matt and I would be married. For protection, we hired undercover police officers who dressed in nice suits to look like wedding guests, in case he showed up. I never knew if he came or not. I figured it would be painful either way.

I never told my father my new name after I got married, and I covered my tracks well. I desperately wanted to stop worrying. I wanted to stop having an escape plan in every environment. But nothing could change these habits. The logical side of my brain said, "You have moved three thousand miles from all the dangerous people in your life," but this did nothing to change the concrete, obsessive, desperate actions of the scared little girl who still controlled my mind. I hated her.

When I went to a restaurant, I needed to be able to see the exit. In each of the apartments I lived in, I always had an escape plan if someone broke in. I felt jumpy and tense when I couldn't see the front door, and I checked it often to make sure it was locked. If I lived in a ground-floor apartment, I never opened the windows, and I'd put an extra security bar in each of them to block them from opening. If I lay in bed and stared at my bedroom door for too long, I could convince myself that I saw a shadow of a man walking down the hallway, and I'd freeze in a pool of sweat. When I went grocery shopping, I always planned what I would do if someone became violent. I outlined my choices in my mind: run, hide, scream, and never stay in a corner for too long. I stayed constantly aware and always on guard.

On and off for years, I felt drawn to reach out to my father. I wanted to hear his voice, to truly forgive him, and discover if we could have a relationship as adults.

What if confronting him was the secret to making myself feel safer, better, and more at ease? I ignored these instincts over and over again, telling myself, *You're insane. After all of the work you did to get away, calling him would ruin everything.*

Then one day, I came home from work, sat on my couch, and draped a warm comforter over my body. I dialed the last phone number I had for my father. I was thirty-one years old, but once the phone began to ring, I immediately felt like a child. The sick feeling in my stomach returned, my back hurt, and I began to sweat. My body shook like a petrified puppy. *You're stronger than this, Laura*, I thought to myself. I tightened my core, took a deep breath, and focused on the texture of the comforter on my fingertips. I tried to ignore my sweaty palms. I threw the blanket off my legs. I felt feverish, like my blood was boiling, as waves of heat engulfed my face, head, and neck.

As the phone rang, I tried to imagine his reaction to hearing my voice. *Would he even believe it's me? Would he be angry? Would he hang up? Would he be happy?* Thanks to years of therapy and supportive friends, I felt wiser, stronger, and more in control than I ever had before.

"Hi, Dad. It's Laura," I announced.

"Laura! How ya doing?" he gasped. The excitement in his voice filled my eyes with tears. My voice vibrated, mirroring the intense emotions and confusion in my heart. I felt unexpectedly safe, which caught me off guard. *Was I making a huge mistake?* I silently asked myself.

"I'm doing okay, Dad. How are you?" And in that

moment, a new relationship with my father began.

"I'm better now," he said. "It's so good to hear your voice. It's a dream come true. It really is," he said. I heard excitement and honesty behind his words. I believed him.

I smiled. "It's good to hear your voice, too. You sound the same. It's cool. Is this a good time to talk?" I asked.

"Of course. You can call me anytime you want. Anytime." He sounded so happy to hear from me. It surprised me that I didn't hear any anger or danger in his voice. The disgusting feeling that I was used to had disappeared.

"So, what's new?" he asked.

"Well, a lot has changed." I began telling him about my life over the previous twelve years, including my wedding, moving around the country, my divorce from Matt, my career, graduate school, and my crazy hobbies. I learned about his family; I was shocked that he and Maria were still married, and his stepdaughters were now in their twenties. He seemed to choose his words very carefully, treating me like a scared cat that was about to bolt at any wrong move.

For several years, we spoke weekly. Some of our honest conversations caused us both intense emotions, but each one led to more and more forgiveness. Mostly, we talked about daily activities and the weather. Ted always loved to ask about the weather. We discussed the past, and he apologized for being a scary and bad father. We didn't discuss any specific memories—I think we were both too terrified to bring them up. He said he didn't do drugs or drink anymore, and that he had quit six years earlier. I sighed with relief, and a huge weight disappeared from inside my heart. I floated and shook intensely when I heard this news.

I apologized for disappearing from his life. He acknowledged that I did what I needed to do to move forward. We forgave each other and agreed to start fresh. Neither of us cried, but we started to understand each other in a new way.

Five years after making that first phone call, I visited my father. My boyfriend, Mike, and I traveled from Seattle to New Hampshire to see his family for Christmas. Since his family lived only a few hours' driving distance away, I conjured up the courage to see Ted for the first time in almost sixteen years. And since I hadn't visited my mother in a very long time, I thought it would be nice to see her as well. I decided to visit both of my parents in one day and keep both visits short. I did not tell my mother my plans; I had never even told her that her ex-husband, my father, lived only a few miles from her house.

When I told friends about how close my parents lived from one another, inevitably someone would ask, "And they don't know it?"

"Nope."

"What if they run into each other in the grocery store or something?" they'd ask.

"World War III would start," I'd respond while chuckling. "Actually, who knows if they would even recognize each other."

The night before our three-hour drive from New

Hampshire to Connecticut, I couldn't stop bouncing my leg or biting my nails. I wanted to drink a lot of wine, but I stopped myself after two glasses. I wanted to share with Mike's family how anxious I felt, but I didn't want to be a burden. I didn't want to seem needy or weird. I sat in a blue chair with my legs draped over the side, and did my best to be social, positive, and charming. I took two melatonin and tried to sleep, but I tossed and turned all night. I tried to picture my father's face. I wondered if he would still have the same blue-green-gray colored eyes like mine. I envisioned his soft, brown hair puffed up on top of his head. I could still smell his horrible sweet, musty cologne.

The next morning, I didn't speak much. When I did talk, my words were brief, even harsh. I wanted to get on the road, and nothing else mattered. Time stalled no matter how hard I pushed. "Let's just go!" I said to Mike. I had lost the ability to be pleasant and funny.

He said, "I'm coming." He stomped his feet as he carried his shoes into the living room. I hated the sound of feet stomping; as a child, this equaled noise, and noise equaled punishment. Mike drove his mother's car, knowing that my emotional state would distract me from driving safely. Simply being near Mike was comforting. When I first met him, I was immediately attracted to his dark eyes, fantastic smile, lean and athletic build, and his sporty but mature style. But the biggest draw was the calming effect his presence, his voice, and his touch had on me. I felt safe around Mike immediately. While it took some time, I learned that I could be myself completely around him.

We traveled to my mother's house first. I remembered the place well, despite having spent minimal time there in high school. When my mother left me, she moved here, to a small hunting lodge with her boyfriend, Pete. Pete had winterized the cabin so that it could be lived in year-round. The dark brown wainscoting on the walls made the 1,200-square-foot home feel even smaller. Dead animals and fish mounts that littered the entire home acted as trophies for Pete's hunting achievements. The drawing of Pete's dog that I had made for him as a Christmas gift almost twenty years earlier hung on a wall in the kitchen. I enjoyed seeing her remodeled kitchen. She had installed new cabinets, appliances, and counters. She had changed the kitchen layout completely, and she had a huge closet full of food. "You have a ton of food, Mom!"

"I now have a place to store everything. It's so nice," she explained.

I instantly remembered the bare shelves and empty refrigerator when she lived with me. I steadied my footing and changed the subject.

"Where was the soot when your heater broke?" I already knew the answer, but I asked anyway, since I couldn't think of anything else to talk about.

"It was everywhere! We had cleaners in here for a week to help get rid of it." They had recently replaced their gas fireplace insert after the previous one malfunctioned and covered the entire house in black soot. She told me about it over the phone about a year earlier. It acted as the main heat source for the home.

I rushed us all out to lunch. "I'm hungry!" I announced.

We took two cars, which pissed off my mother. But I insisted. This was my visit, so things would be done my way. My boundaries always upset her. We each ordered a drink and searched the menu. Per my usual, I resorted to humor to overcome the nerves I felt. I looked around the Italian restaurant and saw several large Italian men wearing very expensive suits and watches. "What, is this a mob gathering or something?" I said as a joke.

My mother laughed as she put her finger in front of her mouth and said, "Shhhh, it really might be. Don't say that too loud."

"You're kidding," I said.

"No, not really," she said, and Pete shook his head. We all giggled. I wanted things to be different with my mother so badly. I had all of her good qualities: strength, humor, talent in art and dance, wit, intuition, and people skills. I loved those parts of myself, but I could never let my guard down. Even though Pete and my mother had been together for almost twenty years, he was still a mystery to me. He had kind eyes behind think-framed glasses, and the gray in his soft hair and full beard made him look distinguished. He spoke with intention, he was very smart, and he collected stamps. He was not the epitome of health, surviving on a diet of red meat, buttered food, and Chunky Monkey ice cream. And he had gained quite a bit of weight over the years.

As we all talked cordially, my mother finished her

drink rather quickly. She started slurring her words, and she tried to start an argument with Pete. This surprised Mike, but Pete and I worked on changing the subject to redirect my mother. Pete and I had spent very little time together over the years, so it surprised me that we shared the same techniques for dealing with my mother's mood swings while she drank. She only had one drink, but her behavior changed drastically. I guessed that either she had been drinking that morning or the alcohol was interacting with her medications.

We ordered our food, and I turned to my mother. "Mom, you're acting funny. What's going on?" I asked, trying to put her on the spot so she would calm herself down.

"I'm in a great mood! Isn't life funny?" my mother asked.

"What's funny?" I asked.

"Life, you know. Life! You're here. But you're already trying to leave. Where are you going to take Mike?" Her tone made it clear that she disapproved of our short encounter, and that she felt I owed her a longer visit.

"He's never been to Connecticut, so I thought I'd show him around. And then we have to get his mom's car back to New Hampshire, because a storm is coming," I explained.

"You could just stay here, you know," she said, sounding more and more irritated.

"Thank you for the invitation, Mom. Next time I'll plan some more time to stay. This visit just has to be quick. I hope you understand." I remained calm, and I managed to control the shaking in my voice.

"I guess," she said.

I disappointed her. I knew that the longer we stayed, the more likely we were to get into an argument.

I hugged her and said goodbye. "We really have to go. I'm sorry it's such a short visit." I felt guilty for letting her down. I felt guilty that I couldn't explain to her that I was building up my courage to see my father. I felt guilty that I never told her that my father and I had been speaking for years. I felt guilty.

We didn't have enough time to drive by all sixteen apartments in Connecticut that I had lived in as a child. But I showed Mike where I went to high school and a few of the apartments I had lived in during my teenage years. My voice tightened as I pointed to the apartment inside the house where I lived alone for the last few years of high school. "I lived on the second floor of that house. The attic is haunted," I said. I couldn't get out more words. I couldn't take a deep breath. I put my hand on my chest and tried to rub away the spasms. "I hate chest pains," I said.

"What do you mean, haunted?" he asked.

"There's a ghost in the attic." I enjoyed this topic. "We used to keep camping gear up there, and the huge space was full of old, dusty things, including an old pool table. There was an old mattress, boxes, lampshades, just junk scattered all around the dark space. The light from the dormered windows would reflect off the dust as I moved things around. I'd cough and need my inhaler up there.

Anyway, one day, I cleaned as much as I could. I swept the floor, washed the inside of the windows, moved all of the old stuff to one corner, and put all of our camping stuff near a window. That night after I finished, while battling my brain for sleep, I heard someone moving things around in the attic above my room. The next morning, I went up the creaky staircase and realized that everything had been put back exactly the way it had been before I cleaned, except for our camping stuff. That was all put near the top of the stairs. It was like that was the only space we were allowed to use. It was creepy!" I explained.

Mike looked at me with a smirk.

"You don't believe in ghosts, do you?" I asked.

He stared at me and shook his head.

"Well I wouldn't either, but until you feel something like that, you really don't know. There were several times I'd go up there and feel like I was being watched. I'd turn around quickly, just as I felt like someone was about to touch my shoulder or my neck. I thought I saw a glimpse of her a couple of times, but the image never lasted long enough for me to be sure."

I continued, "Oh, and I have a picture of that house. And I think you can see her in the window! I didn't notice it until I blew up the photo for a photography project for school. But there is definitely someone standing in the attic window looking out. It looks like her, like the image I saw those times I was up there. Gives me chills!" I shook my shoulders and quivered for effect.

For the photography project in college, I took

pictures of all sixteen apartments in Connecticut where I had lived. I blew them up to eight-by-ten size and developed them myself in black and white in the art studio. On the back of each photo, I wrote a little about what I had experienced in that apartment. I used crayon for the stories when I was really young, and pen for the stories when I was older. I only let two people see this writing, and I never reread what I wrote. I swallowed hard, reflecting back to being so alone and lonely in that house. I remembered the constant fear. The ghost in the attic never bothered me that much; so many other things caused so much more stress and fear. I looked over at Mike. "It feels weird to be here. I don't like it," I said.

He gently put his hand on my leg to comfort me. "I can't believe I lived there alone as such a young teenager. I see our friends' kids now who are that age, and I realize how young fourteen really is. It's so young, so innocent, so dependent still." I started to feel tears form, but I put my fingertip against my sharp thumbnail to stop myself from crying. The distraction worked well. I asked him to turn left at the next stop sign. We had to get back on the highway to head toward my father's house soon.

"I know. It's amazing how well you did," he said.

I looked at him. I had focused so intently on not crying that it took me a second to understand what he meant. I guess he spoke the truth, but I never thought of myself in that way at the time. I survived. I found a way to get free food. I got myself to school every day, unless a migraine prevented me from leaving my dark room. I earned very high grades and got accepted into a good college, the only school I applied to. The tightness in my chest reminded me of the challenges, the overwhelming days when I felt like the most hated girl on the planet, when I felt like I would never build a good life out of that mess, when thinking of a future overwhelmed me so much that I had to count to a hundred a hundred times to get through the day. I took another deep breath.

I thought quietly to myself, so grateful for Mike's support during this visit with my father. My workouts resulted in a very strong, muscular body, which meant I could fight back if I needed to. I imagined myself in a fighting stance, ready to defend myself and ready to strike at the same time.

We stopped at a bar near my father's house, and I drank two glasses of wine to calm my nerves. "I'm about to see my father for the first time in sixteen years," I announced to the bartender.

"Wow, that's incredible," he said.

"Yeah, I guess it is! I'm a little nervous," I said. "I've talked to him on the phone for a few years, but we haven't seen each other since 1998. It's going to be weird."

The bartender nodded, raised his eyebrows, and walked away. Clearly, he didn't know how to respond. I had learned to anticipate this kind of reaction when I shared little stories about how I grew up. People usually had no idea what to say. I smirked and took another gulp of my wine.

I called my father a few minutes before our meeting time. "Hi, Dad. We're close by. Where do you want to meet?" I know my voice sounded strange.

He asked, "Why don't you come by the house, so Janice can deal with her baby, and we can all go to dinner?"

I said, "Okay."

"Do you remember where it is?" he asked.

"Yup, we're actually on your road, just a few minutes away. See you soon."

I hung up the phone and my mind went blank. Another skill I had mastered over the years was emptying my mind, feeling nothing, and going through motions. I saved this for times when I couldn't handle my thoughts, when I couldn't anticipate an outcome, or when I had no options. Sometimes it would happen on its own. I'd feel absolutely nothing.

Ted's stepdaughter, Janice, had a three-year old daughter. My father's other stepdaughter, Renee, had two children. I always avoided thinking of Ted as a grandfather or imagining him around young children. I felt myself sweat and shake on the inside. My stomach ached, and my back tightened. *What could they possibly think of his biological daughter who left her own father? Did they hate me? Did he hurt them too? Did they blame me?* I had so many questions.

I dreaded seeing the place where my father abused me. I scrunched my nose slightly in response to the foul vomit I tasted in the back of my throat as we pulled into the driveway of the row of rundown townhomes. I trembled. The pains in my chest seemed to get worse with each breath. "His is the third from last on the left.

Park in space number eleven," I directed Mike.

I couldn't feel my legs as I struggled to pull myself out of the car. Mike placed his hand gently on my lower back as we walked up to the door. My father stood behind his screen door staring at me. His hair, while slightly longer, looked as healthy as I remembered. His blue-green-gray eyes looked much older.

"It's a really cool thing that I got from my dad," I always tell people when they ask about my crazy eye color. They change colors depending on my mood or what I'm wearing, and they're different from each other. "I'm an alien," is another fun response.

He opened the screen door and gave me a long, strong hug. "It's so good to see you!" he said. I felt him shake anxiously.

"It's good to see you, too," I said. I wondered if he could feel my heart pounding as he hugged me. I wondered if he felt my apprehension. I inhaled a little more breath through my teeth and kept my spine and stomach tight. My sober dad's hug felt mysteriously safe. I stepped into the living room and avoided looking to the right; I did not want to see the spot on the floor where I had slept as a child. I did not want to relive the memories of my father on top of me.

I noticed that he had a new recliner, which was placed in the same location as the old light brown one—at the base of the stairs, straight ahead as you walked into the room. Commercials played loudly on the television. Thankfully, Christmas commercials were over. I hate Christmas.

"This is Janice," my dad said, motioning toward his stepdaughter. I heard pride in his voice. I shook her hand. "And this is Allana." Allana, Janice's daughter, quickly hid behind her mom. We all laughed. "She's shy," my dad said, even more proudly. He had a family. I knew this. I heard it on the phone many times. He'd talk to them, giggle with them, put them on speakerphone, and force us to communicate throughout the last few years. But seeing it felt heavy, deafening, like a knot in my chest, and the ringing in my ear made me dizzy.

"Let me show you around. I've made a lot of changes," my dad announced.

"Okay. I remember a lot about this place," I said, immediately realizing I made a huge mistake. I didn't want to think about my memories. I always avoided thinking backwards; this protected me. *Only focus on the future. Only focus on the future*, was a lesson I had taught myself. It helped on the hard days.

I noticed that the walls desperately needed a coat of paint. Scratches and dirt scuffed them from eye level to the ground. As my father showed me the space in the attic that he had converted to two bedrooms for his stepdaughters, he said, "They needed their own bedrooms." At the time, only one of his step-daughters lived there with her children. I couldn't remember which one, but that much I knew.

"Yes, I see. This space is great, Dad," I said. The room spun, and the ringing in my ear got louder. I put my hand against the wall to hold myself up and tried to smile. I looked down. I thought of questions that I wanted to ask him in that moment. *Why did they deserve their own bedroom, but I didn't earn one as a child? What the hell did they do to earn that? Why were they so fucking special?*

I caught myself and stopped my crazed thinking before I spiraled too far. *Never let them see you sweat,* I thought. Instead of saying anything to make him or his daughters uncomfortable, I positioned my feet in a boxer stance. I envisioned the rest of my body prepare to strike, if needed. I let go of the wall, and I walked solidly while touring his home. "Where's Renee?" I asked. Renee had planned on joining us for dinner.

"She's at work. She should be home any minute and then we can go to dinner," my dad explained. "There's a restaurant down the street that I think you'll like."

"Sounds good," I said.

Maria was in Brazil visiting the rest of her family, including her son. Janice, Allana, Renee, and her husband, Tim, joined us for dinner. We sat at two different tables across an aisle from one another. Ted attempted to order a mixed drink, but when they didn't have what he wanted, he just drank water. I naively accepted this as a good sign. As a child, he wouldn't have turned away any alcohol. *It means he's better,* I thought to myself and smiled a little.

"Did you get my Christmas present?" I asked my dad.

"Yes, I did. It was very nice. But seeing you is the best Christmas present I've ever had," he said.

I smiled. His family stared at the table. I wondered what they were thinking and what they thought of me in general.

We awkwardly talked about Brazil and Seattle for about an hour and then drove back to his house. I sat in the front seat of my father's car on the ride back. He always had large cars. At age four, I was leaning against the open window in the back seat of his Cadillac when it started to close. I let my arm ride the glass until it reached the top. I didn't pull my arm back into the car in time, and the window began to grind against my bony elbow. My mother yelled at him, saying that he nearly cut my arm off. I cried and screamed in terror. The window only bruised my arm, but I had nightmares about my father cutting off my arm or my head in his car window for years. No matter how much I tried to stop them, memories flooded my conscience. My confusion grew while I tried to link my memories to the nice man sitting next to me. He was showing me the features on his car and said, "There are buttons on here that I'll never use. It's so complicated!"

"Well, we have a really long drive back to New Hampshire, so we better get going," I said, after we all arrived back at my father's house.

"I'd offer to let you stay here, but I have a full house tonight. Renee and Tim are staying here until their new home is finished. And Allana is staying here tonight, too. Her dad is picking her up in the morning," my dad explained.

"That's okay, Dad. We have to get the car back, and it's supposed to snow tomorrow. It was really nice seeing you. I'll make an effort to visit more often, okay?" I wanted to visit him more. I wanted to be around the safe, sober father that I never knew.

"That sounds great. I love you, Laura."

"Love you, too, Dad."

I rushed to get into the car. "I'll drive," I said. I needed to take my mind off my feelings, my confusion, my regret, my sadness. I didn't want to cry or be weak. I couldn't let my father see me weak. I started to back out of the parking space, and my chest tightened so much that I couldn't take a deep breath. My eyes filled.

"Are you okay?" Mike asked.

"No." I tried to breathe and make my chest top hurting. "Was I wrong about everything? He's so nice." And just as I said the word "nice," I started to sob. I couldn't hold it in.

"Were all of my memories fake? Were they just stories my mother had told me to make me hate my father and make her look better? Did I cut him out of my life for no reason? Was I wrong about everything? Did I hurt him for no reason?" I asked question after question while sobbing and trying to drive Mike's mother's car. He listened intently and put his hand on my leg, my shoulder, and my arm, doing his best to comfort me. The visit had felt awkward, but I hadn't sensed any danger. I didn't feel that nauseating disgust that I had felt as a child, or whenever I thought about my father over the years. I didn't taste metal in my mouth. I didn't feel the lower back pain that I had felt when he was around. All of my body's physical responses to my dangerous father had disappeared. *What did that mean?*

I drove for almost three hours. I didn't speak much

after my initial meltdown. "I'm fine," I reassured Mike. "I just need to calm myself down." I counted to a hundred a hundred times in my head.

We made it to Mike's family's house a little after midnight. The living room glowed, while the rest of the house slept. Mike's brother-in-law, Sam, played a video game in the warm living room. Mike and I quietly walked into the house. I looked at Sam and nodded. He nodded in return. I walked into the dark, mostly remodeled kitchen. I placed a plastic grocery bag lightly on the counter. It held two bottles of wine that my mother had given me earlier in the day. I looked around the kitchen. Mike's sister had installed gorgeous gray cabinets and marble counters. And they were in the process of putting in new floor tiles that were almost all grouted. I heard the plastic bag make a noise and quickly looked in that direction. As if in slow motion, the bag of wine tilted to the side and tipped over. One of the bottles slowly rolled out. I hustled to try to get to the counter to stop the bottle from falling on the floor, but my legs felt like lead. I couldn't propel my body fast enough, and the bottle of wine crashed onto the newly tiled floor. Red wine seeped in between the tiles where grout had not been placed yet. Wine sprayed across the floor, splattering all over the entire room. My eyes widened and my mouth dropped open. I wanted to scream, "NO!" I had ruined their new kitchen!

Sam and Mike quietly scurried into the kitchen to see what I had done. No one spoke. Sam patted me on my shoulder, and the three of us started to clean up the spilled wine. We used paper towels and extra-absorbent baby wipes to wash the entire kitchen floor and absorb wine from in between the tiles. It took three of us two hours to finish. Luckily, the loud crash did not wake anyone, especially Mike's four-year-old nephew, who had trouble sleeping.

I lay in bed that night thinking about how safe I felt around my father, for the first time. I wondered if I had misconstrued my entire past. But I chose to focus on the positive, which was another skill I had taught myself to get through tough times. *Focus on the good; ignore the bad.* I could visit my father now. He could visit me. I could show him the house Mike and I had just bought in Seattle. I would hope to see the look of pride on his face, like I saw when he talked about his children and grandchildren. I thought about a future with my dad.

16
duped

What future? I had no fucking future with my father. I learned the secrets that everyone kept from me so I wouldn't leave him again. In the hospital, my father was suffering from severe alcohol withdrawal. Maria did not know the word *withdrawal*, so she couldn't explain to me what was going on. "He's drunk! He's drunk!" really meant, "He's going through withdrawals; he's never stopped drinking! He's been lying to you!" In fact, Ted drank more than ever, every single day.

The safe, clean, sober dad I thought I knew disappeared in an instant. I hadn't incorrectly remembered the abuse in my past. I hadn't been wrong when I described my father as a dangerous man. It was all true. It was all real. And that intense fear that always lingered in my heart returned with a vengeance. I always worried about the huge gaps in my past. *What didn't I remember?* I had blocked so much time from my earlier years, save only a few memories.

In the next twenty-four hours, while I sat helplessly three thousand miles away, the doctors diagnosed my father with COPD, atrial fibrillation, pneumonia, and sepsis—all in addition to the original diagnosis of congestive heart failure. The alcohol withdrawal was the most concerning. The staff intubated, sedated, and restrained him. Each time he started to wake up, he pulled at his ventilator tube or tried to fight with anyone around him. He suffered from delusions and hallucinations, and he struggled violently.

"I quit drinking and doing drugs. I quit drinking and doing drugs." I know I remember him telling me that over the phone in one our first conversations after we reunited. I know it. I know I didn't make that up. *Did I?*

I recognized within myself that this news, his condition, and learning about the lies began to affect me in many ways. The nightmares, flashbacks, sweats, mood swings, suicidal ideation, numbness, inability to trust anything or anyone, feeling unworthy, feeling unloved, loss of confidence, and feeling unsafe all returned from long ago. But the lessons, the therapy, and the strategies I practiced through the years all made me a much stronger person now. I had beaten all of this before: depression, anxiety, and PTSD. I had the tools to overcome it again. But I needed support. I had a wonderful relationship and great friends. But I didn't want to burden them with these thoughts. My old therapist and I had worked for over a decade together on various techniques to heal from my past. I already knew what he would say.

"It's another layer of healing, because it means you're ready. Acknowledge the perfection of it, feel it, and then let it go. Don't force yourself. These things take time. Take your time, but don't deny your feelings." These were things I would say to a friend or one of the students I used to advise when I was a School Counselor to help them.

So, I started giving myself the same advice. *Accept yourself as you are while you handle this*, I thought to myself. A new therapist would require too much backstory to meet my immediate needs, so I did not want to try to find one. Instead, I decided to look up Al-Anon meetings and give one a try.

Two days passed since Maria and the doctors revealed my father's secrets. He had been lying, and forcing his family to lie, about his drinking for more than eight years. I walked into the Al-Anon meeting with a small piece of paper. On that piece of paper, I had written a few sentences about why I chose to go to a meeting that day. I didn't want anyone to see me as weak. I would not allow anyone to see at me as a victim. I wanted to portray myself as someone who had the tools to handle this, but who just needed a little support to get through the next few days, until he died.

I had a plan. "My name is Laura," I would say to start.

I imagined they would all say, "Hi, Laura," in return.

I would continue, "The reason I'm here today is that I'm surrounded by alcoholics, grew up in an alcoholic home, both parents, abused, on my own for the most part at fourteen—you get the idea—and I managed to create a really wonderful life. Two degrees, great job, I own my home, which was a dream I had since I was seven, all without any help from any of them, or anyone." I'd ramble to get them all up to speed quickly. "I thought that my father was sober for the past eight years. We didn't speak for about ten years before that, and he told me he quit drugs and drinking when we reunited. But I just learned two days ago that it was all a lie. He's dying because of alcohol, and I need support. I need to be around people who understand how it feels to be less important than alcohol and drugs." I prepared my words carefully, so that I could simply read them aloud. And after I spoke, I would be able to just listen and hope for the best.

At the beginning of the meeting, the group leader read an introduction from a white plastic binder. She asked if anyone was there for a first, second, or third meeting. I raised my hand. Another person then shared her story about how Al-Anon had helped her feel better. "I just felt better," she said. She said she didn't know why she felt better. But she felt better. My eyes filled with tears, but I didn't let them fall. I pressed one of my fingertips into my sharpest fingernail to stop my emotions. I avoided looking at anyone as she spoke.

How nice it would be to just feel better right now, I thought to myself. I envied her. *Maybe these meetings really could help me.* I listened to everyone during the meeting, and the clock was moving way too fast. I was running out of time. I searched deep within my gut and found the courage to share what I had written on my little piece of paper ten minutes before we were scheduled to adjourn.

As I spoke, my eyes filled with tears, but I continued. As I read my words, "dying because of alcohol," my tears fell.

"I don't cry, so I don't know why this is happening," I mumbled, interrupting my own story. I tried to remain strong, but my face turned red with embarrassment. I hated myself for letting them see me weak. I continued reading my words, and the group members accepted me unconditionally—tears and all. Several people nodded as I spoke. Some smiled lovingly. Some stared at the floor, as if they could clearly imagine and feel my story and relate to my words in a way that not many could. Several people talked to me after the meeting and encouraged me to continue attending. I found the support I needed for this difficult time. I promised to keep going back.

I hoped that I would feel better, just like that woman talked about, as I drove to work that day. A few minutes after arriving at my office, I went into a private room and called the hospital to get an update about Ted. I didn't realize it yet, but a daily pattern had begun.

"His body is tense, and he's making strange noises, like gurgling," the nurse told me over the phone. That didn't sound good.

"Can I please speak to the doctor?" I asked.

"He isn't available. But I have your number, and I'll ask him to call you." The doctor never called.

I called again that night to get another update.

"He's sedated and still on a ventilator," a different nurse explained.

"How is his heart rate, blood pressure, and oxygen level? Should I come there?" I asked my questions without a pause.

"He is stable, but he is relying on the ventilator almost entirely."

It sounded like he was going to either be there for a very long time or die very soon.

I called the hospital several times a day to get updates about Ted's condition from the nurses and doctors. "We like to have one person that we give the information to, and that person is then responsible for sharing the information with everyone else," they would tell me over and over again, sounding annoyed. "We're telling Maria everything. You should talk to her."

Each time I called, I had to explain that I was Ted's daughter, I lived far away, and I was having trouble getting information from Maria because English was her second language, and she didn't understand a lot of the words they were telling her about his condition. In any given day, I heard several different stories. "His tube is coming out today." "There is no chance his tube is coming out." "His oxygen levels are looking good." "His oxygen levels are looking worse." "He might be able to breathe on his own soon." "He's relying on the ventilator too heavily for us to try removing it today."

Some of the hospital staff confronted me as to why I wasn't with my father while he suffered in the hospital alone. "You're his daughter? Your father is really sick. You should be here," one nurse scolded.

"I want to be there. I live in Seattle. I am planning to

visit when he is more aware of his surroundings, out of ICU, and off the ventilator," I explained, like a broken record.

"Hmm." I sensed judgement in the tone on the other end of the line.

"Plus, we have an estranged relationship because of his drinking. It's difficult for me to visit. I've only seen him once in eighteen years. He's been lying to me. He was dangerous when I was young. It's not simple. It's not easy."

"I understand, ma'am," the nurse responded with a kinder tone.

"Can I call back again tomorrow?" I asked.

"Yes. I won't be here, though. You'll have to talk to Angie, another nurse."

"Okay. Thank you so much."

Several weeks went by, and this pattern continued daily. I strived to learn my new job as a medical education manager for the United States, meet and make a good impression with new people at work, and smile and carry on as if nothing was wrong. Meanwhile, I searched for privacy and space each day, in multiple cities, and on many business trips, to sneak away to call the hospital and check on my father.

In private, I wrestled with my thoughts about my father's deceit and addiction. I intertwined the fingers on both my hands tightly, and tried hard to pull them apart. Numbly, I forced myself to go through the motions of my daily routine. I had appreciated having a stable parent in my life so much, and it no longer existed. I had spent years second-guessing the trauma of my childhood, rewriting the past to match the story of the current "nice guy" whom I had learned to love and trust. And now I was questioning my second-guessing. *How could I be so wrong about his condition, his health, and his honesty? How could I have misread him so badly? Who else was lying? Who else was unhealthy? Was I just as out of control? Was I just as dishonest with myself about my own demons? Were things even worse than I remembered? Was I okay?* So many questions rattled my brain.

I continued to attend Al-Anon meetings one to two days per week. I learned more and more about how much my parents' alcoholism and addictions shaped my personality. Other group members told me that rewriting one's past and second-guessing emotions due to growing up with an alcoholic parent was common. I never realized how much I worried about everything, how much I protected my parents, how hard I tried to make everything okay for everyone around me, how much I felt that I had to earn love (it's not just given), how many battles I fought on my own, and how much the lack of predictability and safety affected me as a child, adult, friend, partner, employee, and person. I learned so much about who I was, how strong my past had made me, how harsh I could be, and how my moments of weakness were not my fault.

If you knock me down, that's your fault. If you come back in ten years, and I'm still down, that's my fault. I'm not sure if I had heard that phrase somewhere or made it up myself, but I thought this way daily.

17
attempts for escape

As I began puberty, I wanted to escape the pain in my heart and the numbness in my body. *If my own parents don't like me, no one else ever would*, I kept thinking. The neighborhood bully joined me in my apartment after school one day when we were both thirteen; our birthdays were a few weeks apart. Elena's father was black and her mother was white. Elena had beautiful light-colored eyes and medium-dark skin. But she told me that it was difficult for her to go to a school with a nearly-100 percent white population.

We were drinking my mother's vodka, and she looked me in the eye and drunkenly slurred, "Your mother doesn't love you. I know because my mother doesn't love me either." She rolled up her sleeve and showed me her forearm. Scabbed lines formed four letters: "H A T E." I reached out to touch her skin, and she quickly pulled away. She walked into my kitchen and started going through my drawers, touching the tip of each knife that she found. "None of your knives are sharp. Does your mother not cook?" she complained.

"Not really," I replied. Actually, my mother was an excellent cook, when she was home.

"Here. This'll do. Go ahead," she said, as she handed me a knife with a brown handle and a jagged edge.

"What do you want me to do with this?" I asked.

"Do it. It feels good. You probably aren't strong enough, are you?" She laughed.

I stared into her eyes and wanted to scream, "Fuck you. You have no clue how strong I am!" I started to scratch the word "fuck" into my arm. But I couldn't break the skin. I didn't want to. *I'm strong enough to not do this*, I thought. But I didn't want to say those words aloud. "I can't" is all I could say.

She laughed and laughed. She wouldn't stop. I had thought she and I could relate. I thought and hoped we had some common ground. But she kept laughing at me. I went into the bathroom, tied my hair dryer cord to the shower curtain rod, and wrapped the other end around my neck. Hanging myself didn't work since the cord was attached to a cumbersome hair dryer, and the rod didn't hold my weight. I laughed it off as a really stupid idea and went back out into the living room for more drinks.

At the time, I lived for three things: I still had hope that my mother would be nicer to me; I had a great relationship with one of my uncles, Timmy, who had moved into our neighborhood after one of his divorces; and I loved my cat, Toby.

On bad days, I would climb up onto the roof of the parking garage in the apartment complex and debate jumping off. I would then think about the three things that kept me from jumping: my mother, my uncle, and my cat. I would sit on this roof several times a week and think. *Would anyone even care if I jumped? Would I even die? I wasn't up that high, so I probably would just break my leg or something.* One night in my living room, I wrote the initials TTC on a piece of notebook paper, which stood for Toby, Timmy, and Cara. As long as I could spend time with them, I was okay. I glued this note at the top of the roof, so I'd have a fixed reminder of the loves of my life. This note would prevent me from doing something stupid.

"I need to talk to you, Laura," Timmy announced one day while we were riding in his truck. "I'm moving to Colorado. I need a change. I have too many bad memories here. It's too stressful. I find myself tense all the time. Do you understand?"

I started to cry deep inside, and I nodded. "I understand."

He had just gone through a second divorce, and he struggled to find steady work.

"I can't take a deep breath here, you know? I look down sometimes, and my hand is always pressing against my leg like this, all tense." I followed his gaze down to his hand. His thumb pressed against his leg so hard that it was turning white, like the blood had drained out of it completely.

"I know what you mean. I do this," I said, and I held

my hands in a tight grip, intertwined my fingers, and pulled them away from each other as hard as I could. "I catch myself doing this all the time."

He looked at me and said, "I know you have it kind of rough around here. My sister.... I mean, your mom is pretty tough."

Tears filled my eyes. *She hates me*, I thought. "Yeah. Can I come with you?"

"How about this. Let me go there and get settled, and I'll come back for you. Okay, Laura? I'll come back and get you."

"Okay," I responded, doubtfully. Timmy was moving to Colorado to build a new life with his son. That night, I wrote a long letter to Timmy. On his last morning in Connecticut, I put the letter under the windshield wiper of his truck, as I walked past it on my way to the bus stop. He never came back for me. I thought about my note on the garage roof. I had lost one out of the three.

A few months later, my mother and I moved to another apartment a couple of miles away in the same town. I left the garage and my note behind.

I forced my cat to stay in my room every night. I would put him under the covers with me and not let him out. I suffocated him with my love. He was my one constant through several moves, changing schools, and all of the craziness with my parents. Toby didn't hate me. His moves were predictable, and I wanted him close all the time, especially at night.

Two weeks before my fifteenth birthday, I started working at the local pharmacy. When I returned home after my first night of work, my mother and my cat were missing. I assumed my mother had gone to Pete's house. She had been staying there for a few weeks. But where was Toby?

"Toby!! TOBY!!!" I frantically called my cat. I panicked and searched everywhere in the apartment. I looked in the yard out back and the garage near our building, but it was too dark to see much. Toby had vanished.

I heard my mother stumble into the kitchen. "I got rid of your cat. He wasn't happy with you. He deserved to be with better people who treated him right."

I roared, "How could you?"

"You'll get over it," she said, as she walked into her bedroom and closed the door.

I opened her door and followed my mother into her walk-in closet. "I'm not going to get over it!" I yelled as I sensed the emptiness in her part of the apartment. "Where are all your clothes?" I asked.

"I just left some things at Pete's house," she said.

"All of your stuff is gone, Mom," I stated.

"I don't want to hear it, Laura. I don't need a lecture!"

I hadn't met Pete yet. All I knew was that he was a veterinarian who loved to hunt large animals. He lived in a hunter's lodge on a small lake in Connecticut. I guess that's where she officially lived at that point.

The next day, I envisioned myself jumping off the roof over the garage in that apartment complex. I had no way to get there, but I visualized the feeling of adrenaline while sitting on the roof and looking over the edge, desperate to remind myself of things to live for. But I had lost all three. Screw it. I pictured myself hitting the ground. I imagined the abrupt ending to a short freefall, arms flailing, legs kicking, and my body hitting the ground in an awkward, twisted position with a loud thud. I wanted to go back, climb back up onto the inclined roof, find my piece of paper, rip it off, and throw it into the woods. I needed to make a new list of reasons to live.

18
another secret's out

Three weeks before graduating high school, my chemistry teacher overheard me saying to a friend that I had not seen or heard from my mother in several weeks. Dr. Snyder asked me to stay after class.

"Sure, but I can't stay for too long, sir; I have to get to work," I replied.

"When was the last time you saw your mother?" he asked me.

"Oh, I don't know, it's been a few weeks, maybe a month," I said casually, almost giggling. No adult had ever cared to ask before, and I had been used to not seeing my mother for weeks or months at a time. I had several unexcused absences at school, resulting in minute decreases in my grades each quarter. But no one had ever bothered to dig any deeper. "Why do you ask?" I inquired.

"I   have   to   report   your   mother   for   child abandonment," he remarked.

I laughed nervously, and my voice shook when I said, "Uh...sir, you can't do that."

"I have no choice," he said.

"Please hear me out. She's been gone a lot for the past three years. I am doing fine. I have food, I have a roof over my head, and my bills are paid. I have been accepted to the University of Connecticut. I have an apartment lined up for next year with my boyfriend. My parents are required to help me pay for school due to a court order. I'm not sure if they'll adhere to that or not, but if you do anything to make them angry now, I could lose what little support I may get. Please don't say anything," I begged him. I looked him dead in the eye.

"I have no choice," he said again. "I really need to do my job and report what I heard you say about your mom. Then the counselors will ask you questions. That's all that will happen." He tried to reassure me.

"But that's not all that will happen. If she finds out, if she gets into any trouble, she will be angry with me, and I'll lose everything. I understand you have a job to do, but what you're trying to do was what I needed three years ago. It's too late now. Now, it would do more harm than good. Please just think about it for a day before you report anything. Please talk to me again tomorrow before you do anything. Give it one day. A day won't change anything. But please just think about what I said for one day." My voice was firm, assertive, and strong. I felt more confident than I had ever felt before. I just hoped he really listened to me and didn't just brush me off as a stupid teenager trying to get attention. "Sir, I really have to get to work. Please, let's talk again tomorrow before you do anything," I said once more and left the room.

The following afternoon, I met with Dr. Snyder.

"I thought about what you said." He paused and looked around the empty room. It felt like an eternity before he spoke again, and my heart raced. "I will not do anything with the information I have about your mother. I realize that it would do more harm than good for you. You have clearly made a path for yourself, and I don't want to get in the way of that. You are mature beyond your years," he stated.

I breathed a sigh of relief, blinked quickly to stop tears from forming, and I whispered, "Thank you."

Before I could say more, Dr. Snyder continued, "Also, I saw your unexcused absences. I imagine they were unexcused because you live alone. I will not penalize your grade for the absences you have had in my class this year. You've been dealing with this for a long time."

"Oh, thank you so much," I said. My grades were very important to me.

"And," he continued, "on behalf of this school, all of your teachers, and the administration, I deeply apologize for not paying close enough attention to what you've been dealing with. I'm sorry no one tried to help you earlier. You shouldn't have had to do all of this alone."

Tears filled my eyes, but I didn't let them fall. "So, you're really not going to do anything? You're listening to me, right?" I asked to be sure.

"That's correct," he said, and he smiled.

I smiled back. "Do I owe you any money, or chocolate?" I joked.

He laughed and said, "Just get an 'A' on your final."

"No problem," I said.

I did very well in school. I would have had a 4.0 average had I not had unexcused absences. My teachers treated me like a comrade; I had more in common with them than the children in my classes. Each quarter, I found a teacher who would allow me to eat lunch in his or her classroom. While he or she graded papers, we would talk about life and goals. I wouldn't discuss feelings, but I conveyed my determination to graduate and go to college. I wanted a piece of paper that would help ensure that I never needed to rely on donated food ever again. I wanted a healthy life. My teachers would never know about the obstacles that stood in my way. I'd slip under their radar completely.

I didn't care about fashion or cliques. I got along with kids from every group at school. I also walked the halls like I owned them, even though I was a poor, lonely kid who wore used clothing surrounded by rich kids. I began to understand and appreciate my strength more and more. I could handle anything. I hid all my secrets. *Never let them see you sweat. Never let them see you weak.* My mother had taught me well.

19
scars

I had learned to hide my pain. A scarf wrapped around my neck, or a jacket zipped all the way to my collar, felt like a chokehold. Rubbing it hurt, no matter how gentle. Manny's punches had jolted my head to one side or the other, resulting in permanent stiffness and tension in my neck that I could never calm down. If I turned my head too quickly, half of my skull and face would go numb and tingle. I'd have to rub my head to get feeling to return to those areas. Without warning, pain would shoot down my arms.

I "dislocated my neck," for lack of a better way to describe it, a month or so after I turned fourteen. I was watching a movie while lying on my side on the floor. I rested my head on my hand with my elbow propped up onto a large pillow. This position kinked my neck, but I felt no pain. After staying in the same position for a period of time, I heard my mother call my name from the kitchen. I bolted off the floor quickly, heard a loud pop, felt a sharp pain in my neck and left shoulder, and froze with fear. I could not move my head in any direction, and it felt twisted and stuck.

I yelled out, "Something's wrong! Something's wrong with my neck!" I panicked.

My mother came into the room. "What do you mean? What did you do?"

"I just got up off the floor, and I heard a pop, and now I can't move my head!" I felt my eyes glaze with tears.

My mother stared at me and said, "Stand up straight and look at me."

I did as I was told.

"Your neck is out. Let's go see Dr. Davis. He can put it back. It's going to be okay."

"Okay. Is it going to hurt?" I asked.

"No, he's really gentle. I gotta call Rick and let him know we're going to be late in getting to the lake. Also, I have a neck brace that should help. Wait right here."

"Okay."

I heard my mother on the phone. "Laura hurt her neck. We're going to be late. Yeah, I know. Yeah, we'll be there. Not sure how late, but we'll be there."

We went camping a lot, but this particular annual campout party was at my mother's friend's house. I believe my mother was a little bit in love with Rick, and I knew she didn't want to miss out on the weekend because of my injury.

The chiropractor asked me to stand up straight and look him in the eye as he stood in front of me. He was uncomfortably close to me. He had me line up my toes on a line of tape that stuck to the carpet. Then he asked me to close my eyes and keep them closed while I turned my head from side to side, which I could barely do. Once I returned to center, he had me open my eyes again. He smirked. "Your neck is misaligned, quite a bit, actually. And you say this happened while getting off the floor?" he questioned me.

"Yes, I was leaning against a pillow on my arm, and I got up quickly and heard a pop," I explained.

"Has your neck been injured before?" he asked me.

I looked at my mother, who glared back at me before I said, "Well, it hurts from time to time." I knew I couldn't say that I had been punched by her boyfriend years earlier. It wouldn't matter at this point anyway. Manny was long gone.

"Have you been in a car accident?" he asked.

"No," I replied.

"Yes," my mother chimed in. "We were in a car accident when she was four."

"Ma, that was a minor fender-bender. It barely dented the bumper." She looked annoyed that I had clarified for the doctor.

Dr. Davis had me lay down on the table, and he wrestled with my neck to put it back into place. He made three adjustments on each side, and all six of them hurt badly.

"I'm going to have to see you twice a week to get this all fixed up," Dr. Davis recommended.

"Twice a week? Really?" I asked.

"Yes, see, it's back in place now for the most part. But over time, it will slowly go back to where it was when you got here. So, I'll have to put it back into place. We'll have to do that twice a week for a while. Then we can drop down to once a week," he explained.

"That's going to cost a lot," I said.

"Laura, don't worry about that. Just make sure you listen to Dr. Davis," my mother replied.

I tried to nod, but it hurt, so I said, "Okay."

After we got in the car, my mother instructed, "I need you to work really hard to get rid of this neck thing. Our insurance doesn't cover chiropractic. Just do whatever Dr. Davis says you can do to make it better quickly."

"I know," I replied.

My mother and I went camping that weekend, but I didn't see her after that for several weeks. I think she spent that time at Rick's house. I had no way to track her down.

I continued to see Dr. Davis for several months to adjust my neck and work on my back. I would remind him, "I haven't been able to relax my neck in years. It's always tight."

He'd crack it anyway, and sometimes it wouldn't release. A tear would fall against the side of my face onto the sheet beneath my head.

"If you relax the muscles, it won't hurt," he warned me each time.

"I'm trying. I can't relax those muscles," I said at each visit.

My back ached often, and pain would shoot down my

legs if I carried something too heavy or twisted awkwardly. I had to be very careful when putting on and taking off my backpack full of books. I had to be very careful in gym class, even though I loved to play sports. I slept with a pillow under my knees. I used a heating pad almost every night on either my back or neck to ease the pain. I became accustomed to having spine issues define me. I never complained or told anyone the story of my injuries until the worst episode occurred.

In January of 2006, I was twenty-eight, and fitness had been part of my daily routine for over seven years. I had just returned from my first vacation, and I had not worked out for two weeks. While getting ready to return to work, I leaned over to place a jar of pickles on the bottom shelf of the refrigerator. I must have bent down incorrectly, because I found myself on the floor a split second later. I had no time to catch myself or control my fall, and my body crashed onto the tile floor, awkwardly. And then my biggest fear came true. I had no feeling in my legs.

I knew I had herniated a disc or two in my lower back. Previous scans had shown the extent of this injury four other times since Manny's kicks to my lower spine. But I had never lost all feeling in my legs. My limbs would not respond to even the most basic command. Using my forearms, I dragged myself along the floor in the kitchen to my carpeted living room. I strained my neck to look up and around searching for my phone. I called my job to say I would not be in. Then I called my Aunt Connie to ask for help. Connie had moved to

Washington State a few years earlier.

I began my routine of carefully and slowly setting up pillows and couch cushions on the floor in the living room, and tried to situate myself into my "back-recovery position," as I called it. I could not lift my legs into position, so I rolled my body onto the pillows carefully and swiftly, breathing out in hard puffs to censor the pain a bit. I leaned against the firm couch cushion at just the right angle, and I stuffed two pillows under my knees.

Connie watched me pull myself across the floor to the bathroom. Using my arm and shoulder strength, I pulled myself up onto the side of the tub, and then positioned myself over the toilet so I could pee. After I dragged myself back into the living room, she tried to convince me to go to the emergency room. I explained to her that I knew this injury very well, and that I would be fine as long as I didn't move for a couple of days.

The pain became more excruciating over the next several days, as the numbness in my legs started to subside ever so slightly. This revealed intense, sharp, relentless pain in my lower back and down both legs like strikes of lightning. I could gather myself into a standing position, but my body stayed hunched and twisted significantly to the left. I could hobble a few inches at a time. And I felt as if I would collapse at any moment.

After I called in sick to work for the fifth day in a row, my boss pressured me to return to work. "My back hurts sometimes, too," she said.

I decided to go to the doctor, but three flights of stairs blocked my path to my car. And I had no idea how I would drive since my legs didn't work very well. I called a friend and asked for help down the stairs and a ride to the hospital. It took roughly thirty minutes to get me down the stairs and into his SUV. Once I was in his passenger seat, he used the handle to tilt the seat backward a little to try to help. I screamed in agony and saw spots of white dots in my darkening vision.

"Don't move anything!" I yelled, unable to control my voice.

"Sorry," he said.

At the hospital, the doctor gave me an injection of morphine for the pain and scheduled another MRI. The MRI showed degenerative disc disease and four herniated discs: three were severe and almost ruptured, and one was moderate. In the past, my MRIs had shown degenerative disc disease and two herniated discs. It was discouraging to learn how badly my back condition had progressed. Several specialists, neurosurgeons, and spine surgeons advised me to have surgery to remove the discs and fuse four vertebrae in my spine. But I knew better, despite my doctor and my mother's constant advice.

I narrowly avoided a painful procedure called a discogram, where a surgeon injects dye into the already-injured herniated discs to determine which caused pain. I had scheduled an appointment with a spine surgeon after several doctors reviewed my MRI. Connie drove me back to the hospital. The spine surgeon asked me if I had intended on having surgery within the next three months.

I said, "absolutely not. I know I can recover from this

since I've done it many times before." The determination in my voice was unmistakable.

"How did this injury start? How many times have you recovered from it?" Dr. D. asked.

"It's from when I was a kid, and this is the fifth time it's been this bad. Well, each time it's been worse than the last. But I've always been able to get better without surgery. I don't want surgery," I explained, while still keeping my secret.

"Was it a car accident?"

"Um. No, it wasn't. That's what everyone thinks when they see my MRI." I did not want to reveal my secret. I had only told two people about my beatings: my father and my mother. I worried that if I hid the truth, my recovery could be jeopardized, so I caved. "I was punched and kicked when I was younger, and I'm pretty sure that's when this started. But I didn't have my first MRI until years after all of that."

Dr. D.'s tone changed slightly, and I resented the sorrow in his eyes. I only wanted him to know the truth so that he could help me recover in the best way, and so he could understand my motivation to not let this injury define my life.

He leaned toward me and explained, "This is the most painful procedure I do. It's torturous. It reinjures you to the worst your discs can be. It is a presurgical tool to help me decide the best way to approach the spine for surgery. And it's only useful if you're planning on having surgery within the next few months." He paused.

I felt my body temperature rise. I told every doctor

that I had no intention of having an operation.

Dr. D. continued, "The only thing worse than having one discogram in your life is having to have two. If you are not having surgery, particularly, if you are not having surgery soon, there is no reason to do this to you."

"Then why would that other doc order it for me?" I felt anger radiate through my words. "I'm sorry. I'm not angry with you. I just never wanted surgery, and I've been very clear. I feel like a fool."

"You're not a fool. You listened to your doctor. There's nothing wrong with that. I don't know why it was ordered. But I can tell you that if all my patients were like you, I'd have a lot less business. You're weight-height proportional, clearly determined, you listen to your doctors, you take good care of yourself. You don't need surgery, at least not now."

"So, what do I do now?" I asked. I appreciated the compliment, but I wanted the facts quickly.

"Have you had injections within the last two years?"

"No, never."

"You've never had injections? That would be the logical next step. Let me see what I can do. Maybe we can get that done today. How does that sound?" Dr. D. asked.

"I'm worried about cost," I admitted.

"I'll work with your insurance. Let me go make a few phone calls. Are you comfortable waiting here?"

"Yeah, I'm okay." Connie and I waited in the sterile, chilly hospital room for about thirty minutes.

Dr. D. returned and said, "Good news, Laura. We can

do the injection right now, and your insurance has approved the procedure at ninety percent. You wanna give it a try?"

"Absolutely!" I was elated that I had another option to help my recovery.

About an hour later, Connie wheeled me out to the parking lot, and she and a nurse helped me into her car. My legs were completely numb from the injection, and I felt loopy from the medication they had administered to help me relax.

Over the next few weeks, the pain began to subside. I walked slowly, twisted and hunched, but movement was getting easier.

I received short-term disability income and secured my job by using the FMLA rules. My doctors estimated that I would be out of work for six months. A team of physicians and therapists worked with me for two to five hours per day. By committing to physical therapy, acupuncture, relaxation techniques, and pain management, I returned to work part-time within three months.

I continued therapy with my psychologist, whom I had been seeing for many years. He taught me visualization techniques. While lying on the floor, I'd imagine what I thought a healthy disc looked like. Then I would envision all of my discs in this way. I also worked on resolving anxiety and depression surrounding this injury. I worked on letting go of my anger, forgiveness, and self-love. I worked on getting more sleep, and I ate healthier.

I went back to work by the end of March of that year. I did my first very short but somewhat difficult hike up Tiger Mountain near the end of April. I went back to my gym in June. I committed to making my body strong in order to compensate for a weak spine. I learned how to lift weights in proper form, and I learned specific exercises that helped my lower back. I proved to myself that any movement was better than no movement. A still spine is a spine that will never fully recover. Manny's beatings would never stop me from doing anything I wanted to do ever again; I just had to do every move perfectly for the rest of my life. And I could never take that much time off from working out again.

This constant reminder of the kicks and punches haunted me, infuriated me, and motivated me. I did everything possible to strengthen my spine, take care of myself, and prevent flare-ups of my injuries.

20
holding on to hope

After hanging up the phone with one of my father's nurses, I thought about how different I was from my father. My determination to have a healthy and strong body motivated me every single day. When a doctor told me that I couldn't do something because of my injuries or my past, I'd find a way. While I fundamentally understand that addiction is not a choice, and that it should be treated as a disease, I could not relate to what I viewed as my father giving up. He never tried therapy or Alcoholics Anonymous. He never learned about addiction or admitted he had a problem. In fact, he lied constantly.

I wanted him to get one more chance to live a healthy life. I wanted to motivate him and help. I knew the odds. Statistically, only twelve percent of alcoholics and addicts get clean and sober. And since he never had done the work, the odds of him starting anew at his advanced age were even lower. But I had so many questions. I wanted to have an honest relationship, even if that meant I had to forgive again. I wrote him a note and posted it for the world to see on social media.

> Dear Dad,
>
> As a child, I went from loving you more than anything, thinking of you as my protector and teddy bear, and using your belly as a pillow, to being completely terrified of you and confused by you when you got drunk or high and violent. As a young adult, I had to make the decision to cut you out of my life for my sanity and safety. As an older adult, I had the joy of reconnecting with you, believing you were clean and sober, and I loved every moment of our honest, raw, and quiet conversations. To now—I am back to being completely terrified that you may die, completely confused that alcohol withdrawals are contributing to you being so sick that you cannot breathe on your own, and I more than I've ever wanted anything to see you smile again and swing a golf club with you again. Please keep fighting. I love you, unconditionally.

I didn't realize that posting my feelings publicly would haunt me later. It would be viewed as a sign of weakness, a reason to judge, to pounce, to hate. I broke my rule. I let people see me weak.

"Your father is ready for a visitor. I think this would be a good time to visit." Three and a half weeks of constant phone calls and updates had passed, and I finally heard the news that I had waited for. I had a small window of time to fit a visit in between work trips at my new job. I planned to fly from Seattle to Boston on a red-eye on a Thursday night and drive to Connecticut early Friday morning. I wanted to visit him as much as possible and do some work remotely on Friday and have dinner with my mother nearby. I planned to stay at a hotel a few miles away from the hospital on Friday night and visit my father as much as possible and do some work remotely on Saturday. On Sunday, I'd have to drive back to Boston and fly home.

I needed to return to work for mandatory training on Monday. As I sat at my desk and booked my flight, hotel, and car, I felt that familiar numbness, dizziness, and disgust. The pain in my back and churning in my stomach had returned. In my mind, I desperately tried to iron out the dark, jagged, crumpling, metallic paper that I visualized taking over the room, my desk, and my mind. I stared at the keyboard and doubted my every decision.

"Did you hear that a blizzard is on its way to CT this weekend?" A text from my mother lit up on my phone. *Crap*, I thought. I logged onto the internet and navigated to the Weather Channel's website. Sure enough, a huge blizzard was heading toward the East Coast. I put my head in my hands and rubbed my forehead and my eyes. I felt feverish, cold, and sweaty. I swallowed and it felt as though sandpaper was scratching my throat; it screamed in pain, like I was coming down with a cold or flu.

"Are you okay, Laura?" asked a coworker whom I had met just a few weeks earlier.

She startled me. I didn't hear her approach my desk. "Oh, hi. Um, no. You know what? I'm sorry. I'm not really okay. I'm flying to see my father. He's not doing well. There's a blizzard hitting the East Coast right as I get there. And I think I'm getting sick. It's kind of a mess." I hadn't revealed any of my internal demons and constantly acted like the eager, funny, charming new employee I wanted to be. But I needed a kind word, so I risked opening up just a little.

"Wow. Um. Well, why don't you go get some orange juice, vitamin C, from the cafeteria. Get away from your desk for a minute. You're probably just really stressed. Get some fluid. Get some rest tonight. Try to relax the best you can." She was so kind.

I nodded at the good advice. I walked down to the cafeteria and bought some orange juice and a juice smoothie with extra vitamin C. I sipped them both. It stung each time the bitter, cold liquid passed my tender, raw throat. My stomach churned and gurgled deep down into my core as acidic molten vomit tried to escape, but I kept drinking anyway. I was determined that this would cure my ailments in that moment.

I went back to my desk and continued to work. I stiffened my upper lip and tightened my core. My boxer disposition returned. I visualized my wide stance and anticipated a fight. I have to do this. I'd regret it for the rest of my life if I didn't see him one last time. I need to look into his blue-gray-green eyes and see if any connection with my father remained. I booked the trip.

"Your daddy is very angry today, Laura," Maria told me over the phone as I drove home from work that day on Interstate 5. I quickly pulled the car over to the side of the highway. Cars shook my little Subaru as they flew past at speeds of seventy miles per hour or more.

"Did something happen?" I asked.

"No, he just doesn't understand. I think the medication makes him not understand," Maria said.

My father's history of lashing out while in the hospital forced the doctors to keep him lightly sedated. Each time the medication started to wear off, he became angry and violent again. "Can I talk to him?" I asked.

"Yes, but he doesn't have a voice. His throat is too sore from the tubes."

"Okay, I'll talk to him, and he can listen," I explained.

Maria then switched the phone over to FaceTime so my father could see my face, and I could see his. He looked gray, and his eyes squinted so small that I couldn't see their color. An oxygen mask covered his nose and cheeks.

I smiled and brightly said, "Dad. Hi! I just want you to know that I will be there in a couple of days. And I have a work trip there in a couple of weeks, so I will be back again in a couple of weeks too! If everything goes well, you should be home by then. Wouldn't that be great?"

He nodded.

"I'm going to try to visit you more often, okay?"

He nodded. I think he tried to smile, but the tubes and swelling hid his reaction.

"So, Dad. I need you to listen to your doctors. And relax as much as you can. I know you aren't comfortable. But they are taking good care of you. You just have to be patient. If you start to get nervous, I need you to take long deep breaths in and out and do your best to relax. That's all you need to do. Just breathe in and out. Nothing else matters now. The more you relax, the sooner you will go home. Okay, Dad?"

He nodded again and tried to whisper. Maria looked into the phone and said, "He said he understands."

I smiled and said, "I love you, Dad. I'll see you in two days."

He nodded again. His body looked a little bit less tense. I hoped that I had helped.

21
going through the motions

As I sat at the gate for my flight, I learned that all flights to the East Coast that followed mine were cancelled because of the storm. I was lucky that I would make it to Connecticut. I felt numb, nervous, and sick. I wanted to turn to the person next to me and share my story. But even if someone looked nice enough to actually listen, I wouldn't know what to say. A woman one row in front of me and two seats to my left got air sick and vomited in the sick-bag on and off all night.

I did not sleep. I tried to read a book, but I kept rereading the same paragraph over and over again. I tried to do the crossword puzzle in the back of the airline's magazine, but I couldn't figure out any of the answers. Nothing made sense, and I held my pen over the page, motionlessly. I stared at the seat in front of me and looked at the people around me as they slept peacefully. *Did they all have parents who loved them? What did they do to earn it? How hard did they work to make them smile, to make them laugh, to make them proud? What made them so damn special? Did they have family? That disgusting word.* I hate that word, *family*. Just thinking of it made me tense, angry, resentful, and queasy. *Who could relate to these thoughts?*

I wondered if seeing my father, now that I knew his secrets, would obliterate my strength. I had created a hard, protective shell over the years. While I was sometimes too hard, and people described me as harsh sometimes, I liked being strong and independent. No one crushes you that way.

The plane shook from side to side and up and down simultaneously. I thought about how I had overcome my intense fear of flying. Being around airplanes terrified me so much that I couldn't pick someone up at the airport without having panic attacks and needing Xanax to control my anxiety.

Planes flying over my head frightened me. I couldn't handle anything that was remotely out of my control, and flying was the epitome of that. If I needed to fly, I'd spend hours choosing my flight, my seat, the specific airline, type of airplane, airport, location within the terminal, and even the food and drink options. Everything had to be planned in order for me to purchase a ticket.

Then I'd spend days before a flight in and out of the bathroom with diarrhea and stomach cramps. For nights before my flight, I'd dream about plane crashes. They'd either crash with me aboard or crash into me from above, while I was on the ground. No matter what people told me about the physics of flying and the safety of airplanes,

I believed that flying was dangerous.

I overcame this by exposing myself to flight in the most dramatic way. I celebrated my thirtieth birthday by skydiving for the first time while I lived in Colorado. The initial motivation for this was to overcome my phobia around airplanes. I didn't expect the permanent smile on my face to last for nearly a week afterwards. I wanted to jump again and again.

I moved back to Washington State for graduate school and continued my new sport. I excelled at skydiving and earned my A-license in twenty-five jumps, much faster than the average of forty jumps. The progression begins with static line jumps, where a line is attached to the plane and it pulls your rip cord for you as you fall away from the plane. You have to climb out onto the strut of the plane and hang in the arched position before the coach instructs you to let go and fall. Your instructor then observes and critiques your ability to get into position and go through specific motions, while remaining aware of your altitude. Climbing out onto the strut was the scariest and most exhilarating part.

The more advanced stunts include a routine of belly turns, barrel rolls, front and back flips, and a delta move. Students were required to remain on heading before pulling their rip cord at or above a specific altitude. Additional requirements included calculating jump location, figuring out the ideal distance between jumpers based on wind conditions, and proving that you can get into and out of formations with other skydivers without hurting them. The A-license allowed me to jump alone at most drop zones in the world.

Leaping out of small Cessnas, floating in freefall, doing stunts, and making formations in the air with other jumpers freed my mind of everything else. The horizon always looked beautiful. On some days, I could see from the Pacific Ocean to the Cascade Mountains. On other days, I'd float just below gorgeous clouds. The loud wind in my ears drowned out my worries. And the air pressure on my cheeks forced my face to smile. I'd feel a rush as my parachute unfolded and opened. Under chute, I'd drift slowly to the ground, turning and spiraling as I wished. When I reminisced about my skydiving days, I could still hear the nylon parachute flutter in the wind.

I smiled in my airplane seat, and the jet steadied. I looked at my watch as everyone else slept. We were scheduled to land in two hours at 5:30 a.m. I closed my eyes and continued thinking about my crazy adventures. I had explored many sports and hobbies since my illness. Each endeavor served a purpose. And when I met my objective, I let go and moved on to something else. I used the excuse that I stayed so active and pushed so hard in order to keep my spine from relapsing. While I'm certain that activity and movement is great for my back and has likely prevented several flare-ups of old battle-wounds, I learned to be honest with myself. I pursued extremes to prove that I hadn't died, that I hadn't been broken down, and that I could do anything. I wanted to show anyone who ever felt sorry for me that, not only was that a waste of their time, they had absolutely no chance of keeping up with me now. *Never let them see you sweat. Never let them see you weak.* "Them" referred to anyone and everyone, since I learned that I could trust no one. If someone saw me as vulnerable, that meant getting hurt was inevitable. So, I wouldn't slow down long enough to be caught off guard.

I climbed rock faces, frozen waterfalls, and mountains. In climbing, all that matters is your next move. Whether you move an inch or a foot, it was all progress. I became addicted to the feeling of defying gravity on a rock wall and the sense of accomplishment at the top of each pitch I climbed. Occasionally, I struggled to get past a harder move. I would try and try and eventually make it. My belayer once called me "the most determined person in the world." He said this to me after it took me nearly forty-five minutes to get past a hard move on the first pitch of a climb, called Mosquito, in the Squamish Smoke Bluffs. I admitted defeat on climbs and descended only a few times. I still recall the exact moves on the exact climbs that I have given up on all over the continent.

I hiked as much as I could, even if that meant I had to go alone. I'd sometimes hike for seven or eight hours by myself, and I wouldn't see any sign of another human being for most of that time. I found the most remote hikes that I could, and soloed some of the most beautiful peaks in Washington State and Colorado. I logged my miles and hiked at least twenty miles per week, every week, for several years. I felt unstoppable.

With hiking and snowshoeing, all that is important is your body's condition and location. *Am I warm, safe, and dry? How far from the car or another person am I? Will I make it to the top and down before dark? If not, do I have a headlamp and extra batteries? Do I have enough water and food? Do I have extra clothes, just in case?* I didn't think about my failed marriage, my work stress, my family, my health issues, or my financial troubles. I concentrated on where I existed in space and time.

Hiking and climbing gave me the same sense of escape, calm, and achievement. Both allowed me to focus only on my body at precise moments and nothing else. The movements were meditative, simple, deliberate decisions. After each climb or hike, I would anxiously check the forecast for the following weekend or day off from work in order to plan my next adventure.

"What's next?" I eagerly asked my climbing friends at the end of each trip.

"Oh shit. We created a monster," my climbing partner replied.

Weightlifting increased my strength and sense of empowerment. I applied the lessons from physical therapy to body building techniques that I learned about through a friend. I wouldn't allow myself to think that I couldn't lift something because of my old injuries. I cautiously tried my best with every exercise until my confidence increased. I carefully warmed up on lighter weights and gradually increased my repetitions and weight load on each move. At five-foot-four and 125 pounds, I lifted more than most people in the gym. My boxer image from childhood changed to a more muscular vision of myself fighting off pain, stress, injury, and anyone who tried to put me down. I attended kick-boxing classes, so I could learn how to utilize my strength. I kicked higher and higher, punched harder and harder, and lifted heavier and heavier weights.

I pursued any hobby that peaked my interest. I guess that's what a person does to prove they are alive.

When asked "What do you do for fun?" my answer usually took a long time.

"I climb, hike, run, lift weights, skydive, race cars, ski, dance, draw, and write. What do you do?"

Graduate school involved a full-time class schedule and a part-time internship, all while working full time. I worked out each morning before my internship. Each day started at 5 a.m. and ended at 7 p.m., and then the homework started. I attended classes on weekends and some weeknights. I couldn't fit in all of my hobbies, but I never slowed down. If I stopped moving, I worried I would become depressed, stagnant, in pain, or sick again.

I spent almost ten years pushing too hard, going too fast, and doing too much. And the enjoyment eventually dissipated. *What am I trying to prove?* This thought haunted me constantly. I needed to be honest with myself. I had spent eight years trying to outperform others' expectations of me, to be able to say, "I did that crazy thing that you could never do! Ha!" I forced myself to climb even when I didn't like it anymore, just because I was too scared about what it would mean to stop. I forced myself to jump out of planes, even though the joy that used to compensate for the nerves had morphed into boredom.

One day, it hit me that pushing so hard all the time shifted from feeling accomplished to feeling resentful about my life. I lacked balance. I no longer felt the need to prove anything to anyone. I survived abuse, neglect, serious illness, depression, and extraordinary pain and disappointment. I stopped caring about what others thought about my abilities, strength, and resilience. I decided that simply existing needed to be enough. I struggled to define what gave me joy.

"I don't want to climb anymore," I said to Mike one day. "I don't enjoy it. I only do it because I feel like I have to. I don't want to do things for the wrong reasons. I work too hard to not have fun on weekends. Climbing isn't fun anymore."

"Okay," he said. "You said the same thing about skydiving before."

"Yes, and I stopped. I feel like I've been doing these things to prove something. To prove I'm alive, or something. To prove I'm not depressed anymore. To prove I'm strong. I'm tough. I can do anything. But I want to focus on things that I enjoy now."

"Okay," he said again. "But I just bought this camping grill for our climbing trips to Squamish."

The guilt hit me like a Mack truck. Even though I knew that my decision to quit climbing disappointed him, I never looked back.

I continued hiking, running, weight-lifting, and dancing. I let go of the pressure to be the best. I began to get to know myself, not as a survivor, or as a bulldozer pushing through life, but just as myself. My chest didn't feel as tight. My voice softened, and I stopped dreading the weekends. I felt lighter and happier. As a good friend once said, "If it ain't fun, why do it?" Plus, doing physically strenuous things for the wrong reasons almost inevitably leads to injury. I had experienced that and seen it in others. I wanted to be healthy. I had accomplished so much; it was time to be the healthiest person I could possibly become. And that included having balance.

I watched the sun rise above the glowing city of Boston as we descended. The plane glided peacefully, and the pink sky glowed against the purple-tinted buildings. I shivered thinking about how cold it looked outside, but also due to lack of sleep and food. I couldn't remember the last time I ate.

I had no idea where to find my rental car in the Boston airport. I struggled with my rolling bag, laptop, and purse. I blinked my eyes repeatedly. My eyes screamed as I opened and closed them against my contacts, which had been stuck to my eyes for far too long. I stumbled through the airport and followed the signs for the rental cars.

"I need to pick up my rental car. Can I get the thingy for the tolls?" I asked the agent.

"Are you in town for business of pleasure?" he asked, as he typed on a keyboard.

"Neither. My father is very sick, and I'm going to see him," I replied.

"I'm sorry to hear that, ma'am. Don't fall asleep behind the wheel of my car, okay?" he said, and he handed me some paperwork.

I must have looked like hell. He indicated that our conversation was finished. I didn't figure it out right away, and stood there lifelessly. Exhaustion had set in, but I had to keep moving.

"Where d-do I go?" I stuttered.

He pointed toward a long hallway and said, "Pass that escalator, go out the door, turn left, and go to the parking garage. Choose any car on the third floor. The key will be in it."

The old me, before sickness, divorce, extreme sports, overcoming phobias, graduate school, and moving around the country alone could never have handled such uncertainty, especially within the middle of the turmoil with my father. Such vague instructions on finding a rental car in a strange city after no sleep on a bumpy flight would have set the old me into a tailspin. But the new me didn't bat an eyelash. I just needed to get my tired ass to a car and start driving to the hospital, which was about three hours away.

I chose a small, red Chevy and plugged the hotel address into the GPS program on my phone. I managed to make my way out of the parking garage just fine, but a large truck almost crashed into me while I tried to merge onto the highway. There were not a lot of directional signs on the East Coast. Either you knew exactly where you were going and what you were doing, or you were toast. The close call barely affected me. I haphazardly waved my arm to say "sorry" to the truck driver and kept going.

"Oops, not a good way to start this shitty day," I said

to myself, and I laughed.

I struggled to find something positive to focus on for this trip. I had a talent for finding the positive, the humor, the lesson in everything. If I thought too much about the unknown of everything I was about to face, I'd suffocate with emotion, shake violently from my core to my fingertips, and drift into a daze.

"Just pay attention to driving, Laura. You can do this," I said aloud.

I planned to visit my dad and then go to my mother's house for dinner. I hadn't seen her since Mike and I had lunch with her a few years earlier. And that visit upset her immensely. Cara was unpredictable. I worried about my visit with her almost as much as my visit with my dying father.

22
strained relationship

My relationship with my mother always felt like a roller coaster ride. I wouldn't visit and neither would she, but I always sent a Christmas gift, a Mother's Day card, and birthday flowers. We talked on the phone once or twice a week. Strangely, she sent me gifts at the strangest times. I received an email on September 7, 2010, stating that my package needed to be picked up at the Sears Warehouse on 1st Avenue in Seattle. "What package?" I said aloud. As I read the email, my phone rang.

"Merry Christmas!" my mother celebrated.

"What the heck? What are you talking about?" I asked.

"I ordered you something, and I got a great deal on it. You'll love it. You just have to go pick it up! It's at Sears."

"Oh! I just got an email from them. What is it?" I asked.

"You have to go and find out." She giggled as she spoke. I couldn't tell if she had been drinking, but she was definitely in a great mood. "It's big. You'll have to get Mike to go with you."

"Okay, we'll try to go get it today," I said.

Mike and I drove to downtown Seattle to pick up the package. The large box barely fit in the back of my Subaru hatchback, even with all the seats down. My mother had bought me a large gas grill. We managed to get the box into my car and haul it to my apartment. We got it upstairs and immediately realized that it needed to be assembled.

"Are you kidding me?" Mike seemed very frustrated. We had nothing else to do that day, but he was always grumpy on weekends when he was too injured to climb. And this just made his bad mood worse.

We spent the next four hours putting together the gas grill. I called my mother and thanked her several times, but it never felt like enough. The grill took up the majority of the space on my small deck. Christmas came early that year, I guess.

I spent years in therapy learning how to set boundaries with my mother. I kept most of our conversations short and on positive topics that were not too emotionally draining or potentially vulnerable. If she slurred her words when I called, I'd make an excuse and get off the phone. To avoid catching her after she'd been drinking, I learned to call her in the morning on my way to work. I told her that I didn't want to talk about my childhood, because I was focused on moving forward and living a healthy life. I'd warn her that if she insisted on bringing up the past, I'd hang up the phone. I faced my past in a healthy manner, in therapy, with a trained psychologist. Talking about that bullshit with her only fueled the depression, anxiety, and anger. She had a tendency to lie to make herself feel better, and we'd end up arguing about the truth. This accomplished nothing. If it wasn't a productive conversation, I wouldn't allow it. If she was negative, I'd end the conversation. There were many unwritten rules and boundaries. But I either enforced them or we wouldn't talk.

She would occasionally threaten to visit me in Seattle, but would back out for a variety of reasons: illness, dental work, a busy schedule. She had retired years earlier and didn't have any hobbies, so I never understood her "busy schedule" excuse. But I never pushed.

In October 2015, she flew to Seattle to spend ten days with me at my new house. I wanted her to be proud of me for buying my first home with Mike. I had saved money from my divorce in 2002, invested well, and worked very hard. I always dreamed of having a yard, caring for a house, painting colors on walls without having to talk to a landlord first, and feeling secure in knowing that I didn't have to leave with very little notice at the whim of a landlord or anyone else.

I heard rumors that she disapproved of this decision. She told everyone in the "family" that I had made a huge mistake by putting all of my money into a house. I blocked her negative comments from my mind and prepared for her visit. I spent three days cleaning the house and weeding the yard, and I painted the entire upstairs during the weeks prior to her visit. I spent $200 on groceries that I knew she would like, and I planned recipes I would cook for her. I made a list of things to do and places to go. I would keep our conversations on positive topics, and keep her happy; if I did everything right, it would be a great visit.

"We can walk around the lake and Discovery Park. We can go to the zoo, farmer's market, wineries, Ballard Locks, beach, and I can't wait to show you my neighborhood. There are a bunch of restaurants and antique stores within a few blocks of the house!" I told her on the phone the night before her flight.

"I don't know if I can do that much walking. I'm old," she replied. My mother was sixty-seven years old at the time, but she had smoked since age nine, and her health problems worsened every year. I thought walking would help her.

"We can start with a short walk in the neighborhood, and go from there," I suggested.

"Okay, that sounds good. I just want to have time to relax and have a cocktail, too."

The taxi pulled up, and my mother looked very tense. She got out of the cab, slammed the door, and lit up a cigarette, as I rushed out to greet her. The taxi driver looked overwhelmed, as he made his way to the trunk to retrieve her luggage. His face frowned, and his body looked exhausted. "Did you have a nice flight?" I asked my mother.

To my surprise, the taxi driver responded, "Your mom has had a stressful trip."

Oh shit, I thought to myself. "Mom, are you okay?" I asked, as I gave her a big hug and tried to avoid getting burned by her cigarette. I remembered the scars from the red-hot tips of those things as a kid.

"Oh, I'm just happy I made it. There were no bathrooms on the plane, and we were delayed. And then there was traffic. Seattle traffic is awful. Why do you live in this city?"

"Because it's beautiful, Mom. Let's go inside. Do you want a cocktail?" I knew how to make my mother happy. And I no longer cared about trying to stop her from drinking. I learned that I did not have the power to prevent an alcoholic from drinking.

"That bag is heavy. Don't hurt your back!" she yelled, as I lifted her larger bag to carry it into the house.

"I'm fine, Mom. It's okay." I carried the bag up the three steps into the house. She limped up the steps behind me, rambling something about her hip and her back hurting from the flight.

"What do you mean there were no bathrooms on the plane?" My curiosity was stronger than my experience in knowing that I should just let it go.

"They broke!" she replied

"All of them?" I asked.

"Yes, can you believe it?"

"That's insane, Mom. I'm really sorry." I didn't believe her, but challenging her would accomplish nothing. And I sensed her effort to shake off her bad mood.

We entered the living room and she said, "Wow, this room is really cute!"

Inside, I lit up. She finally liked something of mine. "This is where we hang out a lot, Mom. Do you want a tour now, or a cocktail?"

"Yeah, let me see your house! It's cute!" I contained my excitement, but I felt myself shaking inwardly.

We walked through the rest of the upstairs, and she made several positive comments about the windows, the light, and the open layout.

I said, "It's small, but it's laid out well."

She agreed. I showed her the stairs that led down to the finished basement. "The stairs are steep because the house is about a hundred years old. Do you want to go down there now, or wait until later?"

"Let's go see!" she said. She seemed excited. I carried her large bag down with us, since she'd be staying in the guest bedroom. She made it down that stairs and commented about the steepness. "It *is* an old house, huh?"

"Yep. It still has its charm, I guess." I said, sarcastically. We both laughed.

After showing her around, I asked her, "Do you want a cocktail here, or should we walk to the local pizza place and get a drink and some food there?" I had already bought her favorite vodka and various mixers that I knew she liked.

"Let's go out! That sounds like fun," she said.

I chose to take her to the pizza restaurant on my street because I knew the staff, and I had warned them that I would be bringing in my mother for a visit. I didn't know what to expect, and I wanted to know that I had support, just in case. My mother and I had a nice talk over a few glasses of wine and some pizza. I kept the conversation on positive topics, and I continued to make her laugh all evening.

The next day, we drove to Redmond, Washington, which is about forty-five minutes away, to visit with her sister, Connie. Connie is an inch and a half shorter than me. She has short, wavy, reddish-brown hair, and we have very similar profiles—with our chins slightly sunken in, high cheekbones, and small noses. At lunch, my mother acted very drunk after one margarita. Her behavior changed so quickly! I couldn't figure out if she had been drinking without my knowledge, or if the margarita was interacting with her medications.

She brought up her childhood with Connie including the beatings and the baseball bat. She turned to me and aggressively said, "You should be thankful that your childhood wasn't worse, and that I protected you so much!"

Connie tried to change the topic, but it didn't work. My heart hurt, my temperature rose, and I couldn't find any constructive words to say. *Yes, my childhood could have been as bad as hers. Yes, it could have been worse. But why would my mother display this as some kind of competition?*

I felt the urge to share all of my secrets about my father. I wanted to remind her of all the beatings I had endured that she ignored. I wanted to reveal, in front of her sister, that I was left alone at age fourteen, not seventeen like she told everyone. I wanted to yell that I had gotten free food from the town hall because I was hungry and alone, not because I wanted to help her with bills. I wanted to scream, but I resisted engaging in her pissing contest. I took a deep breath and a large drink of my margarita. In my head, I started to count to a hundred. In a hundred seconds, my emotions would go away. Counting always helped. *One, two, three...*

"And when you were in Connecticut last December and only had lunch with me, that wasn't right. You really hurt my feelings. That wasn't right at all," she scolded.

I looked around the restaurant and hoped that no one overheard my mother's angry, loud voice. I excused myself and went to the restroom. I leaned against the wall in the hallway for several minutes, so I could catch my breath and collect my thoughts. I dug my sharp fingernail into the soft flesh of the fingertip of my thumb.

Don't let her get you down, I thought to myself. *She sees things differently because she has to. It's how she copes. Just let it go. You're stronger than her. You've had more help. You've taken care of yourself better. She's doing the best she can with what she knows.*

I couldn't hear what my mother and Connie were talking about when I returned. But as my mother looked out the window, her mood suddenly changed again when she saw the Bed Bath & Beyond across the parking lot. "Let's go shopping!" she gasped. Connie and I looked at each other, shrugged, and agreed to go to the store. While we waited to pay our bill, my mother became more and more antsy, like a child waiting to go to an amusement park.

While we walked through the store, Cara laughed, talked loudly, and pointed to things that I just "had to have"! She kept telling me to pick out anything I wanted. My mother enjoyed purchasing things for people, but I didn't want anything. I wanted her to calm down. I wanted to go home. She raised her voice, and she insisted that I "go shopping"! I hate shopping.

Eventually, I picked out a ceramic cat toilet brush holder and a new set of silverware. Cara seemed satisfied that I had picked out some things that she deemed useful. I appreciated the gifts, but I craved quietness and calm. Connie pulled me aside and said, "I'm sorry you have to deal with this."

I smirked and nodded in response.

"Aren't you having fun?" my mother asked me, slurring her words.

"Yes, Mom, this is great. Thank you for everything. I think I'm all set. And I'm tired. Can we get going?" I asked.

"Oh, you always kill the fun, Laura. I guess we have to go. Laura said it's time to go. Time to be miserable again," my mother said, sounding extremely disappointed.

I turned the radio on in the car ride home, and I tried to find upbeat songs that I knew she would like.

The next day, my mother woke up with a cough. It sounded like a bad chest cold. "I need to go to the hospital," she demanded, as she made her way up the stairs from the guest bedroom.

"What?" I asked.

"I need a doctor. I have pneumonia," she declared.

"Mom, I can probably get you in to see my doctor, or we can find a walk-in clinic. I don't think you want to go to the ER, do you?"

"Well, if you can't get me an appointment, then yes. Yes, I do!" she insisted.

"Okay, let me try."

I scheduled an appointment for her with my doctor for later that day. She continued to cough as she smoked on the front porch. "Maybe you shouldn't smoke, Mom," I suggested.

She rolled her eyes and said, "It calms me down."

My doctor diagnosed her with bronchitis and prescribed antibiotics, several inhalers, a decongestant, and cough syrup. I made six trips to the pharmacy to get her everything she needed. She continued to smoke, and I believe she continued to sneak her drinking. I did not go through her luggage to confirm this. But in the past, she always traveled with a large plastic jug of vodka. "It's the only size they make in plastic, so it won't break on the plane," she would say.

That afternoon, she came inside from smoking a cigarette. As she held her stomach, she said, "I don't feel good."

"Do you think you're going to be sick?" I asked.

"I don't know. I think it's the cough medicine. Or maybe it's the cigarette. I feel really sick. I'm going to lay down. I can't go to dinner with you and Connie tonight."

"That's okay, Mom. Go lay down. Do you need me to stay here with you? I can call Connie and cancel," I offered.

"No, no, I'm just going to go to bed," she replied.

"Okay, I'll leave quietly in a few minutes. I'm

supposed to meet her at the Mexican restaurant down the street in a little while. I'll be really quiet. Do you need anything before I go?" I asked.

"No, I have everything I need. Thank you." She made her way down the steep stairs, and I turned on the television in the living room. After a few minutes, I started to hear strange sounds coming from downstairs. I could tell she was vomiting, but I couldn't tell where she was. I immediately flashed back to when I was young and she would vomit after drinking too much. I remember taking care of her, holding her hair, serving her water, bringing her a cold washcloth, and cleaning up afterwards.

I shook uncontrollably, and tears filled my eyes. Through therapy, I had learned many tools to handle triggers when bad memories arose. I needed to remember the steps: acknowledge that I'm being triggered, take responsibility for how I respond, become aware of my body and its responses, and replace negative thoughts with positive self-talk. *I am not there anymore. That is no longer my life,* I thought. *My life is calm and predictable now.* I took slow, deep breaths and tried to clear my mind of all thoughts. I attempted meditation, but her noises interrupted me. I relaxed my arms and imagined warming the center of my body. I thought of one emotion that I would like to replace this feeling with, and I focused on it. I wanted to feel safe.

Her vomiting interrupted my strategies. Each sound created a new trigger. Each cough re-created the memory. So, I quietly put on my jacket, picked up my purse, and left through the front door. I didn't have to meet Connie for another forty minutes, so I called her as I walked up the block.

"Where are you?" I asked.

"I'm just leaving now. What's up?" Connie asked.

"My mother is vomiting all over the house. She said it's the cough medicine. I think she's drinking, but I don't know. It could be the medication. Anyway, I started to get upset, so I snuck out. When will you be here?"

"Probably not until six. I'm sorry you have to deal with this," she repeated what she had said in the store the day before.

"Okay, I'm going to hang out somewhere. I can't be in that house," I said.

I walked the six blocks to the pizza place where I knew I'd run into people from the neighborhood. From the looks on their faces, I could tell that I was not hiding my discomfort well. I walked up to the bar and the bartender asked if I wanted my usual.

"Can I just have some water?" I asked.

"Water? Sure. You okay?" he asked.

"Um, not really. Can I just hang out here for a few minutes? I can't be home right now."

"Of course!" the bartender said.

I sat at the end of the bar and sipped my water. I saw several people that I knew. Many waved. Several people said "hello." I waved back and briefly said "hi." My stomach felt nauseous and shaky. I focused on being warm and heating my core to calm myself. My logical side felt as though I was overreacting; my emotional side couldn't stop shaking. I thought to myself, *You're safe, Laura. You don't have to feel guilty for leaving her. She'll be fine. She said you could go. She isn't your responsibility. You helped her all day. You'll check on her when you get back home. I should be giving myself positive self-talk.* I was really struggling with that concept. It was all about her. I silently struggled with my thoughts.

My mother was sick for the rest of the visit. Anytime she smoked, she vomited. I tried hard to help her, and I brought her whatever she asked for: water, Pedialyte, a cold washcloth, new cough medicine, a specific brand of tissues. I noticed my throat getting sore and my head throbbing. I ignored it and pushed through.

"I'm starting to feel better," she said after seven days. "But I don't know if I can go to Texas. I don't want to get anyone sick down there. I also always feel like I'm leaving you when you're sick." She had a booked flight to Texas to visit two more of her sisters and her parents.

"I'm fine, Mom. I just have a cold. I just need to sleep. I doubt you're contagious anymore. But you need to decide if you want to go to Texas or not. It's up to you," I advised.

"I just got off the phone with Lisa. I guess Brenda got another DUI," she began. Her sisters, Lisa and Brenda, lived in Texas on a ranch with her parents.

Lisa and Brenda both drank more than their fair share. Alcohol was there go-to-solution for everything. Brenda had already wrecked a few cars in drunk driving accidents. Lisa drank every day, but she managed to hold down a job.

"What else is new?" I asked my mother, feeling quite impatient and sick of the drinking stories.

"Well, this time it's different. She was so drunk that she assaulted the police officer, and then she shit in his car!"

"She shit in his car? You're kidding!" I exclaimed.

"No, I'm not. She really did. And then they cleaned her up, and she shit in the holding cell—the drunk tank. She's facing some serious charges."

"Holy shit, Mom.... Literally." We both laughed. "That's really serious!"

"Yeah, I know. She's really embarrassed, so you can't tell anyone."

"I'm embarrassed. I don't want anyone to know either!" I replied.

"Well, I'm not sure I want to go down there."

My mom and Brenda always argued, usually after a lot of drinking. They got into a fistfight at the party the day after my wedding in front of everyone, and they had several other physical altercations over the years.

"Actually, this might be the best time to go! She'll probably be on her best behavior. Maybe this will be a wake-up call for her," I suggested, secretly hoping my mother would hear the same call.

"Yeah, you're probably right. But do you think I can drink around her?" she asked.

"You know what? You have to use your judgment on that one," I said, appalled that she was even thinking about drinking in that moment.

"Let me see if I can change my flight and just stay the

weekend to take care of you," she said. I just wanted to be left alone, but I couldn't say that and hurt her feelings.

She logged onto my laptop and tried to access the airline's website. "I guess it's meant to be," she said, and she turned the laptop toward me. It showed an error message saying the website was under construction.

"Ma, I'll be fine. Go to Texas and see your parents if you feel well enough. I just need a good day or two to rest and I'll be fine," I reassured her.

I drove her to the airport, went home, and slept for the next three days. The visit did not go as I had hoped. As I lay in bed, I remembered something Mike had told me on the phone the night before, and my eyes filled with tears. He said, "It's okay to wish things were different." Tears fell down my cheeks and onto my pillow. I didn't have to pretend to be so strong in this moment. No one would see me weak.

23
reunited

I wished things were different today, too. I was about to
see my father for the second time in almost twenty years,
a few weeks after learning that he had been lying to me
about absolutely everything. I entered the hospital and
searched for an elevator to patient rooms. I found room
405 and entered. He was sitting in a chair with his head
slumped over his body, and he looked gray. His belly and
chest were swollen with fluid; his legs and arms were
pencil thin. He looked up and his eyes lit up. He
whispered my name and tried to smile. He recognized
me. I smiled back. "Hi, Dad!"

He tried to talk, but he couldn't speak since his throat
was still healing from the ventilator tube.

"Are you doing okay?" I asked, knowing he couldn't
do more than shake his head yes or no. He nodded.

I kissed his forehead. His blue-green-gray eyes were
barely open. He couldn't hold his head up for more than

a few seconds. The nurse entered.

"Hi. I'm Betty." Betty was a black, heavy-set woman, and she had a huge smile. Her personality lit up the room instantly.

"Hi, Betty. I'm Laura. I'm Ted's daughter...from Seattle."

"From Seattle? Did you just land?" Betty asked.

"Yeah, well." I took a deep breath, still adjusting to the stench of antiseptic. "I landed in Boston about three hours ago. I drove here from the airport. How's he doing?"

"He's stable. He's doing good! We're trying to keep him awake. And we want him to cough whenever he can. Ain't that right, Ted?" She looked toward my father, and he nodded in response. He tried to cough, and his body jolted painfully. "Three times," she commanded.

He tried twice more. My heart started to break as I watched his body struggle, and then I got mad at myself for being weak.

"Are you going to stay long?" the nurse asked me, disrupting my confused thoughts.

"Yes, I'll hang out for a few hours. I brought my laptop to do some work, if that's okay."

"Sure, sure. There's a plug over by the window. Stay as long as you'd like." The nurse sounded pleasant and upbeat.

My father struggled to stay awake. "Wake up, Dad. Wake up!" I said, leaning into him. Flashes from when I was little cluttered my brain.

I sat back down in the cold, crusty chair and rubbed

my throat, almost protecting it from the hands that could choke me at any moment.

By raising his arm slightly and pointing to the bed, my father indicated that he wanted to go to bed. But it was important that he stay in an upright position. "Dad, you need to cough. Can you cough three times for me?" He tried to cough. His body jerked. He looked like he was in pain, and nothing would loosen the concrete within his swollen chest. "It's my job to remind you to cough once in a while, Dad. Why don't you rest for a few minutes, and I'll do some work?"

He nodded. He pointed to the bed.

"Dad, you can't lie down right now. You have to stay sitting up. It's better for your lungs. It'd be great if you could sit while I visit."

He opened his mouth and moved his lips as if to say, "Water."

"Water?" I asked, to be sure I understood.

He nodded again.

I walked out into the hallway to try to find the nurse to get my father some water. As soon as I was out of sight, my eyes filled with tears. My father was dying. I touched my throat again. I felt fear, but I knew he couldn't hurt me now. I shouldn't be here. I swallowed hard. I turned toward the nursing station, and I almost ran into two people near the doorway next to my father's room. I vaguely recognized the older couple standing in front of me. The man was very tall with thinning gray hair and glasses. The woman was petite, with dark hair and a small face. The stood close to each other and looked at each room number as they approached my father's room. They looked lost.

"Can I help you?" I asked.

"We're here to see Ted," the man said.

"Oh, you're here to see my dad. I was just trying to get him some water."

"Laura. Laura, is that you?" the woman questioned, looking me in the eye.

"Yes. Do I know you?" I asked.

"It's us. It's Eloise and Les. We remember you from when you were young," the man said.

"Oh. Wow. Yeah, I remember you. Wow. Hi!" I reached out to shake their hands. They shook my hand and frowned. The look of judgment in their faces sucked the air out of the hallway.

"It's been a long time. I can't believe you're here," Eloise said with a condescending tone.

"It has been a long time. I've grown up. And yes, I'm here *now*. Have you been in to visit my dad?"

"Every day," she said, looking down her nose.

"Well, I live in Seattle. I flew in last night. I just started a new job a few weeks ago and this was the only time I could be here," I said defending myself.

I remembered that these were his drinking buddies. They believed it was perfectly acceptable for him to be a drunk father who never remembered what he did to his daughter each night. "How have you been?" I asked. I worked hard to insert kindness in my voice.

"We're good. Our kids grew up, too. They're both working. They're still here in Connecticut. Do you know where your dad's checkbook is?" Eloise asked me.

"Oh, that's so nice for you," I said. "No, I don't know where his checkbook is. Have you asked Maria? I haven't seen her yet, but I think she is on her way."

"Oh, she wouldn't know." I heard more condescension in her words. "He said it was missing, that someone stole it."

"I'll be sure to ask Maria when I see her. I'm sure it will turn up. Well, I have to find the nurse to get my father some water. Excuse me," I said, as I started to sound just as cold as they did.

They entered my father's room, and I heard excitement in their voices as they greeted him.

I found Betty and said, "My father is asking for some water."

"Okay, I'll be right there," she replied.

The nurse brought in some thickened water. "Why is it thickened like that?" I asked.

"So he doesn't choke," she explained.

My dad's friends refused to look in my direction, even when I spoke. "Ted, we will see you tomorrow. There is a storm coming, but we will make sure to stop by, okay?"

My father nodded, and they held his hand. "Goodbye, Ted." My father nodded again.

They held hands for a moment longer, smiled, and turned to walk away. I looked at my father and said, "I remember them from when I was a kid."

His eyes lit up again, and his eyebrows raised in surprise.

"Long time ago," I said with a sneer.

My father's friends had only stayed for about fifteen minutes. A few minutes after they left, Maria arrived.

Maria looked just as beautiful as I had remembered from their wedding day. She's still thin and curvy, and her hair looked shiny and healthy as it cascaded down her back. She hugged me for a long time, which surprised me.

I watched my father slurp his gel-like water. Maria explained that the doctors kept giving him medication to make him sleepy so he wouldn't become so upset.

"I understand," I said. I noticed the horrible bruises on his arms; it looked like he had been in a bad car accident. "Do your arms hurt, Dad?"

He shook his head no. "He says no, but they must hurt. The bruises are from the straps," Maria explained.

When my father detoxed, he experienced delusions and hallucinations, and he fought the staff. They were forced to restrain him. I couldn't stand to see the bruises, the effects of a writhing, panicking old man.

At one point while Maria and I were talking, my father's catheter must have moved out of place, because urine spilled all over the floor. I called the nurse to help clean it up. He looked so humiliated, powerless, and vulnerable. His blue-green-gray eyes were teary as he looked around, trying to assess his surroundings. His oily, gray hair made him look so much older than the last time I had seen him, just two years before.

The nurse cleaned up the urine. Another person came in to fix his catheter. He drew the curtain in between us and finished in just a few minutes. Maria and I watched television and awkwardly talked quietly. She asked about my life in Seattle, and I asked about her children and her family in Brazil.

My father indicated that he needed to use the bathroom. He held up two fingers. Again, I asked the nurse for help, and she brought in a bedpan. Maria and I went out into the hallway. A few minutes later, everything smelled like shit. I gagged several times. Maria went into his room, and I paced the hall, trying to catch my breath. I didn't want to gag in front of my father. I didn't want to embarrass him.

"He made a mess," Maria said, frowning. He had missed his target, and shit ended up all over the bed and floor. The smell filled the air and overwhelmed me like a hot, thick cloud. I continued gagging. The nurse went behind the curtain to help him. I felt so helpless. I caught myself weakening.

"I'm going to give your father a sponge bath. You're welcome to go get some coffee or something. We should be done in about twenty minutes," the nurse explained.

Maria and I uncomfortably talked about the condition of the hospital as we made our way to the cafeteria. "You work in a hospital, right?" she asked me.

"I used to. I just started a new job a couple of weeks ago. And I worked in a much cleaner hospital than this," I responded.

"Your daddy doesn't like this hospital, but I had no choice," she said as we helped ourselves to coffee.

We sat down at a small tan and red particle board

table near the window. "I found him on the kitchen floor. He was in his robe and underwear and he was shaking everywhere, kicking."

"Like a seizure?" I asked.

"Yes, seizure. That's the word. I called 911, and ambulance came to get him. I was with him in the ambulance, and they came here because it was the closest. I know he likes the other hospital better, but I had no choice." She was determined to make sure that I knew that she wanted to bring my father to the hospital he liked and not to Waterbury.

"That must have been very scary for you," I said.

"He drinks every night. You know, the big plastic bottle with the handle, vodka, with cola. Always same thing. He drinks one bottle every week. Sometimes more."

"That's a lot. Did he ever stop drinking?" I asked.

"A couple of times, yes. When he got your letter. I didn't read your letter." She paused. That seemed like an important point for her. "He stopped then. He tried to kill himself. He was in the hospital for three weeks. I don't know what your letter said. He always talks about you and your mom. He gets so drunk and so angry. He calls the police on me all the time. He says he will call immigration on me all the time. I learn we just don't talk to him after eight o'clock every night. He only drinks from eight o'clock until he sleeps in his chair. That's it. He doesn't drink during the day so he can work."

I started to shake inside. She talked so fast, and said so much. *He still sleeps in his chair. He still drinks vodka. He drinks the same vodka that my mother drinks. He still drinks until he passes out.* I listed all of the commonalities in my mind. "Has he ever hit you?"

"Oh, no. No," she said. I could tell by her eyes that she was lying. "But I teach my children, and their children. No one talks to Grandpa after eight o'clock at night."

"I'm so sorry. I didn't warn you." I swallowed my tears. I tasted vomit.

"You were a child. You were so young," she said in a comforting tone.

"My mom drinks a lot, too. I started going to Al-Anon. Do you know what Al-Anon is?" I asked her.

"Your mom too, really?"

I nodded slowly.

"Al-Anon? No. What is?"

"It's for family members of alcoholics. It's to help them learn about how their loved ones' drinking has affected their lives. It's to learn how to live a better life while knowing that someone you love has a problem with alcohol. You might like it. It might help you." I did my best to explain, but she stared at me skeptically.

"Oh, no, I don't need that. It's not me. It's just him. It's only him. Not me," she said.

"No, I know that. I mean, things like counting his drinks, or worrying about his behavior, or how you act even when he's not around. It changes how you are without you even knowing it. It did for me. I'm learning so much. It's helping me. I can leave you one of my books if you want," I offered.

She nodded and continued talking about my father.

"You can't leave him again. He won't live. He'll kill himself. I know it. He's going to get better, but you can't leave him again."

She looked at me, desperately. I paused for several seconds.

"I won't do that. I just didn't know he was still drinking. He told me he stopped. He lied. I was so shocked that he was drinking. Does he still have nightmares? Does he scream at night?" I touched my throat again.

"Oh, no." I didn't believe her. "We were told to not talk to you. He thought you would disappear. He loves you very much. He talks about you every day. You can't leave again," she said.

"I won't," I responded. My stomach began to tighten and ache. I rubbed my chest to stop the sharp pains. I felt sweaty, sick, nauseous, disgusting, inappropriate, just like I did when he treated me like his partner. When Maria arrived, he no longer needed me. I had taken my mother's place; Maria took my place. And now I was staring my replacement in the eye, and she was telling me all he could talk about was me.

"I wrote that letter after I got sick. Did he tell you I got sick?" I asked.

"No. When did you get sick?"

"I got sick when I was in college. I promised myself that if I survived that I would write him a letter to confront him and forgive him for everything he did when I was a kid. I didn't mean to hurt him. I'm so sorry I hurt him. That wasn't what I meant to do. I just needed to move on with my life and be healthy." My eyes filled with tears, but I didn't let them fall. I looked away.

"He felt guilt. You didn't do anything wrong. He would drink and then get mean and say bad things and then feel guilt and say sorry and cry. He does that to me. He does that to everyone. He would go play golf and go to bars and be with his friends and drink. Like those people who were just here—them. I don't like them."

"Oh, you saw Eloise and Les?" I asked.

"I pass them in hallway. They come every day. I don't like them," she repeated.

"I don't like them either," I agreed.

"And then he'd come home drunk and be very mean and angry and do bad things. Then he would feel bad and cry until everyone forgive him."

"That sounds familiar. I'm so sorry for what he's done to you," I said quietly, as I looked her in the eye for as long as I could muster.

"I'm sorry for what he did to you," Maria said as she tilted her head to the side. Neither of us spoke again for a few moments.

24
the woulds and the would nots

I made a lot of decisions toward the end of my illness. At twenty-two, my life changed in every possible way. I had been married for three months, and I thought things would finally be stable and happy. Matt and I had been together for almost seven years. He was attractive, with light brown hair and blue eyes. He was smart, having recently landed a job at one of the largest software companies in the world. He was quiet and shy, which gave me room to ramble on and on. I loved him very much, and I believed he loved me.

During the first week of my last year of college, I had recently competed and won a seat in the advanced graphic design program at the University of Washington. Only twenty-two out of 121 students were chosen that year, based on three designs. I loved my classes, and I worked full time at a local pharmacy as a manager.

I took a lot of medication growing up, and I knew

what to ask for to cure each and every symptom. When my breathing squeaked, I needed a steroid inhaler. When I felt pressure in my face and chest, I needed decongestants. When my mucus turned yellow, I needed antibiotics. My body, unlike others, did not have the ability to fight infections on its own. I often got sick with sinus infections and bronchitis. I took antibiotics every time, and I knew the routine well. Being sick all the time felt familiar. I started my second round of an antibiotic, called Keflex, in order to treat a sinus and bronchial infection, and I waited for the medications to do their job. Fix it.

In the middle of the night, I woke up with strange stomach cramps and chills. I opened my eyes and couldn't focus on anything; the spinning room made me nauseous. My new husband breathed heavy as he slept next to me. I ran to the bathroom, threw up, and had diarrhea for about an hour. *I must have eaten something that didn't agree with me,* I thought to myself. I had eaten a ham and cheese omelet—breakfast for dinner—earlier that evening. Maybe the cheese, ham, or eggs were bad. I felt worse and worse by the hour. "Matt, Matt." I tried to wake my husband. "Something's wrong. I'm sick."

Matt grunted in response.

We had known each other for eight years, and his patience for my health problems ran thin. I got myself a hot washcloth, put it on my head, and tried to get some sleep. I had three classes the next day, including a three-hour graphics lab, and I had to work a seven-hour shift at the pharmacy after that. I hoped a few solid hours of sleep would do the trick, and I would feel better by morning.

The next day, I missed my classes, and I called in sick to work. "I think I have food poisoning," I told my boss. I thought I just needed to rest and wait for the bug to work its way out of my system. After eight days in bed with no improvement, I went to my doctor. He suspected that I had the flu and advised me to go home and continue resting. I spent another weekend in bed. I continued to sneeze and cough from my sinus and bronchial infections that were not going away. I sneezed hard, arched my body, and felt a surge of intense pain in my lower back and down my legs.

The familiar pain was a permanent reminder of Manny's hatred for me. My repeated MRIs over the years showed several herniated discs, and they liked to pop out whenever they felt like it. I had angered my back with that sneeze. *Great*, I thought.

When I tried to eat, I'd have to rush to the bathroom almost immediately. I had a low-grade fever. The stomach pain, chills, and spins were relentless. I alternated moving the heating pad from my stomach to my back, searching for relief from the pain in both areas. I took Tylenol and Pepto for the fever and nausea. I was desperate for relief, but the medicine did not help. I had stopped taking antidepressants, anti-anxiety medication, and mood stabilizers only three months earlier, and I craved the warm relaxation that Xanax could give me. If only I kept a bottle, I'd be able to find some comfort. I tried all foods, but everything made me sick. The pattern continued: eat, vomit, diarrhea, sleep, dizzy spells, back pain, heating pad, sweating, cough, sneeze, hunger, eat, and repeat. I felt hungry, but I couldn't keep food down.

I fell asleep with the heating pad on my back one night; it was set to high because the spasms would not stop. I woke up in the middle of the night, and I felt intense itching on my lower back. I reached around to scratch it and felt liquid on my fingertips. It felt like blood. I yelled for my husband to come in and help. He had been sleeping in the living room for the previous week, since any movement in the bed made me sick. He ran in, and I begged him to help. He turned the light on, and my eyes burned and teared from the brightness.

I rolled over. "You burned your back," he said.

"What?" I yelled, panicking.

"The heating pad burned your back. Did you have it on high?"

"Yes, I need it on high. It's the only thing that helps!" I sobbed. I melted a two-by-three-inch circle of skin with the heating pad. He found some cream for burns in the bathroom and rubbed it onto my open wound. I screamed in pain. He put bandages on my back and did his best to comfort me.

I called the doctor the next day. My symptoms had persisted for over two weeks. I was in jeopardy of losing my job and having to withdraw from school. I rapidly lost weight. I remember thinking this part wasn't such bad news, since I had gained a lot of weight over the years. I did not eat healthy food; McDonalds and Burger King provided regular meals for me. And I didn't exercise at all. At five-foot-four, I weighed over 165 pounds. I had no energy. I fought hard to do the simplest things each and every day.

The doctor advised me to go to the hospital for testing. The ER waiting room was spinning, I was sweating, and I had trouble standing upright and walking since my stomach and back hurt so badly. The admin entered my information into the computer, and asked me to have a seat. I felt faint as I walked across the lobby. Matt arrived after I had been taken into a room.

After I undressed so they could perform a CT scan on my stomach, the nurse noticed the bandages on my back. "Miss, what's this on your back?" she asked.

"Oh, I threw my back out sneezing the other day. It happens all the time," I replied, factually.

"Sir, can you leave the room, please? We'd like to talk to your wife alone," the nurse addressed Matt.

Matt looked worried as he walked out of the hospital room. The nurse closed the door behind him. "How are things at home?" she asked me.

"Everything is fine. We're newlyweds. But I've been so sick. I feel bad," I replied.

"Did he hit you?" she asked me.

"What? Oh, no. No, never. He'd never do that. Oh my god, no. My back really is an old injury. I've just been in bed sick for so long that when I sneezed, I threw it out. It's something that's happened to me several times since I was a kid. I have herniated discs S4 to L3. They act up whenever they feel like it," I explained.

"And how did you hurt your back, initially?" she

asked, prodding for more information.

"I was abused as a child," I said, knowing very well that this statistically increased my chances of being in an abusive marriage, so I continued. "I've had a lot of help over the years. I'm doing really well. Matt has been very supportive. He'd never hurt me. He's been there for me and helped me get out of a bad situation at home when I was younger—when we were both younger. My back injury is just old wounds that won't go away."

That seemed to satisfy her. "I just have to check," she said.

"I appreciate that very much. Thank you for caring and being so kind. Can Matt come back in now?" I asked.

She opened the door and called for Matt to come back. He looked concerned. After she left, I explained our conversation to him. He was a little irritated, but I assured him that she was just doing her job.

They took urine and blood and ran every possible test. They asked me to bring in a stool sample the next day for more testing. I slowly got my stuff together and got dressed. Just then, the doctor came back in and said, "I have good news, Laura. We figured out what's going on. You have a kidney infection. It explains the back pain and most of your symptoms."

"A kidney infection? But I don't have a bladder infection. Don't you have to have both?" I asked. I had a kidney infection before, and it started with a bladder infection. I thought the two had to go together.

"Not necessarily," he said. "I ran an instant dip-stick test for a kidney infection, and it came back positive. I'm going to write you a prescription for some antibiotics and something for your back pain, and you should feel better very soon."

"That's great news! Thank you!" I needed to get back to class and work.

I started taking the new antibiotics right away and waited for relief. I could hardly move in bed since my back hurt so badly, and I kept the heating pad on my stomach. The next day, I did my best to collect a stool sample, and I asked Matt to drop it off at the hospital on his way to work. The doctor still wanted to run the labs on my stool to be sure nothing else was going on. The only foods I could eat without getting sick were plain toast and Crispix cereal.

Unbelievably, I felt worse. I took pain pills for my back and tried to make myself sleep. The next two weeks was a blur of antibiotics, pain pills, feeling awful, and sleeping. I stopped eating completely. I watched cooking shows on TV and felt jealous of people who could eat without getting sick.

At about 2 p.m. one day, I woke up suddenly, sat up quickly, felt alarmed, and disregarded my back and stomach pain. Something felt much worse than it ever had before. My heart raced, sweat soaked the bed, and the room spun worse than I had ever experienced. I stumbled around the bed to find the phone. I tried to stand and collapsed, weakened by the twenty-pound weight loss.

I called 911, "I'm not sure what's happening. My heart is racing, and the room is spinning. Something is wrong. I've been sick for several weeks. I can't calm down." I couldn't say more than a few words without gasping for air.

I told them my name and address, and they said they sent an ambulance. I crawled to the front door to unlock it for the EMTs and struggled to crawl back to bed. I called Matt's office and asked him to meet me at the hospital. I could barely speak; I shook badly, and the pounding in my chest terrified me. I could feel my pulse in my neck, my chest, my arms, my legs, my hands, and my fingertips.

The ambulance arrived, and the EMT checked my heart right away. "Pulse: 222," he said. "Did you take anything?" another man asked, as they shined a tiny light into the slits of my eyes.

"I'm on antibiotics and Percocet for my back. I've been sick for about three and a half weeks. They said I have a kidney infection," I explained, a few words at a time.

"Who's they?" the EMT asked.

"I was in the ER like a week ago. I don't remember. The doctor did some test, said I had kidney infection." I struggled to talk.

"What's this on your back?" the first voice asked.

"I burned my back on the heating pad."

"Did someone hurt you?"

"No," I whispered. "I think I'm going to pass out."

The room went dark. "We're going to take you to the hospital, okay, Laura? Laura?"

I tried to move my head up and down. Blackness

overcame me.

I woke up in the hospital. I looked over and saw Matt sitting in a chair in the corner. He stared at the ground, his arms folded, his body slouched. "Hi," I said quietly.

"Hi," he said, looking at his cell phone. "I'm missing a meeting right now."

"I'm sorry," I said. I blinked a flash of white fluorescent light, and the room went black again.

I woke up to the nurse standing over me, inserting more fluids into my IV. "Hi, Laura, how are you feeling?" she asked.

"I'm okay. Matt?" I searched for my husband.

"He's in the restroom. He'll be right back. Do you know where you are?" the nurse asked.

"Yes, hospital," I mumbled.

"Do you know what day it is?" she asked.

"Yes, Tuesday." I wasn't sure.

"Great. Do you know your birthday?"

"August 10, '77. What's going on?"

"You fainted. The doctor will be with you in a few minutes. Just try to relax. Here is the remote for the television. Would you like another warm blanket?" she offered.

"Yes, please," I said, as I shivered.

She grabbed another warm blanket out of the cupboard and laid it over me. The warmth comforted me, and I closed my eyes. Matt walked into the room. He put his hand on my leg and asked, "How are you feeling?"

"I think I'm okay now. Can we go home?" I wanted to minimize everything, feel normal, go home, and go back to work and school.

"We need to talk to the doctor first," he said.

"I'm sorry you missed your meeting," I said.

"It's okay. I'll have to go back to work later, though." He didn't seem angry anymore.

The doctor came into the room and told us both that I did not have a kidney infection, and I needed to stop using the antibiotics right away. He said my stool sample did not show anything. He suspected that I had E. coli or Salmonella, even though those tests had come back negative the first time I was at the hospital. He ran the tests again and sent us home to wait for the results.

Matt and I did not speak in the car ride home. I hate silence. It usually means someone is angry. But I couldn't keep my eyes open. I went to bed immediately, and Matt went back to work. I didn't see him again until the next evening.

The lab results were inconclusive, so I continued to suffer with no answers. My doctor referred me to a gastroenterologist for further testing. I called and made an appointment for the following week. The days blurred together as I watched TV; listened to the hunger cries from my stomach, but was too terrified to eat; sipped water slowly to not increase the nausea; pet my cat, Amy; and slept. Amy would not leave my side while I lay in bed. She stayed with me and stopped eating and drinking water. Matt noticed and moved her food, water, and litter into the bedroom. Although it hurt when she walked on my stomach, I appreciated her company very much. I called her my little angel kitty, even though I don't believe in angels.

The gastroenterologist had received a copy of all of my test results before I arrived. He sat on his doctor's stool as I sat on the table. He looked kind. He was almost bald, with dark hair and blue eyes. He smiled warmly and said, "Laura, you're twenty-two. You're too young for colon cancer, but we need to run some more tests. Are you taking any medications, supplements, anything at all?" the doctor asked me.

"Just Tylenol for the fever and Pepto for the nausea," I replied.

"You need to stop taking both. The fever is not that high, so it's not something to worry about. And with not eating much of anything, the Tylenol is not good for your liver. The Pepto may be causing the lab results to be skewed, so you need to stop taking that for a few days so we can run the tests again. Okay, Laura?"

"Okay. But I know I'll feel really sick."

"We'll prescribe something else for the nausea that won't interfere with the testing. I need to get a clearer picture of your labs. It takes a good twenty-four hours for the Pepto to get out of your system. Can you drop off a stool sample tomorrow?" the doctor asked.

"Yes, I can do that."

"I also want to schedule a colonoscopy to see what's going on inside. If we don't see anything there, I'll want to schedule an endoscopy. But we should see something in the colonoscopy," the doctor explained.

"Do I have to do that if the labs show something?" I asked.

"Yes, I think we should schedule it. It will probably take some time to get you on the schedule. We can always cancel it if the labs show something definitive."

"Okay," I responded, nervously. "What does a colonoscopy entail. What do I have to do?"

He explained the entire procedure. He said that I'd be knocked out, and a tube would be inserted to view my intestines. And beforehand, I would have to drink a gallon of laxatives in order to make sure there was nothing in my system.

"Oh, there's nothing there. I'm barely eating," I insisted.

"What exactly are you eating?" he asked.

"A piece of toast here and there. Maybe a handful of Crispix cereal. If I eat any more than that, I get really sick."

"That's not much food at all. You'll still need to stop eating for forty-eight hours before your test. Because you're eating so little, when you are drinking the laxative, you won't have to drink all of it. You will only have to drink it until your stool comes out clear. It probably won't take very much," he explained.

I worried about the laxatives. How could I get through drinking laxatives when my body was already so weak? I had lost over thirty pounds.

I scheduled the colonoscopy for several weeks away. I hoped that I had bought myself enough time, and I wouldn't have to drink the laxatives at all. We just needed to learn what was wrong with me before then.

Two and a half more weeks went by like a slow haze. I

got out of bed to go into the kitchen to make some toast. I woke up on the floor in the hallway several hours later. I could tell time had passed based on the way the light came into the window. I tried to get up off the floor, but I couldn't get my footing on the moving floor. I crawled toward the closest phone in the living room and dialed 911. Matt worked long days, so it could be many hours before he came home. I was alone and terrified.

"I think I passed out. I've been sick for a long time. I don't know what happened. I need help," I told the dispatcher. My neck and shoulder ached from laying in an awkward position on the floor for so long. The responder took my name and address and sent an ambulance.

I called Matt at work.

"I had to call an ambulance again. Can you meet me at the hospital?" I asked.

"I'll get there when I can," he replied.

I stayed in the hospital for several hours on an IV of fluids. Matt arrived about a half hour before the doctor discharged me. On the ride home, Matt said, "I don't think you understand how much stress you're putting me under. I'm the only one who's working. I have a lot of pressure at work."

"But I don't cost much. I'm not eating anything," I said, trying to make a joke.

He did not laugh. "And you think you're the only one who's scared? I'm scared too."

"I know. I'm sorry." I didn't know what else to say. He worked longer and longer hours, sometimes not getting home until after midnight. I felt so guilty for adding to his stress.

Since I was too weak to drive, Matt begrudgingly brought another stool sample to the hospital the next day. I had little hope that another round of testing would result in an answer. The phone rang a few days later, and again, the test results were inconclusive. The lab tech asked me to bring in another stool sample in a week. By this point, I had lost forty pounds, and I had lost count of how many weeks I had been sick. Time stood still. I hadn't worked or gone to a class in a very long time. I lost my job and my seat in the graphic design program at school. No family called. And my friends lost patience with my sluggishness and my lack of responding as they wished to when they vented to me about the problems in their love lives or work situations. Everything drifted away.

I did not think I could survive drinking the laxatives before the colonoscopy. My fear grew more and more as my appointment date moved closer. More weeks blurred together consisting of collecting stool samples, lab testing, hospital and doctor phone calls, watching cooking shows, losing weight uncontrollably, sleeping, ongoing stomach cramps, dizziness, and sweats. But I had a new heating pad, which had a handheld "on" switch to avoid burns. I held it against my stomach at all times. Christmas, my least favorite time of year, quickly approached. I was excited for New Year's Day, however, because the year 2000 awaited! Matt insisted on spending Christmas with his family while I waited at home to die. I was over fifty pounds lighter, and I couldn't imagine that

I could get better anymore.

Matt brought another stool sample the hospital on the way to the airport. My colonoscopy was scheduled for the Monday after Christmas. He would have to cut his trip short since I needed him to drive me to and from the appointment. But my mind raced with horrible thoughts: *What if I actually did have cancer, even at the young age of twenty-two? What if I didn't make it?* Honestly, there had been times in my life where I believed my life didn't matter much to anyone, so death didn't scare me. But suffering worse and worse until the moment it was all over terrified me. For weeks, I secretly wished I would die in my sleep each time I took a pain pill or fell asleep for the night.

I also decided that if I did survive, I would not waste another day feeling sorry for myself. I wouldn't waste any time with people who hurt me, and I wouldn't let anyone stand in my way. I promised myself that I would no longer reflect or obsess about my childhood or focus on negativity. Instead, I would search for humor and positivity in everything. I would try new things. I would truly forgive my mother and father, and I would move on and let go of the pain. I would laugh more and cry less. I would finish school and find a career I loved. I would never be depressed again. I would never slow down.

I began writing a letter to my father, confronting him and forgiving him for what happened in the past. I also wrote a list of the "woulds" and "would nots" if I survived. All I had to do was breathe in and out until I either died or got well. It was simple.

25
the diagnosis

On a Friday afternoon, my phone rang. It was the hospital calling. I figured they were going to tell me that my tests were inconclusive again, but they had different news.

"Hello, Laura. This is Dr. Jones. We have some results from your labs. We have some findings that could, that *do*, explain all of your symptoms."

"Really? What is it?" I asked, hoping he would talk faster. *Did I have cancer? How could he tell that from labs? What did I have? Was it curable? Talk faster, talk faster, talk faster.* My brain felt as if it would explode with anticipation.

"We found evidence that you have a bacterial infection called C. diff., Clostridium difficile, colitis, in your intestines. It's caused by antibiotic use. It can make you feel really sick and cause rapid weight loss."

"Antibiotics. But I haven't been taking them. Well, I

took them months ago for a sinus infection. Is that all it would take to get this sick?" I asked as fast as I could.

"Yes, it's very possible that that's all it took to get this sick," Dr. Jones confirmed.

"I took more antibiotics for a kidney infection after I was in the ER months ago too, but I never had a kidney infection. Did that make it worse?" I asked, speaking even faster.

"Yes, that probably didn't help."

"Oh wow! So, what do I do? How do I get better?" I felt more energy and hope than I had in months.

"Well, the funny part is, we need to give you an antibiotic to make you better. It's a really strong antibiotic that treats this infection, that kills this bug, but you should feel much better soon. We'll call it in right now. It's called Flagyl. Which pharmacy would you like us to use?"

I told them which pharmacy and gave them the phone number. I knew it by heart from all the medications I had taken over the years. I asked a friend to pick up the prescription for me, since Matt wasn't back from his Christmas holiday with his family yet. I called Matt to tell him the wonderful news. I was going to survive. I started taking Flagyl right away.

The Flagyl made me feel even sicker, which shocked my very weak body and even weaker emotional state. The antibiotic created a battle within my body. The thing that caused my illness was antibiotics, yet I was taking antibiotics to kill the bug that moved in after antibiotic use. It was poison, as far as my body was concerned.

After a few days, I begged my doctor to give me something else. He prescribed Vancomycin, which is the only other antibiotic in existence that kills C. diff. I drove to the pharmacy and picked up my new medication. I hadn't driven in a couple of months, and it made me very nervous.

Vancomycin did not make me feel as sick as Flagyl, but the internal disgust didn't quit. After two weeks, I felt a change. The fever had gone away, and the dizziness and cramps lessoned. I could eat rice with a little salt, in addition to the dry toast and Crispix that I had been living on for months. I weighed 105 pounds.

A week later, I thought I was out of the woods. I could walk around without feeling dizzy. I started to think about going back to school. I was getting excited about living again. I felt lighter, changed, happy. Like a blink of an eye, it all shifted back. I felt very sick, dizzy, feverish, and I vomited up my rice and broth.

I called my doctor and told him.

"Laura, the C. diff. could have returned. Let's run another stool sample and check it out." The test for C. diff. came back positive the next day. I went back on Vancomycin for another two weeks, and I lost another eight pounds. I read online that the relapse rate for C. diff was thirty percent, but I didn't allow myself to think that this could happen to me. My body had been through so much. How could I survive two more weeks on poisonous antibiotics? I couldn't imagine losing more weight. After the second treatment, I felt well for three weeks before relapsing again. After the third treatment, I felt well for a week before the bug took over my body again. My frustration boiled over.

I didn't realize that in one of my delirious conversations with my mother, I told her I was going to die. She then talked to Matt, and he told her she should visit, "just in case." She took two weeks off from work, and arrived during my third treatment. At that point, I weighed under a hundred pounds.

Eating was a trial and error process. Most food failed and made me sick. "This soup cures everything," my mother said, as she boiled chicken breasts. "I usually use dark meat, but I think the chicken breasts will be lighter on your stomach." She took the chicken out of the water and put it aside. She added carrots, celery, and onion to the water and continued to let the water boil until the vegetables were soft. She added a touch of salt, pepper, and oregano. Then, she chopped the chicken and added it back into the broth. She cooked some instant white rice on the side.

As I sat at my small dining table in my small apartment, she brought over a bowl of soup with rice. "This will taste good," she said.

It tasted wonderful. But almost immediately after eating a few bites, I ran to the bathroom to get sick. The Vancomycin didn't help keep food in my system, but I was almost done with my third treatment. She put the soup in the fridge and said, "We'll try again when you're off the medication."

I agreed. She put the soup in the fridge, and I lay on the couch to watch television with her. I was trying to keep her company since she flew so far to see me.

After my third treatment was over, I started to feel better again. I didn't care. Something changed this time. Deep down, I convinced myself that I'd never be well again. I didn't trust my own body to heal. I didn't trust the medication to work. I figured that this pattern would repeat itself until I died. I hardened. I felt surges of anger deep inside me every single second that I was awake. My marriage strained under the pressure of my illness and lack of income. *Who gives a shit if I do get well? What do I have to live for anyway? Not that it's gonna happen,* I thought to myself.

I tried the soup again, and I didn't get sick. My mother's eyes teared, but she blinked quickly to hide them. "Thatta girl," she said, smiling. I smiled back. Hours passed, and I didn't get sick. But I didn't trust it. She cooked different things over the last few days of her visit to see what I could eat. Most food stayed in me, as long as I didn't eat more than a few bites. Anything greasy, heavy, fatty, or with too much fiber, sugar, or acid did not work. I felt pretty good for a few days in a row.

However, the hospital called and told me that my latest stool sample showed that the C. diff. had returned. I'd have to do the treatment again. My mother was at the grocery store when I got this call; she was buying more food for me. I shook with fury, allowed myself to scream in frustration, and felt what little strength I had leave my body. I knew I would not survive. I noticed dirt and crumbs on the off-white carpet in the bedroom in our small apartment. I found the vacuum and started to clean the carpet. I couldn't walk for more than a few steps, but I worked the vacuum like a mad woman! My mother walked in, and I collapsed. While I lay on the ground shaking, I told her the bad news and cried. I had learned not to cry as a child, but I couldn't control myself. I couldn't stop.

I knew she had to leave the next day, and I knew I wouldn't survive another two weeks of taking that horrible medication. She knew I'd be fighting this one last fight alone, since Matt hardly ever came home anymore. He had checked out of our marriage. Maybe it was because we got married too young. Maybe he distanced himself to make it easier on himself when I died. Maybe he wasn't around anymore because he had found someone else. I didn't have the strength to care.

I lay in bed and remembered the times that I wanted to take my own life many years earlier. I thought about the times that another person, a man, almost choked or beat me to death. And now everything balanced so delicately. I had a familiar thought. *If I did die of this illness, who would care or notice?* I had said goodbye to so many people, either from moving around, because my family members left, or because my sickness got in the way of me supporting other people, so they stopped calling. Very few people remained. I pictured my funeral; family members would show up to give my mom the attention she craved. Matt would have a pile of paperwork to get through since we had stupidly gotten married right before I got sick. Some of his friends would show up out of respect. My friends from the East Coast and I didn't stay in touch very well, so I doubt any of them would fly three thousand miles to say goodbye. I hadn't met many people in Seattle yet, because all I did was work and go to school before getting sick. Not much would be lost.

I recognized the horrors of my thinking, and I started to use the techniques I was taught in my years of therapy to work on replacing my negative thoughts with positive ones. I read my list of "woulds" and "would nots." I chose to focus on survival and the changes I would make.

I made promises to myself, and expressed my thoughts on paper. It was exhausting to fight to live when it felt like my body had already chosen to die. But I wanted more than anything to experience the person I knew I was despite everything that had happened. All this time, I knew that I hadn't yet experienced myself as a healthy, happy, strong person. I knew she was in there, but I didn't know how to access her. If I lived, this would become my life-goal. I needed to meet her, be her, and share her with the world. I pulled out my letter to my father, and I finished it within a few hours. I fell asleep heavily, as if I had run a marathon.

My mother left the next day. I spent the next two weeks in bed, and I knew I had changed forever. Something clicked. I had no idea who I was, or how I got to this point. I went from feeling completely alone, dying in a bed, obsessing about all the horrible things I had been through, to suddenly focusing on who I wanted to be. I pictured my boxer stance with my gloves up, ready to take on anything: this illness, the next abusive memory I had, the next guilt trip from a family member, the next depressive episode, or the next anxiety attack. It was time I remembered this part of myself. I promised to use it, every day, from this moment on. I would fight. Fuck it.

The fourth treatment succeeded, but it took several months for me to trust my recovery. February 9, 2000 was my last day taking Vancomycin, forever. February 10 celebrated my first day of healing, and of striving for true health. All of my symptoms disappeared, but the burn scars on my stomach from the heating pad would remind me of my illness for three years. The first day I felt the C. diff. take over, I weighed 165 pounds or so. I now weighed ninety pounds. My body changed from a size 16 to a size 0 or smaller. I went down several bra sizes, one shoe size, and even a ring size. "You look like a model," my mother-in-law said when she saw me. "I can't believe it. I'd get sick anytime if it meant I could lose that much weight and look like you!"

I did not allow my in-laws to visit during my illness. Our apartment had one bathroom. I needed it often and without warning. I would not have been able to accommodate Matt's father's forty-five-minute trips to the bathroom to escape his wife's rants. "We just want to help you, Laura," they said. But their constant questions and other comments proved to me that they wouldn't be visiting out of concern for my well-being. After all, I could not work for eight months; therefore, I had no value.

"You look fantastic. I guess you really were sick," my father-in-law said. "Wow, if I was twenty years younger,

I'd be flirting with you." I smiled at the comment, but I felt deeply insulted. *Yes, I really was sick, and I should slap you for saying what you just said*, I thought to myself. "So, when are you going back to work? You can't be a freeloader forever," he said.

"As soon as I am strong enough," I replied. "I am not eating much regular food yet. I can only eat bread, rice, bananas, and chicken and rice soup. If I eat much else, I still feel very sick. I have to reteach my intestines how to digest food."

"So it's like starting over. Almost like you need baby food?" he asked.

"Yes, kind of like that. I heard it can take some time. I hope to enroll in school next semester and go back to working in the pharmacy in a few weeks or so."

"That's great, Laura. You and Matt seem to be getting along better than ever, too!" he exclaimed.

"Yes. Things are good," I lied.

26
ptsd

Although I healed physically, I suffered from constant panic attacks and anxiety. Every time my stomach growled, felt full, felt empty, or had any sensation at all, I panicked. The room spun, I felt nauseous and sweaty, and my heart raced. I struggled to leave home, go to the grocery store, visit my husband's friends, or go to dinner. I freaked out if I was away for too long, if I got stopped at a traffic light, or if I got stuck in traffic. I convinced myself that I would get sick in the car. I felt fear, dread, terror every single day. I had re-enrolled in school, and classes started soon. I needed to find a way to fight the battle in my brain.

I called my therapist and made an appointment. I met Dr. V. in 1998, when I restarted therapy for my depression and anxiety after moving to Washington State. He was almost seven feet tall, and his stature was very intimidating. But his eyes were warm, and he approached me with kindness. He never asked for details about my abuse—something that nearly every other doctor wanted to know. I respected and slowly learned to trust Dr. V.

"You're a shadow of your former self!" he said, as I walked into the office. I had gained some weight back, but I weighed only 105 pounds, much less than the last time he or anyone other than my doctors or the EMT's had seen me. In fact, some of my husband's friends didn't recognize me at all.

"I need to get back into school, and go back to work, but being sick really screwed me up. I can't leave the house. Coming here made me sick to my stomach. I keep freaking out for no reason," I said, as my eyes darted around the room in fear.

"When did this start?" he asked.

"The first time I tried to leave the house. I couldn't even go into the backyard," I answered.

"What do you feel?"

"Sweaty, dizzy, nauseous, the room spins, I shake, I feel terrified that something bad is about to happen. Like I might vomit wherever I am and make a huge mess."

"And if you vomited, so what?" he asked.

"Oh, I can't do that ever again. And I wouldn't be able to clean it up," I said, as tears formed in my eyes.

After another ten minutes of conversation, he concluded, "It sounds like you have PTSD (Post-Traumatic Stress Disorder) from being sick, which is quite common. People usually think of PTSD after someone has gone to war, or been attacked, but many people get it after being very ill as well. There are many things we can do."

He told me about a technique called EMDR, or Eye Movement, Desensitization, and Repossessing. It is used in patients who have PTSD, usually from war, rape, or child abuse.

"It's risky, Laura. For someone with your past, it's risky. It could bring up memories that you didn't know you had. It could trigger new memories, new effects from your abuse. We really don't know what it will do. But it's a very powerful therapy. It can really help you get past the PTSD and move on with your life. It can help you move on quickly, too. But it's your decision, Laura. I'll be here with you every step of the way."

"Let's go for it," I said. I had very little to lose and so much to gain. He prepared me for what to expect, and we planned to begin EMDR with the next session.

"Here we go!" I said as I walked in the door. I knew about the process: I would move my eyes from side to side as we discussed my memories, both very negative and very positive, from being sick. But I didn't know what the results would be. I nervously took a deep breath, and we began.

"What is the worst memory you can think of from when you were sick?" my doctor asked.

"When I got the call that I relapsed the fourth time. I knew I was going to die. I was sure of it. I got mad and started vacuuming. I didn't want my house to be dirty when my body was found," I replied.

"Tell me a little more, until you feel close to how you felt in that moment."

"Terrified, but numb, defeated. I had given up." I shared more, and he told me to stop a moment later. Dr. V then asked me to follow his finger from side to side with my eyes. Immediately after that, he said, "Tell me about a good memory from the time around when you were sick."

"When I tasted chicken and rice soup after not eating much for several months. It tasted so good. I started to think I might actually get better."

"Tell me a little more until you start to feel the positive emotion associated with that experience."

I shared more and started to feel hopeful and happier, just like I did when I ate my mother's chicken and rice soup. Again, he asked me to follow his finger from side to side with my eyes. This process continued for about forty-five minutes: discuss a negative memory, move my eyes from side to side, talk about a positive memory, move my eyes from side to side, and repeat.

Within eight sessions over a four-week period, I started moving forward with my life again. I attended the first day of class, as scheduled. I remembered everything from being sick, but my emotions were no longer as attached to the memories. I had successfully separated the two.

I lost my seat in the Graphic Design program. I had the option to start over, but that would have meant competing again, and waiting another year and a half before graduating. Instead, I decided to finish school and earn my bachelor's degree in Interdisciplinary Visual Arts (IVA), which I accomplished in three quarters.

Matt asked me to contribute more at home, so I began working again as a receptionist at a mortgage bank. It paid twice as much as the pharmacy. I worked to learn more about myself, and to make sure I upheld all of the promises I had made to myself while I was sick. I read my lists often, and I focused on the life I wanted. I mailed the letter to my father.

Matt worked a lot during the last several weeks of my illness. He also went out with friends almost every night. He said seeing me so sick scared him, and he didn't want to be around it. I didn't have the energy to fight for his attention, so I didn't ask him for his support. Had I died in those final weeks, I would have been alone. More importantly, I would have been lonely. "Alone" and "lonely" mean two different things for me. I had spent a lot of time alone growing up, but in my heart, I had some friends, and even a few teachers, who cared. At this point, I was lonely as well— meaning I couldn't find another person's genuine love within my heart.

"In sickness and in health." I whispered the words aloud as I thought about those moments in the hospital bed. I didn't feel the loneliness that I felt in those moments anymore. I felt angry.

In addition to my own therapy, Matt and I began going to couple's counseling. Through therapy, I learned how betrayed, angry, and hurt I felt. How dare this person who I had made vows to, who I would die for, who I loved more than anyone feel nothing when I needed him the most? I also learned how to access my voice, my strength underneath, the me that I always knew existed under all of the pain.

I honored my promise to myself to not waste my second chance at a happy and fulfilling life. I would no longer live a life of a depressed, subdued, quiet, shy, submissive, un-opinionated, unmotivated, and undriven person who just did as I was told. I wanted to go out there and grab life by the balls. Each time I inhaled, I breathed deeply, cleanly, and fully.

My new outlook on life did not impress Matt. We argued constantly. I started to get more involved in working out and outdoor sports. I had hiked a lot as a child, and returning to the trails felt refreshing, amazing, and authentic. I started rock climbing, racing cars, and kickboxing; and I signed up for dance classes. I spent time thinking about my career and what I wanted to do with my professional life. I found at least one positive thing to focus on every single day. And I laughed often with new friends that I found.

"You're not the person I married!" Matt yelled. The only characteristic that my husband liked about me after my illness was my new healthy, thin, lean, athletic, 120-pound body. The other changes appalled him. Apologizing for not being depressed, quiet, and miserable wore me out. Health became my mantra, my motto, and my passion. I didn't take any medication, drink alcohol, eat any fast food, or waste a single day feeling sorry for myself. I did some sort of workout every single day. I pursued every hobby that crossed my mind.

"You're right. I'm better than her!" I yelled back. "I

am happier. I am healthy. I want to do things. I want to go places. I want to have fun. I want to be strong. I don't want to sit at home every day anymore."

We argued daily. Then we argued weekly. Then we stopped arguing. Then one or both of us stopped coming home altogether. I went for long drives, returning after 10:30 at night, knowing that he'd already be asleep. He went out with his friends, and came home drunk after going to a strip club, or to a female coworker's house to try to make me angry with him. I pretended to be asleep. I felt nothing.

"It is important that you spend the entire weekend not talking about the relationship at all. Try to enjoy each other. Try to remember why you two fell in love," Dr. V. instructed us in therapy one Friday afternoon.

As Matt and I waited for the elevator to open outside of the doctor's office, I said, "I think I should move out."

"Yes, I think that's a good idea," Matt replied.

"I'll look for apartments this weekend." So much for not talking about the relationship.

I moved out three weeks later. I thought about my list of "woulds" and "would nots." After two years, I decided to sacrifice my marriage for my health. I didn't know how to forgive him for leaving me to die alone. But I committed to work on it in therapy for myself. No one should die alone.

27
it's all real

As I stared at my father, I flashed back to the loneliness I felt when I lay in a hospital room, or in my bed at home, dying alone. As much pain as he had caused, I didn't want him to suffer.

"Dad, are you cold? Are you in any pain? Do you need anything? Another blanket? Thick water?" I kept asking him questions. I wanted to be sure he knew that his needs mattered to me.

"Dad, can you do me a favor and cough three times?" I said, remembering the doctor's advice that he needed to cough three times, as often as possible, to try to break up the fluid in his lungs.

That quiet hacking sound caused my throat to tighten. His chest sounded tight and suffocating, as he struggled to break up the fluid. Air barely moved in and out. But I kept making him do it, and he listened every time. His blue-green-gray eyes teared each time, which pulled at my heart.

"Good job, Dad. There you go." He tried to smile in return, as he looked in my direction. Each time he looked me in the eyes, the color of his eyes shocked me. They were the same undefinable color as mine. And just like mine, they changed based on his mood or what he wore. This was still my dad.

As I left the hospital, I called my mother to tell her I was on my way. The frigid wind blew hard, and I struggled to keep my down coat closed. I hadn't bothered to take the time to zip it up before hurrying out of the hospital. I didn't want anyone to see the weakness brewing within me.

"I'm leaving the hospital now, and I'll be there in a few minutes," I said. My mother lived only a few miles away.

"How's he doing?" she asked.

"Um, not good. He's off the ventilator, but it's not looking good. He's stable, but he's really sick. And I talked to his wife. Her name is Maria. I'm not sure you know that." I had never told her about my father's wife, and I couldn't think of any other way she'd be able to find out. "Anyway, it's all real, Mom." And I couldn't get another word out. If I opened my mouth, I knew I would sob. My chest tightened; emotion choked me. I couldn't breathe. I shuffled my feet along the ice-patched parking lot to get to my rental car as quickly as possible. And I had to figure out a way to get off the phone so my mother wouldn't sense my fragility. *I can't let the tears fall. I can't let anyone see me sweat. I can't be weak.*

"Laura, Laura, are you there? Are you okay?… Laura, say something…. Laura!" My mother insisted I speak.

"I'm here. It's all real," I said, sobbing uncontrollably. "He hurts her too. Just like he hurt us. She told me. I hoped it was all not real, all this time. And I thought he had stopped drinking, and lying, and well, none of it has ever stopped. It's all real, Mom," I sniffled. I instantly regretted my words and revealing my pathetic state of mind.

"I'm sorry. I know it's dumb. I know I'm stronger than this. I know it's all in the past. Just hearing her talk about it was hard. I felt like I should have warned her, you know? When I was a kid. But I was a kid. I'm sorry. I'll stop. I'm okay. I'm fine." I took a long, deep breath and calmly said, "I'll be there soon."

"It *is* all real. I'm so sorry, Laura. And no one would ever blame you for not telling her. You *were* a kid. And even so, you weren't given the chance. I'm sorry you have to go through this. You've done nothing wrong. You're being there for him when he doesn't deserve anything from you. You're stronger than I would be in this situation. I'm so sorry you have to deal with this," she said kindly.

She said exactly what I needed to hear at that moment, and it threw me off balance. I sat in the rental car, looked around, collected myself, and said, "Thanks, Mom. I'll be there in a little while. I want to stop at the hotel room and change my clothes. I need a shower. I'm still wearing what I wore yesterday. I must look awful. I also want to call Mike. We've been texting, but I haven't talked to him yet."

"Okay. I'll see you when you get here. No rush," my mother said.

"Hey sweetie," I said to Mike on the phone.

"Hey, where are you? How's it going?" He sounded concerned, caring, and loving.

"I'm back at the hotel. My dad isn't doing well at all." I updated him on my father's condition, and started sobbing again. "All of my memories are real. He has been hurting his family too. I feel so bad for them. I feel…I don't know what to feel. I guess I should be angry."

"You are allowed to feel exactly how you feel. It doesn't matter. There's no right or wrong way to feel," Mike said.

"Yeah, I guess you're right. This is so much harder than I ever imagined."

"I know. You'll be okay. Are you going to your mom's house for dinner?" he asked.

"Yeah, she invited some family over, because they haven't seen me in a very long time," I said. I probably sounded a little irritated about the extra attention.

"That's weird. Are you really in the mood for company?" he asked.

"Well, I haven't slept in over thirty-six hours, and I'm not in the mood to pretend to be happy, but it's better than being alone. And this is one of my uncles, who I spent time with growing up. He's really nice. And his wife is nice, and my cousin. It'll be okay," I explained. "I'm only going to go for a little while."

For all of my adult life, I avoided family at all costs. I

felt safer this way; I didn't have to be reminded of the loss for not having them in my life, and I didn't have to worry that they would be harmful or aggressive in any way. I was not in the mood for company, but I did my best to be social, positive, and funny. I have always used humor to overcome stress. I was proud of myself for making it through the day, and for allowing myself to release some emotions in a healthy way. I didn't deny myself, and I let some of it out. I did have the strength to get through this; I just needed to remember to use my tools in order to navigate the plethora of emotions that seemed to come out of nowhere. "These are all normal responses to a traumatic situation," I kept telling myself, just as I used to counsel my clients.

"It's so nice to see you, Laura. You look fantastic!" my aunt said to me. My aunt was thin with a narrow face and dark hair. She was slightly taller than me. I noticed right away that her belly was very swollen, and I remembered my mother telling me that her health wasn't the greatest anymore. Her liver was failing form alcoholism. My uncle was also thin, and he had muscular arms from his welding career. The gray hairs in his mustache made him look just like my grandfather. He was wearing his usual baseball cap that advertised a commercial fishing company. My uncle loved to fish.

"Thank you! So do you!" I replied. I met my cousin's new wife, and my family members and I caught up about many things. I hadn't seen them in about eighteen years. We shared stories about our lives, and I made a lot of jokes. I definitely inherited the humor in the family.

When I taught special needs children, my students used to say, "Miss Laura—it's not what you say. It's *how* you say it that makes it funny." I guess my tone of voice made my words funny, and I was on a roll that night.

"Why don't you ever come back to Connecticut?" my uncle asked.

"Well, it's been hard to afford to, mostly," I lied. "But now that I have a higher paying job, I plan to be back more." I meant that part. I wanted to make more of an effort to see my parents. This trip was a wakeup call that they wouldn't be around long. But I needed to be careful to not to lose myself, to make sure I stayed safe, and I had to maintain my boundaries.

"Laura, you haven't even been back for Christmas!" my aunt exclaimed.

"That's the most expensive time to travel!" I replied, emphatically. Inside, my holiday rant began. I hate Christmas. I always have; I believe I always will. I begin the holiday season every single year with the best of intentions, and every single year, I struggle.

28
fuck christmas

My mother's best friend's husband died of cancer a few days before Christmas when I was about six years old. Her friend hated the holidays after that. I remember that everyone understood this reaction to such a loss. No one judged or dismissed her feelings; her friends and family took care of her and provided extra support around the holidays every year.

Three days after Christmas in 1984, my mother and I left my father. We had been spending time slowly moving clothes and other personal items to the one-room apartment behind Stew Leonard's in Danbury, Connecticut. We had been sneaking around for weeks, until my mother finally had the courage to tell him about our plans to leave. She waited until after Christmas so that it wouldn't ruin the holidays for me. However, I linked the two. Walking away as my father threatened to kill himself is my first Christmas memory. The

Christmases before might have been nice, but I don't remember them.

I alternated my Christmas breaks between my father's and mother's homes for the next four years. I couldn't tell you which place felt more uncomfortable, because one theme remained consistent—I became the burden that got in the way of their partying and them living their lives. I always tried to save money to buy them nice gifts, make them smile, and make them laugh, but neither one of them wanted me around.

I remember hearing people say that I was lucky because I got to have two Christmases every year—one with each parent. But that is not how it felt. My father would usually give me a few dollars and then take me out to pick out my own Christmas present, to be purchased with the money he just gave me. I usually bought something I needed, like sneakers or baggy clothes to wear to school. I always wore baggy clothes, especially around my father. I did not have toys; we did not play games except for cards.

My mother bought me presents, but she did not have much money. She would give me some cash to buy her gifts, because she knew how much I enjoyed thinking of and purchasing gifts for her. I did not like receiving gifts because of the guilt attached to them. "I can't afford anything on your Christmas list," or "I have no idea what to get for you," or "I don't even know your size" were things I heard every year. I had to do more than ask for presents; I had to teach my parents about myself. And it felt awkward and disgusting. For the parent who was stuck with me for the holidays, the gifts became reminders of how unwanted or insignificant I felt. Those emotions attached to the item, making it hard to enjoy.

My mother wanted to be partying with her boyfriends—yes, she had many boyfriends at times—or drinking with her girlfriends and buddies. She wanted to be out late, getting attention from her friends and the strangers she interacted with. I know this because I watched it. My mother sometimes would take me to bars with her, starting at age eight. She'd order drinks for me, and she was the life of the party. On the drives home, I would wonder how she could be so much fun around other people and so angry in my presence. A whole week hindered by a child at Christmas definitely got in her way.

My father wanted to be sitting home, getting high and drunk, and passing out in his recliner. He didn't know how to fall asleep any other way. He obsessed over the loss of his wife, and stewed over it. He did not want the responsibility of having to care for a child. When I visited him for the weekends, it didn't feel like a father-daughter relationship. He forced me to sleep in the same bed as him. I cleaned his house and comforted him over the loss of my mom. I felt like a substitute wife.

On Christmas Day, my father and I would go to his mother's house. She lived in a trailer park in a bad neighborhood. I loved her cooking. My uncle, Lenny, lived with my grandmother. He suffered from very severe migraines and hardly ever left his dark bedroom in the back of the trailer. I was not allowed to make a noise.

Although my father didn't seem to mind this part of our Christmas tradition, it definitely got in the way of his drinking. My grandmother's house had no alcohol because my grandfather had died from alcoholism many years earlier. He suffered from diabetes, and continued to drink until gangrene ate both of his legs and his heart stopped.

After I stopped visiting my father, my mother took me to my grandparents' house for weekends or breaks from school when she'd "had enough" of me. This became another home, and I spent a couple of Christmases there. My grandmother would bring me to church with her. "Honor thy mother and father," I would hear. *How do you honor someone who hates you?* I thought to myself. I spent a few Christmases completely alone, which depressed me even more.

When I turned fifteen, I met my future husband, Matt. His family enjoyed wonderful Christmas traditions of lavish gifts, amazing meals, and hours of happy family time. They played games, none of which I knew, and told stories and jokes. Several conversations would occur simultaneously, and I struggled to keep up. During this time, I'd find a way to spend some time with my mother around Christmas. But my future parents-in-law resented this. They would ask me, "Why do you want to see someone who doesn't want to see you?" Although they were right, this hurt me deeply. This is when I started to see the differences in my Christmas experiences and others.'

When I was twenty, Matt accepted a job in the Seattle

area. We moved before my last year of college, and I eventually finished my college education at the University of Washington. Matt always needed to be with family for the holidays. For most Christmases, we flew across the country to be with them for at least a week. I could not relate or understand the importance of this. His family transitioned from liking me to deciding that I would not be a fit mother to my future children or a good wife to their son, because I stupidly told them about the abuse I had endured as a child. They saw this as a black and white definition of my character. "How can she possibly have a family when she never has been in one? People who were abused always abuse their own children. You can't possibly have a future with someone who's so screwed up," I heard them say to the person I would marry one day. I did my best to kill them with kindness and buy them very thoughtful, but far from lavish, gifts. Nothing worked. Their subtle put-downs and blatant insults continued. Their opinions about me never changed.

One year, I asked Matt if I could spend Christmas by myself at home. I did not want to travel during the holidays, and I especially did not want to spend another Christmas around people who didn't enjoy my company (no matter how hard I tried). I had had enough of fake-smiling my way through this supposedly cheerful time. I enjoyed Christmas this year, because I did nothing to represent or suggest a holiday. I stayed home, watched movies, played on the computer, ate lot of fast food, and enjoyed the quiet. While I felt healthier and happier because I spent this time of year doing exactly what I wanted, my husband's family used this opportunity to add to their arsenal of criticisms.

We got married the following year, and I loved married life. As Christmas approached, I battled for my life. I had been sick since September 1 of that year. As of Christmas Day, the doctors still had not diagnosed me. I had already lost more than fifty pounds from my illness. I had lost my job and withdrew from my classes. No doctor could figure out what I had as I disintegrated and suffered. For Christmas, my parents-in-law wanted to visit my husband for a week. I declined since I did not feel well enough to handle visitors. They said they would "take care of me," but I knew they would impose, use our only bathroom constantly, and judge how sick I "really was." They insisted that my husband spend Christmas with "his family" and he went to their house for a week. I spent the holiday alone and fighting for my life. *Another shitty Christmas*, I remember thinking.

Being sick for so many months isolated me more and more, forcing my mind to race and reflect. I compartmentalized all my pain, abuse, loneliness, fear, anxiety, and angst about my childhood into one thing: Christmas. Screw it. Why celebrate such bad memories? And what is this whole thing about having to spend time with family all about? Family, for me, equaled loss, pain, disappointment, and danger. "Family" is an F word, a reminder of the hole in my heart, and a reminder of what I had never experienced: a safe place to fall—unconditional love. Every single symbol of Christmas became a trigger for the effects of the abuse and neglect I had suffered through. I'd feel tense, stressed, furious, fearful, depressed, and resentful at the sight of Christmas trees, lights, cards, movies, or commercials, or if I heard the stupid songs.

Two years later, my husband and I divorced. I spent the next few Christmases by myself. I went hiking, backpacking; or I stayed home to draw, write, or watch non-Christmas movies. I felt lonely, but my anxiety level decreased. I did not feel pressured, judged, or looked down upon by others. My exposure to triggers decreased.

Occasionally, I would spend Christmas with a friend's family or with my Aunt Connie's family. Seeing other people's families experience such joy together warmed my heart and also created resentment. I never wanted to feel this way, and I never expressed it. But hearing people complain about their family drama, and then seeing their loving family dynamic and unconditional acceptance of one another frustrated and confused me. I did not have a normal family; therefore, I could not be normal, right?

I remember a particularly paradoxical experience. I spent Christmas at my friend's house. They were married and both sets of their parents had flown to the Seattle area to spend a week with them. I could not relate to the amount of effort their parents had made just to see them. Even the thought of someone doing that for me would make me extremely uncomfortable. What would I owe them for that? I witnessed laughter, love, conversations, and smiles. While I imagined that their relationships weren't perfect, the unconditional love was evident. I focused on the joyous energy in the room, rather than fixate on my usual sense of loss. I achieved this quite well that year, but pain and confusion lingered moments away.

Years earlier, I had moved across the country and cut off all communication with my father, with one exception. I kept an email that used my old name that I could use once in a while to ask him a question and vice versa. We barely communicated. He hated me for not having a relationship with him. And I needed to protect myself by not having a relationship with him and maintaining very strong boundaries.

He remembered my birthday incorrectly, but he remembered every year. On a day around my birthday, he would send a quick message that said, "Happy Birthday." Every Christmas, he would send a curt message that simply stated, "Merry Christmas." But in 2005, no birthday message or Christmas message ever arrived. Sensing something might be wrong, I spent weeks calling all the hospitals in his area to see if he had been admitted. I looked up county records to see if he had been arrested or imprisoned somewhere. I had to be careful not to reveal who I was, since I had been hiding from him for years. But I could not find my dad.

My mother called me on the way to my friend's house for their Christmas celebration.

"I called your father," she said, coldly.

"You did? What did you say? Where is he?"

"He's been ignoring your emails. He's fine. He just wanted attention, Laura. Feeling sorry for himself. I think he might have tried to kill himself. You know, the usual crap."

"Seriously? All this time? Did you tell him where I was? Did you tell him my last name? He doesn't know any of that, Mom," I explained. I suddenly shook with worry and regretted that I never told her about my hiding. I had chosen not to tell her because I didn't want her to feel worse about things. I had to protect her feelings at all costs.

"Of course, I did. He knows you're in Seattle. He already knew your last name. Why are you asking me these questions?" She sounded confused and angry.

"Wait, Seattle or Redmond. He didn't know my last name, Mom. Did you tell it to him? My actual last name? Did you say my name?" I trembled, my heart raced, and I felt sweat bathe my entire body.

"I don't know. Maybe. I don't know. You sound paranoid, Laura. Just getting attention again."

My mother gave away my cover; she revealed my identity and location. I immediately felt more paranoid than usual. But I also hoped that his lack of motivation and the three thousand-mile distance between us were big enough barriers to keep me safe.

At the Christmas dinner, I smiled and joked around, but I couldn't stop ruminating about the dysfunction in my life. I felt resentful toward the family in the room. *They couldn't possibly handle my thoughts right now. They didn't do shit to earn their happy family or their happy Christmas. How dare they flaunt their family in front of me?* I battled with my thoughts. I pushed my feelings down as deeply as I could. I kept my secrets.

Each year, I dread the holiday season, especially all things Christmas: Christmas lights, Christmas cookies, Christmas cards, Christmas commercials, ridiculous Christmas TV movies, stupid Christmas clothing that people wear, and Christmas music. Everything about Christmas triggers very severe anxiety and hostility in the depths of my soul. I work on overcoming this. In the past, I broached the topic in therapy, and we discussed coping strategies. I use these strategies every year. Usually, I barely make it through.

No therapist ever forced me to enjoy the holiday. "You're allowed to feel however you want to. It's how you react to those feelings is what matters," Dr. V. told me. While my friends mean well, the pressure to "enjoy the most wonderful time of the year" is palpable, deafening, and heavy. When I express how I truly feel about Christmas, I am judged. I overwhelm people. I get dirty looks or comments like, "We all have crap in our families; yours is no different." The people who judge did not watch and worry about suicidal parents, experience violent abuse, endure molestation, suffer from severe neglect, witness drug and alcohol abuse, or face death alone, specifically around—and at a higher intensity during—the stupid fucking holiday. Christmas makes everything worse.

If a person loses a loved one around Christmas, they get extra support and special understanding. I lost my childhood and endured trauma around Christmas. The fucking holiday now represents all of that pain, yet I'm looked down upon for tying these memories to that time of year. The amount of pressure to smile and act as though I feel I belong to whatever family whose presence I happen to be imposing upon at Christmastime has been nauseating and sometimes debilitating.

So, no, visiting Connecticut at Christmas is not an option.

29
surprising comfort

I felt like a stranger in my mother's house, and I didn't sleep for more than an hour that night in my hotel. I spent the night reliving past memories. *Flashbacks are a natural response to a reminder of trauma*, I thought to myself. Each time I closed my eyes, I pictured someone over me, about to strike. I hadn't gone to sleep with those hauntings in decades. I lightly stroked the sharp bristles of my hairbrush that I pulled out of my purse. I learned that rubbing fingertips against various textures can calm a person and even prevent a panic attack. I pulled the covers off and let the cold air of the hotel room wash over me. If I could get my body really cold, it would feel so good when I warmed it up under the blanket that I could possibly fall asleep. I tried meditation. I imagined each muscle in my body tightening. I held it for five seconds, then I released. My body should have melted. I should have relaxed. Nothing worked. I swallowed two

Melatonin, but they didn't help. I succumbed and took a Xanax that my doctor had prescribed for my anxiety. I hated taking medication, and one thirty-day prescription of this medication easily lasted me a year or more. But desperation took over.

The next morning, I rushed to the hospital to see my father again.

The television played quietly in my father's hospital room. I arrived early that morning to spend a second day caring for the man whose honesty, loyalty, and love had eluded me for my entire life. That day, his condition had improved. Maria said that this was because the doctors didn't have to sedate him the night before; she clearly blamed the hospital for most of his problems. I agreed that the sedation made him sleepy and slowed his progress. I also understood that the hospital staff had very few options when patients became confused and aggressive. The calmer my father was, the faster he would recover. But unpredictable, irrational, and scary people are never calmed down.

"You look better today, Dad. Your color is coming back," I said to my father, as he stared at the floor.

"I feel much better today. I'm ready to go home. The doctor said I can go home tomorrow," he whispered very slowly so I could understand each word.

"Tomorrow! That's great, Dad!" I exclaimed.

I knew it wasn't true. My father wasn't lucid. But humoring him was a defensive move. Keeping him happy avoided conflict.

"Dad, I just want to let you know. The storm is

getting bad out there. I'm only going to stay for another hour, so I can be sure I don't get the car stuck. But I'll be back tomorrow, okay?"

"Okay, I understand," he whispered. "Be safe."

I debated and struggled with what to do next. If I went back to the hotel, I'd be alone, with no food, and there were no restaurants nearby. If I went to my mother's house, I risked feeling more pain or having to play more games to maintain my boundaries. The exhaustion started to settle in, and I wasn't sure I had the strength. But she always had plenty of food in her house now, which was so weird to me.

"Dad, I'm just going to go out in the hall and make a phone call, okay? I'll be right back."

He nodded.

"Hey, Mom. Is it okay if I do come to your house today and spend the night? I don't really want to be alone, and I think it'd be fun to hang out with you," I said, secretly hoping we'd get along for another night.

I could hear the smile in her voice, which surprised me. "Of course, come on over whenever you're ready. How's your dad today?"

"Thanks, Mom. He seems a little better today. He's not as tired, and he's not as gray anymore. I'll call you when I leave the hospital," I said.

I walked back into my father's room, as he drank the gross, thickened water. The nurse followed me in with his lunch, which looked similar to the thickened water. His protein shake smelled disgustingly sweet, and he did not look pleased that he had to stomach another one of them. I couldn't help but let my nose curl a little at the stench.

"I just called Mom. I think I'm going to go to her house instead of going to the hotel. I don't have any food with me, and I'll be snowed in until tomorrow morning," I explained to my dad.

"Is your mother coming to visit me?" he asked.

"My mother? You want my mother, Cara, to visit you?" I asked my father, carefully.

"Yes, of course!" He looked confused.

I didn't understand this request. He hated my mother. And she hated him even more. Why would he ask her to visit?

I texted my mother, "Dad is asking if you want to visit. But I don't think that's a good idea. Do you?"

"Not really. Does he really want me to visit? What about Maria? Isn't she there?" my mother responded.

"Maria is too scared to drive in the snow. I don't think Dad realizes what year it is and that you two are divorced. Don't worry about it. I'll tell him you're snowed in." While I texted my mother, my father's confusion became more and more evident.

"Okay. That sounds good," my mother replied.

"Dad, mom's car is snowed in already. She won't be able to visit today. Maybe she can visit tomorrow," I lied. "The snow is getting pretty bad. I really should get going soon. I'll stay until you finish your lunch, and then I'll go, okay?"

He nodded.

It took my father another thirty minutes to finish his

thickened protein shake. I gagged quietly a few times from the stench. "That doesn't look very good, Dad. Does it taste okay?"

He shook his head no and finished the drink.

"Good job, Dad. Do you need anything before I go?" I asked.

"More water," he whispered.

I walked out into the hallway to try to find a nurse. I paced the hallway for about ten minutes. Anxiety was building about the drive to my mother's. The snow was piling up quickly outside. The plows hadn't come through in a while, and my horrible rental car didn't handle well on even dry roads.

"Nurse, nurse...can you please bring my dad some water?" I yelled down the hall.

"Be right there," she yelled back. I felt bad for being impatient with her.

"She's on her way, Dad. I really should go. But I'll be back tomorrow on my way back to Boston."

He nodded and smiled. I leaned over and kissed his forehead. "I love you, Laura," he whispered.

"I love you, too, Dad." My heart definitely broke.

I slid a few times on the hilly roads to my mother's house, but I handled it. *Gently turn into the skid, make no sudden moves, and don't panic.* I thought of the lessons I had learned as a teenager who drove to school in the snow all the time. I lugged my bags into my mother's warm and cozy cabin. She had set the gas fireplace on high, and the television blared. She quickly grabbed the remote and turned down the volume. "Pete can't hear. I get so sick of that noise," she barked.

She gave me a long hug and asked about my father. I told her that he seemed physically better today, but he didn't understand anything. She said she was sorry for what I was going through, and I thanked her. Over the next hour, I revealed my big secret.

"Mom, I've talked to Dad on the phone for a few years. We managed to stay in touch. And I thought he was clean and sober. He told me he was, and I believed him. I didn't want to tell you because I didn't want to make you feel bad about anything." I explained it all.

I continued, "I feel like an idiot for believing him, for thinking he was safe, and that we could have an honest relationship. He's a fucking liar."

She responded by saying, "Your relationship with your father is none of my business. I always hoped you would reconnect with him again." Her words took some weight off my chest. But suddenly, I felt horribly guilty for having so many boundaries with her all of these years and for not making the effort to spend time with her. *Maybe she wasn't as destructive as I thought. Maybe all of the secrets were unnecessary. Had I misread both of my parents? What was the truth?* Confusing questions cluttered my mind.

She shared with me that he had lied to her all the time. He lied about where he was, how much money he spent, how much he drank, whether he stopped doing drugs, or whether or not he went to work. "I'm so sorry he's doing that to you, too. I'm sorry he's so sick," she said.

"I'm sorry, too. I should have been honest with you."

"It's okay. I understand why you did what you did," she said. "Do you want some more wine?"

"I think one is enough. In fact, I don't think I want to drink anymore," I said, surprising myself. I always thought I could drink whatever I wanted, whenever I wanted. Suddenly, the hard reality of having two alcoholic parents who could not, or would not, quit drinking, hit me hard. Alcohol lost its appeal.

"Really? Well, I guess I can understand that," she said.

"Seeing him like that, and seeing what drinking too much can do…it scared the hell out of me," I explained. "I don't want to go out like that."

"I can imagine. I watched Pete when he was in the hospital, and I felt the same way," my mother said.

"He's drinking again, though," I said, assuming the soda on his desk contained vodka since it had no bubbles.

"Yes, of course. After he got out of the hospital, he stopped for a few months. But that was it." She shook her head. "There's nothing I can do. And his leg is infected again."

A year before, Pete almost died. It started with a blood clot in his lower leg. The surgeon put in a stent. The stent then collapsed, causing him to need seven blood transfusions. He almost lost his leg due to an infection. I guess the infection had returned.

"That's not good. He didn't learn anything at all, did he?" I asked.

"Not a damn thing," she said, as she swigged on her cocktail and started to slur her words.

"It must be hard to watch someone you love so much

not care about their own health. It's helpless." I said this, knowing she wouldn't catch on to the irony. I admit my comment was somewhat passive-aggressive, but I didn't care.

"He acted just like your father. He was delusional. He thought we were trying to hurt him. He lashed out at the nurses," she continued.

"Yes, Dad's doing that too. He says the hospital is keeping him, hurting him, giving him the wrong medication, making him sicker. He said he's hired lawyers, and they are going to come get him and take him away to somewhere safe. He said everyone is the enemy, and everyone wants him dead. It's really scary. All I can do is nod and try to reassure him. But not argue. Arguing just makes him angry, which makes everything so much worse," I explained.

"That's how Pete was, too. But it didn't stop him from drinking, at least not for long."

"It's not normal, Mom," I said. My voice started to raise.

"What?"

"None of this. Our family. It's ridiculous. It's not normal for your sister, your boyfriend, my father to go to the hospital and have to go through withdrawals before their medical condition can be addressed. It's not normal for so many people to have so many DUIs that we can't keep track. It's not normal! I'm just sick of it. I don't want anything to do with any of it anymore." I felt myself lose control a bit.

She nodded and tilted her head to the side.

"I'm sorry. I didn't mean to get upset. It's just everywhere. Addiction, alcohol. I hate it," I said.

"I know. You're right. It's really upsetting. Oh, I wanted to mention something. I talked to my sister, Lisa, the other day. She said you should be careful what you post online." She changed the subject.

Her sisters, my aunts, spread gossip like wildfire. All that changes is the target of their stories, their exaggerations, their lies, their bullshit.

"What do you mean?" I asked, cautiously, feeling more irritated with every millisecond.

"My sisters are all talking about what you posted about your dad. They say that you don't even talk to your dad, so you shouldn't care. You're just trying to get attention."

"Are you fucking kidding me? I posted that because I needed support. I am not ashamed of a single word I posted. *That* is their response? To gossip? To judge?" I breathed anger. I felt my face redden. "People I haven't seen in twenty years reached out to me, offered support, and said nice things. But that is how they respond? Screw them." I was furious.

"I know. My family doesn't know how to reach out," my mother explained.

"That's a copout. That's bullshit. They know perfectly well how to pick up the phone and spread rumors and share third-hand stories about people they don't know. They don't even know me! They don't know anything about my relationship with my father! I've been talking to him for the past eight years. I thought he was clean and sober and safe. It's none of their business. And if they're so concerned, why not ask me how I am? Why not call me and ask?" Emotions overcame control. "Mom, they weren't there for me when I got divorced. They weren't there for me when I got sick. They didn't pick up the phone once. I don't need any of them. I never have. I never will. And I will not be ashamed of posting something on my Facebook page about what is going on in my life," I yelled.

"I understand. You're right. I was just concerned, and I wanted to make sure you're okay. They talk about Mike too. They say he's arrogant, and you should find a new relationship. I guess Connie said some things about how you have to walk on eggshells around him. I'm worried," she said.

The level of betrayal and shock increased exponentially. Connie was angry with Mike about something that had occurred over a year earlier. He apologized several times. Rather than let it go, Connie jumped on the rumor train with her sisters. The only female in the family whom I trusted spread more bullshit about my life to people who don't know me and don't give a fuck about me. They place every negative word on a scoreboard of the game *Who's Kid is Shittiest?* Rather than build anyone up, it's a competition to bring people down.

"Oh, that's rich. The people who don't know shit about me, who can't be bothered to ask how I am and just make their own immature assumptions about my life think that I should leave the one person who is there for me no matter what. Honestly, if they don't like him, it's a compliment to him and validates my choice." I smiled, realizing the humor and truth in my words.

She laughed. "You're right. That is true…and pretty funny."

"Anyway, it's been a really hard day. I think I'm going to get ready for bed. Thank you for the talk. Thanks for listening." I calmed down.

"Anytime, Laura. I love you."

"I love you, too, Mom."

I faced another night of no sleep, and none of my relaxation techniques worked. I decided to imagine a happier time. I thought about my future with Mike. We had no plans to get married. Neither of us felt that marriage was necessary; we already felt like family. But I found myself imagining what it would be like if he proposed. I started to feel comforted and warm. I missed my home.

30
memories

I woke up in a panic the next morning. I looked around and recognized nothing. Between all of the traveling for my new job and spending the last few nights in a hotel and at my mother's house, I felt lost. Once I got my bearings, I planned for the day. I would wait for the plows to come through to clear the roads a bit, and then I would head to the hospital again. I would spend a few more hours with my father, and then head to Boston to catch my flight home. I wouldn't rush to get ready, since a foot of snow covered everything, and my mother lived on a dirt road outside of county lines. The private plow wouldn't be in a hurry either. I would methodically approach the day, and focus on anything positive that I could find.

I stumbled down the stairs, exhausted. "Would you like breakfast?" my mother asked.

"Yeah, that sounds great," I said.

"I was going to scramble some eggs with cheese, and makes some sausage. I have fruit, too. And coffee's just about ready."

My mother knew how to cook very well. And experiencing her cooking for those past couple of days comforted me. But it was bittersweet. I also remembered when she stopped cooking, and when she stopped coming home when I was a young teenager. I relied on donated canned beans, canned corn, pasta, and cereal. Those sad memories felt so far away, like they happened to a different person, with a different mother. How does a person remember the past, forgive, move forward, and then also not feel sad once in a while for all that was lost? *This is normal*, I thought to myself. *Of course, it's sad. You're being reminded of what you missed so much. You'll never know why it stopped, you'll never get that time back, you'll never get an apology or even an acknowledgement, and that's okay. Because you're okay. You loved her anyway, and you still do.* I smiled and said emphatically, "Thanks, Mom!"

After breakfast, Pete, my mother, and I talked about a variety of things. I packed my things, and my mother and I cleaned the snow off my rental car. She gave me a long hug goodbye. "It was so nice to see you, even though it wasn't under the best of circumstances. Please come back again soon." My mother sounded genuine, which warmed my heart.

"I will. I'll be back in a few weeks for work. I'll definitely visit again then, no matter what, okay?"

"Okay, that sounds good. I love you, Laura."

"Love you, too, Mom."

"I'm going to watch to make sure you get up the driveway. That hill can be tough," my mother said, as she pointed to the curved hill in front of me.

"Okay, thanks. I'll just put it in low and keep going. I think I got it."

"Okay. Good luck with your dad today. Call me when you get to the airport. And drive carefully," my mother said.

"Okay, Mom. Bye!" I yelled out the window. I made my way up her driveway and over the hilly roads to the hospital. I found a spot in the icy parking lot and went to his room.

"Hey, Dad! I'm back!" I announced as I entered my father's hospital room. He's still sitting in the uncomfortable-looking hospital chair.

"How are you?" He sounded like he didn't remember seeing me the day before.

"I'm good, Dad. How was your night? How are you feeling?" I realized that I kept asking him questions without letting him answer. My stupid nerves got in my way.

"I'm feeling much better. I'm going home today," my dad claimed.

I knew he the doctors had not told him this and that he didn't understand the facts. He couldn't stand. His breathing was shallow. His oxygen was low. He was still on IV fluids. He couldn't eat solid food or drink regular liquid. His bruises needed more time and care to heal. He whispered, unable to talk. He only had the strength to lift his arms a few inches and wiggle his toes.

A tall, handsome doctor who was wearing the usual white doctor's coat walked in and bellowed, "Hi, Ted. How are you doing today?"

My father perked up and said in his quiet raspy voice, "I'm doing great!"

"That's great, Ted. Feel like drinking alcohol?" the doctor asked him.

"No, never again. I'll never do that again," my father said.

I had not heard my father acknowledge his drinking yet. He looked at me, and I smiled. He looked away in shame.

"Hi, I'm Dr. Carter, cardiologist, taking care of Ted." The doctor introduced himself as he stepped toward me.

I shook his hand and said, "Hi. I'm Laura, Ted's daughter."

"Oh, are you related to Maria?" Dr. Carter asked.

"No, I'm his biological daughter. I'm not related to Maria. In fact, I don't really know them at all. But I'm here now. I live in Seattle." I started my usual defense.

"Are you Power of Attorney?" Dr. Carter asked.

"No, no, nothing like that. My father and I haven't been all that close. But I'm here now," I repeated.

"I understand. Do you have any questions?"

"What kind of care will he have when he leaves here, to maybe help him not drink? Counseling?" I asked.

"Well, he'll be evaluated. And a social worker will meet with him to discuss his options. It will then be up to him to decide what he'd like to do. There are places he can go, if he chooses," he explained. I was disappointed that he wouldn't be forced into some kind of program after all of this.

"I'm going home. I want to go home," my father barked.

"Dad, it's okay. We're just talking about options. We know you want to go home. You have to get stronger first. That's all." I tried to calm down my father, again.

"I am strong!" he yelled. He tried to stand up, and he almost fell over. Dr. Carter scurried over to my father and guided him back into his seat. He gently said, "Ted, we just need you to sit still. We don't want to have to restrain you. Please be calm. Take a deep breath for me, okay?"

My dad took a deep breath and looked over at me. I smiled.

"Who is this beautiful lady?" the doctor asked my father, as he pointed in my direction.

"That's my daughter," my father said. I smiled again.

"Yeah? What's her name?" Dr. Carter asked him, as he made some notes in my father's chart.

My father stared blankly and searched the room for an answer. I looked into his eyes and said, "It's okay, Dad. Do you remember my name?" I paused for a moment and then said, "It's okay if you don't."

"It's okay, Ted. How about a guess?" the doctor asked.

"Brenda?" my dad questioned, looking helplessly confused.

"Brenda? No, Dad, it's Laura. But that's okay. You've been very sick, and it's normal to be a little forgetful. You'll be okay," I said.

He nodded and looked embarrassed.

"It's okay, Dad. Brenda's a cool name! Do you remember that I live in Seattle, and I need to fly home today?"

He nodded. "Laura, I remember. I just forgot for a second," he explained.

"I know, Dad. It's okay. We don't see each other that much. But I'll make sure I visit more often, okay? I have a business trip coming up in about a month. I'll be in New Jersey, and I'll take an extra day off to drive up here to visit you. How does that sound?"

"Good. Really good," he whispered.

The doctor listened to his chest as he took a few deep, wheezy breaths. "Good job, Ted. You keep getting better. I'll be back in a few hours."

"Okay," my dad whispered.

Maria walked in after the doctor left. I updated her on my father's condition since we last spoke on the phone. She said that my father's memory was coming and going. She said that he had forgotten her name several times as well. She looked worried. "He's going to get better," I said. He had to get better. He had a family to take care of. Maria didn't earn much money cleaning houses, and they had a mountain of debt. They needed him.

"Dad, I'm going to have to head to the airport soon. The roads are still pretty bad, and I have a three-hour drive ahead of me. But I'll be back in a few weeks to see you. And by then, you'll probably be all better!"

"That sounds good," he said, softly.

I leaned over him, kissed his forehead, and said, "I love you, Dad. I'll see you soon."

"I love you, too." He didn't know my name, and I knew it. I looked into his blue-green-gray eyes and smiled as comfortingly as I could. I gave Maria a big hug and said goodbye.

I made it to Logan Airport almost four hours before my flight. I didn't mind. The three-and-a-half-hour drive blended together in one fuzzy blur. I didn't remember driving at all. At the airport, I thought about my parents. Everything had changed. My angry mother had comforted and supported me. My dangerous father couldn't stand, speak, eat, or drink regular water. Maria confirmed my bad memories and obliterated my ability to minimize the bad times.

I did not sleep on the plane. Each time I almost dozed off, I had a nightmare of my father trying to strangle me, cut my head off with a knife, or molest me. I thought to myself that *this is a normal response to a traumatic situation*, and I tried to focus on my surroundings. *Acknowledge the trigger, center my body and imagine myself getting warm, focus on a positive emotion. Acknowledge, center, focus. Don't fight it, but focus on something positive.* I had learned these techniques in therapy and in grad school. The powers of the mind astounded me.

During grad school, I studied education, counseling, and brain development. I read about the effects of trauma in children. I learned about the four levels of attachment disorders that can begin as early as the first few weeks after a child is born. This disorder is a response to a mother's inability to connect with or adore her own baby. I studied how a child's brain can actually change in response to a stressful home environment, and this can lead to increased stress hormones, alterations in responses to stress, and sensitivity to stimuli throughout the person's life. The amygdala is in charge of how a person responds to violence or a threat. It is responsible for a person's emotions, survival instincts like fight or flight, and memory. The hippocampus is involved in learning and memory, and is highly sensitive to stress. The frontal cortex develops in the late teens to early adulthood. This part of the brain is responsible for decision making, planning, assessing risk, and judgement. The more I discovered, the more determined I became to live a successful life. I just had to define what success meant to me.

I studied counseling theories, and the solution-focused approach excited me the most. It's an empowering, strong approach to solving problems. Focusing on previous solutions, examining previously failed solutions in order to find a lesson or determine a next step, listing what's in a person's control, reminding a person of what is working already, and giving positive comments and compliments were techniques that worked best for me when I needed help. So, I planned to utilize them with my students, especially since I had limited time with each student to address their needs. Some people have described me as being harsh or abrupt in how I help solve problems. But it's my tried-and-true strategy for changing my core from a victim to a successful, happy person.

I wrote a fifty-page paper on EMDR Eye Movement, Desensitization, and Reprocessing for PTSD. It helped me tremendously when I needed to move on after my illness. I learned about cognitive behavioral therapy (CBT), and I used it to replace my negative thoughts with positive ones. The science, theories, and data that I studied in graduate school both scared me and validated my experiences.

31
another fall

Another mantra I learned in therapy was "expect the unexpected." The day after returning home, I received another frantic phone call from Maria. "Your daddy is not doing well. After you left, he was bleeding from his nose and his mouth and they had to put him back on the ventilator. They had to sedate him and he is back in the ICU. They found a spot on his lung," she said, almost all in one breath.

"What? But he was doing so well when I left. What happened?" I asked her, almost sounding accusatory, which I didn't mean.

"I know, I know. He was doing better. And then all of a sudden, he was having trouble breathing again, and he started bleeding everywhere. They rushed to him and tried to help him. They are going to do a scopy to see what is on his lung," she tried to explain.

"What kind of scopy? Endoscopy? Is there a doctor I

can talk to? I don't understand." I'm sure I sounded crazy.

"Yes, his name is Dr. Carter. He's the cardiologist. I think you met him. And there's Dr. Allen. He's the resident who is working on him today too."

"Okay, thank you so much, Maria. Are you doing okay?"

"Yes, I am okay. All that matters is your daddy. They sedated him again. That's not good. Last time he was on ventilator, it took forever for him to wake up."

"I know. But now we know a little bit more of what to expect. It will take him a while, but they need to keep him calm while they figure out what's on his lung. I'll call the doctor and let you know if I find out anything else, okay?" I said, trying to comfort her the best I could.

"Okay, thank you." She sounded heartbroken.

"Talk to you soon."

I called the doctor and got very little additional information. They were determining if my father was strong enough to do a bronchoscopy to check out his lungs. They were putting in a central line in case he needed immediate surgery. In my new job, I learned a lot about central lines, and the associated risk for infection. I asked if they used ultrasound guidance. He said "no."

I minimized my question and explained that I worked in that field. I started calling the hospital every few hours to get updates on his condition, with the additional hope of getting the results of his bronchoscopy.

Nothing changed by the time I got home from work that day. I needed something to get past this anxiety. I touched the texture of the couch, the buttons on the remote, and my cat. Nothing calmed me down. *I could work out again*, I thought. But my muscles and joints protested since they already carried me through a pretty intense workout earlier that day. Exercise helped reduce my anxiety and stress as well. I wanted to iron everything out, and make it all disappear.

Dr. Carter took my father off the ventilator within a few days, and he slowly began to wake up again. He'd sometimes wake up confused and combative, and the staff responded by restraining and sedating him. And sometimes, he sounded quite lucid and could answer complicated questions with ease. I kept asking Maria, Dr. Carter, Dr. Allen, and the nurses about my father's bronchoscopy, but no one ever gave me a conclusive answer. "Did he even have the test?" I demanded to know.

"Miss. Let me check. Please calm down," said the voice on the other end of the line. And the familiar hold music rang in my ears and increased my nausea. After six minutes and thirty-eight seconds, she returned and said, "The doctor will just have to call you back."

"Which doctor? Who? Did he have the test or not? Why can't you tell me that?" I couldn't hold back my impatience, my stress, and my frustration.

"It looks like he did. The doctor will call you back!" And she hung up the phone.

I spoke with my father on the phone a few times. He wouldn't say much during one conversation, and then sounded very angry and threatening during the next. "I'm ready to go home. I'm much better now. The doctors are poisoning me. Why don't you believe me, you bitch!"

"Dad, I do believe you. I just want you to be strong enough to walk on your own before you go home. Maybe a nursing home would be a better choice?" I asked.

"No, I'm fine. Don't talk to me like I'm a fucking child. You're just a bitch like Maria. You don't care about me at all." He sounded furious and hateful. Even though I was three thousand miles away, I shivered with fear.

The next day, I got a text message from Maria. "They're bringing your daddy to a nursing home. He wants to go home. He's mad. I will let you know what the new number is when we get there. In ambulance now."

"Thank you," I texted back.

I could easily imagine the fury emanating from my father as he left the hospital to go to a nursing home instead of going home. Visualizing my angry father made my heart beat faster. I searched for something on my desk to distract myself. I played a mindless word game on my phone for several minutes.

While I drove home from work that day, I received another frantic call from Maria. My phone lit up, indicating that a FaceTime call was incoming. "Laura, it's Maria. Can you calm your daddy down? We're at the nursing home and he's very, very upset. He doesn't want to be here. He's very mad. He thought he was going home, even though I told him no. I told him he was coming to nursing home. He's very mad." I pulled over onto the shoulder of I-5, cutting off a few cars before coming to a stop on the shoulder.

I could hear him yelling in the background. "Fuck you!" he yelled as loudly as he could.

"Yes, sure. Point the phone in his direction." As she aimed the phone's camera toward my father, I could see a lot of movement in the darkened room. With the three-hour time difference, it was obvious that the rest of the home was trying to shut down for the night. "Dad. Dad. It's me, Laura. How are you?"

"How do you think I am? They're keeping me here. They kidnapped me. They have me here against my will. They're all against me," he yelled.

"Dad, everyone wants what's best for you. Everyone is just trying to take care of you until you are better," I explained.

"I'm fine!" he yelled. "I'm going home. I called my lawyers. They're coming to get me. And you'll never see me again. You'll only find my dead body someday. In a ditch or a lake." His eyes were dark, beady, mean, and angry. The blue-green-gray color had disappeared. I recognized the look of contempt, of a hardened soul, of harsher anger than I'd ever seen in anyone else.

"Dad, take a deep breath. You're safe where you are. No one is trying to harm you. Are you in any pain?"

"No, I'm fine!" he yelled louder and threw something across the room.

I heard one of the nurses say calmly, "Ted, the other guests are trying to go to bed. Please keep your voice down."

"Dad, I need you to take a deep breath. You're in a safe place. It's nighttime. You seem to have the most trouble at night. I understand it's confusing and it sucks that you can't be at home right now. All you need to do is breathe in and out and wait until you are one hundred percent better. Then you can go home. Just not yet. That's all."

"Fuck you, Laura. I should have killed you when I had the chance!" he screamed and threw the phone across the room. The screen darkened, as if it landed face-down on a dark carpet.

I sat breathless for a moment. Cars flew past me at seventy miles per hour. I hadn't paid attention to them until this very moment. I had been focusing so intently on comforting him. But in an instant, with those words, I became acutely aware of the loud cars and trucks zipping by only a few feet away, the banging of my pulse, the dryness in my throat, and the stinging tears in my eyes.

Killed me when he had the chance? I thought to myself. *Did he mean when I was a kid? Does that mean he remembers choking me all those times?* I had written off all of those horrible memories as alcoholic blackouts that he'd hate himself for, if he remembered them. *Did he mean to harm me in that way? Who the fuck does that to a child intentionally?* For some reason, believing those nights of terror were caused by an alcoholic blackout made it easier to accept and move past. But if he remembered, if he knew what he was doing, then he really was a monster.

Maria's face appeared on my phone's screen. "I'm sorry, Laura. I gotta go."

"Are you okay, Maria?" I asked.

"I'm okay. It's going to be a hard night."

"Tell them to give him a Benadryl. It used to calm him down and make him drowsy." I couldn't think of anything helpful to say. The nursing home lacked the resources of the hospital. They couldn't sedate him. His heart medication could interact with any anti-anxiety medication that they would have on hand. "Good luck, Maria," I said as encouragingly as I could.

"Thank you, Laura. I love you."

"Love you, too."

I sat still on the side of the highway, assessing my feelings. *Am I okay to drive the rest of the way home?* I thought to myself.

I texted Mike, "I'm on the side of I-5. I've been on the phone with my dad. He's insane. I'll be late getting home."

"Okay," he responded.

I focused on driving, counting the cars I passed, and subtracting one for each car that passed me. I love driving. Don't brake in corners. Brake in the straightway before the corners; accelerate at the apex out of the corner.

As soon as I stepped into my home, I began shaking uncontrollably. I told Mike what my father had said, and he held me until I stopped shaking. I didn't cry, but I shivered as if the room was only thirty degrees. I couldn't tell if it was fear or shock, or both. *Did he remember hurting me like that? Did he actually want me dead back then? Now?* I couldn't shake this thought.

Mike and I cuddled on the couch for nearly an hour. And then, unexpectedly, I felt relatively normal. I had allowed myself the chance to let it out. To feel the shakes. To talk it through a little. If I felt the need to cry, I would have. I didn't fight my emotions or force myself to feel or do anything. Sixteen years of therapy taught me to allow myself to feel and do whatever I wanted in times of need, and not to second-guess myself. Anything other than that led to suppression of emotions, which always led to unhealthy outbursts later.

"What would you like to do for dinner?" I asked.

"Whatever you want," Mike said. I looked at him and smiled. He smiled back and sheepishly said, "What?"

"Nothing," I said with a crooked smile. I could feel so much love. "How about pizza?"

"Sounds good," he said. We went to the local pizza joint, and I ordered a soda with lime. The bartender looked very confused.

"What, you go away on a trip and come back and you're too good for us?" he asked, referring to the fact that I hadn't drunk my usual two to four glasses of wine the last couple of times we were in.

"No, I'm just taking a break from drinking," I said, still shaking slightly.

I didn't talk to Ted or Maria for a few days. I needed a break to take care of myself. I also quietly decided that I would not visit him during my upcoming business trip unless he was in a hospital or rehab center of some kind. I would not take a chance and be alone with him or go to his home. I no longer trusted him. The man I feared as a child had replaced the father I thought I knew for the past several years.

I received another text message from Maria. I didn't see what it said. I turned my phone over and tried to ignore it. After a few hours, I read it. "Your daddy is at St. Joe's now."

I called her and said, "Sorry I haven't called. I needed to take a little break after what Ted said."

"I understand," Maria said. "St. Joe's is a better hospital. He stayed at the nursing home for two days, but he was very angry. He hit the nurses. He called the police and said they hit him."

"Oh wow. Is he in any trouble? Are they going to press charges?" I asked.

"I don't think so. Last night, he said his chest hurt, and he said he couldn't breathe well. They called ambulance to come get him and take him to the hospital. They said it was a perfect reason to take him back to the hospital, which is a good thing."

"How is he doing now?" I asked.

"His oxygen level is low again, but he is stable. He is in Telemetry unit." She had clearly been practicing that word. "Do you want the number?" she asked.

"Yes, of course." I took down the new number and the name of his new doctor. "Just to let you know, I need to go to Los Angeles next week for a business trip. It's a very busy trip, with really long days of training, and I will actually be in hospital emergency rooms where I cannot use my cell phone. So, I won't be near my phone during the day. But I will call each morning and each night. It's a very important training that I need to do for my new job."

"Okay, Laura. Thank you for telling me. I understand. Call them when you can. They know you are going to call. If you get any information, please call me or text me. I will call you when I get information too."

"That sounds like a plan. Thank you, Maria."

"Thank you, Laura. I love you."

"Love you, too," I said. It felt strange saying that each time. How could I love her, and how could she love me? It made no sense. And I hated that she called my father "daddy."

A few days later, my coworker and I drove to the LA County Hospital Emergency Room. We waited outside for our program leader, and my phone rang.

"Laura, you have to talk to your daddy." Maria sounded terrified.

"What's going on now?" I asked.

"The doctor said he can go home. I cannot take care of him. He can't even walk! He's still so weak, and he's not well. He forgets, and then he's fine, and then he forgets again. The doctor is letting him leave the hospital. And he is not going to nursing home." She talked so fast, I struggled to understand her.

"What? How can they do that? Which doctor said that?" I asked above her rambling.

"Not Dr. Allan or Dr. Carter. Some other mental doctor, psychiatrist or something. He talked to your daddy for twenty minutes, and then decided that he was okay enough to determine if he stayed in the hospital or go home."

"Twenty minutes? He decided that after twenty

minutes? He's had lots of times where he seemed fine for twenty minutes, and then he'd forget where he was, or why he was there, or what his name was. And he can't walk! How can he possibly be allowed to go home?" I realized that my new coworkers could overhear me. My secret was leaking out, and I didn't care.

"Is there another doctor there? Someone I can talk to?" I asked, desperate for answers.

"Yes, Dr. Delang. He's right here."

Dr. Delang introduced himself.

"Hi, I'm Ted's daughter, Laura. I strongly disagree that he's ready to be discharged. I'm not happy about this at all."

"I'm not either." I heard him take a deep breath. "I'm the resident in charge of your father's care. I asked that he be evaluated by psych this morning. He had been in and out of being lucid during his time here. He spent twenty minutes with the psychiatrist, and he was told he had the authority to make his own decisions about his care. Once that was signed off, there was nothing more I could do." He sounded defeated. He sounded disappointed. I realized we were on the same team, and that he was just as shocked and disappointed.

"I understand. Your hands are tied. He must have just had a good few minutes, and that's all this is based on. I'm so concerned. Maria can't care for him. He can't even walk. His moods, his demeanor, his cognition, it's all so unpredictable. This isn't good."

"I agree with you. There's really nothing I can do. I've already spoken with your father about his options. I've recommended a nursing home or rehab facility for him to get stronger. But he's not interested. He's very determined to go back home," Dr. Delang said.

"Would it help if I try talking to him? I have calmed him down a couple of times in the past couple of months. I've failed, too. But I can try," I offered.

"Yes, anything. It's worth a try. Can you call his room? Here is the number."

"One sec. I have to find something to write on," I explained. I walked over to my coworkers, who were sitting at a patio table and chairs about fifty feet away from me. The look of concern on both of their faces chilled me to my bones. I had said too much too publicly. I asked them for a pen and paper. No one had any paper with them. I took out my work phone and texted myself the phone number.

"Dad. Dad, please listen," I begged.

"I'm going home, and you and no one else can stop me!"

"I'm not trying to stop you. Do you remember when I told you that I hurt my back so badly I couldn't walk?" I asked.

"Yes."

"Do you remember that I told you how much rehab I had to go through before I could go back to work? I had to do physical therapy for six months and I had to go to four doctors every single day. But then I was one hundred percent better, and I could do everything like I did before. Remember?" I tried so hard to get through to him.

"Yes, I remember." He sounded agitated, impatient, ready to strike.

"That's all I'm asking of you now. To do this right. You've been very sick and you can't walk well right now. Maybe it's best to go to a place that can help you get stronger faster, the right way, so that you can get one hundred percent better and be like you were before."

"I'm going home. Fuck you!" And he hung up the phone.

Crushed, I hung up the phone and called Maria. "I tried to talk to him, but he won't listen. He wants to go home. Is there someone you can call to help you carry him into the house, at least to get him to the couch or his chair? Maybe he'll get there and realize he can't do anything and change his mind."

"He's gonna get hurt. And it's gonna be their fault," she yelled.

"Maybe that's what needs to happen for him to realize that he still needs help. Either way, it's not your fault. You've done everything you can to help him. Can you get help to get him in the house?" I asked again.

"Yes, his friends, who he always drinks with, are coming."

"Great," I said sarcastically. "I don't like them one bit."

"Me neither," she said.

"Okay, well, let them help and then make them go home. Then try to get some rest."

"I'll have to go to work. I can't keep missing work. We're bringing in no money." She sounded so concerned. I wished I could help her, but I was barely making ends meet myself.

"Call me if you need to, okay? I really have to go. We're walking into a hospital right now."

"Okay. Bye, Laura."

I entered LA County Hospital Emergency Room to observe trauma cases and tried not to think about Ted in Connecticut. My coworkers and I observed a car accident victim who wasn't wearing a seatbelt, a stabbing victim, and several patients claiming they had bad chest pains and shortness of breath. Each time a trauma came in, our nurse leader would usher us to the front row, so we could witness firsthand how our ultrasound equipment worked during an emergency. We could ask questions and be as close to the patient as we felt comfortable, as long as we didn't interfere. Having worked in a hospital before, I felt very comfortable, and I watched in awe at how well our machines did their jobs in telling the healthcare workers exactly what they needed to know as fast as they needed to know it.

The doors swung open with a trauma case of an unconscious man with a very bloated belly. "Man found seizing. Alcohol. Pulse, forty-five. BP, ninety over sixty-five," the EMT said.

This is probably how my father arrived at the hospital months earlier thousands of miles away, I thought instantly. I focused on the learning opportunity and watched the healthcare professionals assess his condition and try to save his life. They asked the man many questions, but he just mumbled. They rubbed his chest aggressively to try to get his eyes to move, and he responded angrily. "That's a good sign," the nurse said. "He has a chance."

I couldn't speak. I just watched. I had shared a little about Ted to one of my coworkers. She made her way over to me, through the chaos, without me seeing her. She put her hand on my shoulder, leaned in, and whispered in my ear, "You all right?"

I nodded. I tried to smile, but my face wouldn't stop staring at this poor man. They began to intubate him and he struggled violently. "We will have to restrain you if you fight us," they said. I felt tightness in my chest, and I clenched my jaw. My mouth went dry. The room darkened and went silent, as I watched this man I didn't know struggle just as my father must have. After they intubated him, I faintly heard my name being called.

"Laura. Laura, there's another one in room 11. We gotta go."

I made my way around the crowd of workers who tended to the bloated man and caught up with my crew. I refocused on the next case, ocular trauma. Another bloated man who was found seizing, suspected of alcoholism, came in a few hours later. It was a long day, but I sucked it up and survived without anyone knowing my thoughts.

Two days later, while still in LA, I received a call from my father. "Hi, Laura. It's your dad." He sounded stronger somehow. "I'm in a new place. It's another nursing home."

"Wow, Dad. Where are you?" I jotted down the name of the new place. *Watertown Manor. Room 101.* He sounded so calm. "Dad, have you been drinking?"

"What? No. I don't do that anymore," he replied, sounding insulted.

"Dad, I'm sorry. I just had to ask. What happened when you went home?" I hadn't heard from Maria. I hadn't been near my cell phone early enough to call her.

"Oh, you were right. I wasn't ready to go home. I need physical therapy."

"Do you like the new place?" I asked.

"Yes, it's much better. And they fixed my medication, and it was like magic. I'm all better now. The other place was poisoning me. I called my lawyer and told them all about it, but I probably shouldn't tell you about that," he said.

"Dad, you can tell me whatever you want," I assured him. I knew most of what he said was lies or based on delusions anyway.

"I had to call the police. They abused me," he insisted.

"What did the police do?" I asked.

"Nothing! I think they're in on it. Everyone has been against me. I need to get better so I can figure it all out and sue them all."

"Just focus on getting better, Dad. That's what matters most right now," I said.

"I understand," he said.

32
a final goodbye

In ten days, I was scheduled to travel back to the East Coast to run my first medical conference in my new job. I debated visiting my father again. As long as he stayed at the rehabilitation center, I would visit him. If the nursing home staff discharged him, I would not go to his house. Each day, Maria and the staff questioned his release date. I could not get a definite answer. He worked through several hours of physical therapy per day, he saw several doctors each day, and his condition improved slowly. The day before my flight to New Jersey, I learned that Ted would not be sent home until after my trip. I could squeeze in another visit, safely.

I visited Ted again on Monday, February 22, 2016, almost two months after he collapsed on the kitchen floor. I parked the rental car and searched the nursing facility for his room. I walked in as saw Ted sitting in a wheelchair watching a movie on his laptop. "Hi, Dad.

Nice room!"

He smiled and his eyes lit up. "Laura! You're here!" he said clearly, but his voice sounded different; it had a higher pitch than before.

"Yes, I told you I'd be back to visit. How are you feeling?"

"I feel great. I can walk with a walker and everything!" His legs looked very swollen, but his color was normal, and the beautiful blue-green-gray tones returned to his eyes. His hair looked greasy and messy, and his long, gray beard drooped over his robe. He paused the movie and looked at me. I had no idea what to talk about now that he was cognizant.

"What were you watching there?" I asked.

"Oh, just a boxing movie. Remember, we used to watch boxing together?"

"Yeah, Dad. I remember." I hate boxing. I hated watching people get hit in the head. As someone who was hit in the head all the time, I never understood why a person would put themselves in a position to hit or be hit, purposefully. What a horrible sport, if you can call it that. "I'm glad to see you doing better. You scared me. I worried we were going to lose you, and your family needs you."

"Scared me, too," he said.

"Did this scare you enough to become a health nut like me?" I asked, smiling, and trying to keep the topic of conversation light and positive.

"Oh, definitely!" he said. "Definitely."

I felt my chest relax with hope. Maybe, even at his

somewhat advanced age of sixty-eight, he would grasp his new chance at life, and begin taking his health seriously.

"That operation was really bad," he started to reflect.

"What operation? You didn't have an operation," I said.

"Yes, I did. That's why I went to the hospital in the first place, for an operation." Clearly, he already started to rewrite what had occurred. "And why does my throat still hurt?"

"Dad, you were on a ventilator. You might have some scar tissue that needs to heal. It might take a little time. Do you have any pain?" I asked.

"No, no pain, but my voice feels funny."

"Yeah, you sound a little bit strange, but it will get better with time," I said, trying to reassure him. He sounded very feminine, which bothered me.

"How many surgeries did I have?" he asked.

"None, Dad. You were very sick, and you were sedated a lot. Maybe that felt like surgery to you?"

"No, I had surgery. Then they messed up. That's why I've been gone for so long," he said, sternly. "And my lawyer says I can sue them for almost killing me."

I guess he decided not to take any responsibility for contributing to his declining health.

"Dad, what did you do when you went home a couple of weeks ago? Did you see your friends?" I wanted to know if he drank, but I knew he wouldn't tell me directly.

"I didn't go home. What are you talking about?" he asked. He sounded more and more irritated with me.

"When you left St. Joe's, you went home for one night, and then you came here. Did you see your friends?" I asked.

"I never went home!" he yelled. "They sent me here, because I was doing so well!"

"Okay, I guess I misunderstood. It was hard for me to get information since I was so far away," I said.

"I understand," he replied.

"So, are you going to eat healthier and quit drinking now?" I finally had the courage to ask him directly.

"Yes, oh yes. I'll eat healthy and cut down on drinking." And there they were, the words I hated to hear. The words every alcoholic uses when they have no intention of admitting they have a problem, of admitting they are powerless to alcohol. They were the words that obliterated my hope— "cut down on drinking." My heart broke again. I held my lips tightly together, breathed quietly through my nose, and nodded in silence.

Maria walked in a few moments later. "Oh, hi, Laura! You found your daddy's room!" Bile filled my throat. *Stop calling him that!* I thought to myself. I looked at her with contempt, and then I hid my face so she wouldn't notice.

"Hi, Maria. How are you? Yes, he's looking much better." I tried to sound optimistic, but in my mind, any hope I had left, any feelings at all, had disappeared in a flash. I recognized the numbness inside me, the feeling of no turning back.

"Yes, he's much better. Going home tomorrow, right, Ted?" she exclaimed.

"Yep," he said. Maria handed him an envelope. I

caught a glimpse of the return address on the envelope, labeled "IRS." Their bills had not been paid since December. I saw a dollar sign and the amount as he opened the letter. He owed over $123,000. I knew he didn't have the means to pay this.

"Laura, can I talk to you out in the hall?" Maria asked.

"You don't need to talk to her," Ted barked.

"Oh, okay, Dad. It's okay, Maria. I'll just talk to you later." I smiled, and she half-smiled in return.

Maria and Ted argued over the IRS bill. He thought he had mailed a check, and he asked her for his checkbook. She said she didn't have it. Their voices raised. I spotted the checkbook on the windowsill and pointed it out. "There it is, and there should be a record of the check if it has already been paid," I said, trying to help.

He grabbed the checkbook and thumbed through it. Maria's phone rang. I heard her say a few words in Portuguese. "Janice is coming over. She wants to know what you want to eat, Ted."

"Burger King. Cheeseburger and onion rings and a Coke," Ted responded. *So much for becoming a health nut*, I thought to myself.

"We need to figure out where you are going to sleep when you get home tomorrow. You can't sleep in that chair," Maria said to Ted.

"I can sleep wherever I want! Why can't I sleep in my chair?" he shouted.

"You can't get out of it. When you were home, you got stuck, and you couldn't push the thing down to get out of it!" she yelled.

So, I guess he did go home before coming here. The lies never ended, I thought.

"I'm fine. I know what I can and cannot do."

"No, you don't. No, you weren't!" Maria insisted.

"Dad, what about the stairs? Are you going to be able to get up and down the stairs?" I asked, trying to change the subject.

"They're installing a chair lift on the stairs today, so he can sleep in his bed upstairs, like a normal person," Maria answered.

"I can sleep in my chair!" he yelled.

"Don't worry about that right now, you guys. I'm going to have to get going at five. I'm meeting a childhood friend for dinner. I haven't seen her in about fifteen years. So, I can't stay too much longer. Can we talk about something else?"

I just wanted my remaining time with my father to be civil. The following day, my father had four hours of physical therapy scheduled, followed by exit interviews with each of his doctors, so there would not be time for me to visit him again before my drive to Newark airport.

Even though I didn't have to meet anyone until 6:30, I left at 5:00 due to pure exhaustion. The tension, the lies, the lost hope, the confusion, the fear all swallowed the air in the room. I hugged my dad a little longer than normal, because I knew one thing for certain: I'd never see him again. One of two things would happen—he'd die soon, or he'd continue living his unhealthy ways, which I couldn't witness. I would not cut him off, like I had done in the past. But I would redefine my boundaries and stick to them. I'd restructure my relationship based on the occasional greeting card and phone call of small talk.

I walked out of the nursing home and smelled the fresh winter air. I watched a flock of birds fly through the scarce branches. Streams of sunlight fought to strike through the dramatic heavy clouds. Winter on the East Coast was quite beautiful.

I desperately wanted to feel safe. It took until my mid-thirties to stop looking over my shoulder all the time and to stop barricading my doors and windows with bottles and cans that would alert me to an intruder. I looked around as I sat in my rental car. I felt terrified of every person in the parking lot, as if they'd unpredictably become violent at any moment. *Trust no one*, I thought. My nightmares had returned. The flashbacks haunted me so much that I constantly visualized violence all around me. Logically, I knew nothing had changed in the last three months. But emotionally, I had reverted back to that scared little girl who had learned to trust no one; that violence could happen at any time; that every happy moment could change unpredictably to a crinkled mess of stiff dark paper on the floor that would consume me. I desperately wanted to iron out.

I returned to my mother's house and tried to let go.

"You did more than most people would have by visiting him. He didn't deserve another chance after all he's done to you," my mother said.

"I gave everything I had. I have nothing left to give him. He's lying about everything again. I don't think he's going to change. I think he's going to drink as soon as he gets home. It's sad, really."

"It is sad," she said, as she sipped her cocktail. My mother had a unique way of saying the word "cocktail." It was a celebration and a joke at the same time.

She had loved to try to embarrass me when I was a kid. She'd do things like follow me around the grocery store, dragging her leg, and picking her nose, while making a funny face and screeching my name. When she met my future husband for the first time, she asked me as she shook his hand, "So is he a screamer?" She said she used to do these things to lighten me up, because I worried too much and I ruined everyone's fun.

"Let's go to dinner. Sarah is going to meet us there in about twenty minutes," I suggested.

Sarah and I had grown up together, but we didn't have much in common anymore. She spent most of her time with her family. She wanted to have babies. I avoided my relatives, spent most of my time with friends, participated in sports, and exercised daily, and I had no interest in having children. I worked with special needs children for twelve years, and I loved the work. But I did not enjoy being around young children and babies. I had learned too much about how perceptive young children are to adults who don't truly adore them. I didn't want to be a mother; therefore, I felt I shouldn't ever try to become one. Sarah never moved more than fifty miles from the town she'd grown up in. I moved as far away as I could.

My mother ordered a bottle of wine for us to share,

and Sarah ordered her own drink. "We can cork what we don't drink," my mother said. After one drink, my mother began slurring her words and giggling at ridiculous things like the way the napkin was folded on the table. I couldn't tell if she had been drinking during the day or if the alcohol was reacting with the medications she had taken. She laughed at everything and raised her voice. I amused her by agreeing with her antics and telling jokes. I used humor to prevent her from changing from laughing to yelling, from happiness to hostility, and from liking me to hating me.

Sarah texted me on her phone under the table. "Your mom seems pretty drunk. Is she going to drive?"

"Yes, I think so," I replied to her text.

"Text me when you get home," she texted back. She looked worried about me, just like when we were kids.

We paid the check and stood up to leave. The bottle of wine was almost empty.

"Ma, you okay to drive?" I asked.

"I'm fine!" she barked.

"Okay, I was just checking," I said. I knew that if I pushed, she'd become angry, still insist on driving, and the situation would degrade into an argument and angry driving.

We got on the highway, and cars zoomed past us on both sides. I peeked at the speedometer, which indicated fifty miles per hour. The speed limit for Interstate 84 is sixty-five, meaning people traveled at least seventy all around us. "Mom, you might want to speed up a bit. People are speeding."

"They're just going too fast. I'm okay as long as I stay in the right lane," she insisted. And we weren't in the far-right lane.

"Yes, people drive way too fast around here. I remember when I first moved to Seattle. Everyone thought I drove too fast. But it's only because I learned how to drive here. Like these maniacs!" I tried to stay on her side of the argument, stay positive, and make her laugh. She sped up a little, but she was clearly inebriated. She swerved in her lane. Even though I hadn't understood the rules of the road when I was young, I knew when her driving was not safe.

We made it back to her house, and she laughed loudly as she opened her front door. I kept my thoughts to myself and humored her. I didn't want her mood to change.

"So, what do you want to do tomorrow? I don't have to head back to Newark until about one." I had hoped my mother and I could do something fun together, like go for a walk around the neighborhood, or go to a consignment shop.

"Oh, I can't hang out. I have a dentist's appointment, and I have to leave by nine to get there by ten. It's a long drive, you know."

"Oh, you have a dentist appointment?" I asked to be sure I had heard her correctly. I had visited only four times in eighteen years, but rescheduling a dentist appointment to hang out with me for a few hours was too much to ask. She didn't work. She didn't travel. She didn't have any hobbies. To show her that I felt hurt would be a clear sign of weakness. *Never let them see you sweat. Never let them see you weak,* I thought.

"Yes. You can hang out here with Pete if you want. But he's going to be busy with his stamps." She didn't look up, and she took another drink. "Are you sure you don't want some wine?" she asked.

At this point, I wanted several glasses of wine, to numb myself, to help me sleep, and to stop reliving the past few weeks that had connected me to past traumas. "No, thanks, Mom. I'm good. I'm going to turn in early. I guess I'll head to the airport early then, unless I can think of something to do near the city for a couple hours that would be easy to get to."

"Yeah, I can't really think of anything. New York City is right there, but you wouldn't want to risk being late for your flight," she said.

"Yeah, exactly," I responded as I walked up the stairs.

33
to change the world

The next morning, I woke up after a few hours of sleep. I heard the television blaring from downstairs. I showered and packed quickly. My mother had already left, and Pete sat in the dining room chair in front of a display of hundreds of stamps that littered the table.

"Well, Pete. I gotta get out of here. It's a long drive," I announced.

"Okay, Laura. It was good seeing you," he replied without standing up from his chair.

"You too." I let myself out and scurried to my rental car.

The disgusting feeling in my gut, the burning bile in my throat, and the tightness in my back continued while I drove on the familiar Connecticut roads. *Just get me out of this fucking state*, I thought over and over again. Once I crossed the border into New York, I felt a little bit better. I crossed the New Jersey border five hours before my flight. Even though a major accident slowed traffic for a while, I still arrived at the Newark airport over four hours before my plane was scheduled to depart.

I pulled out my laptop and sat at a table in a restaurant near my gate. I ordered a glass of wine. Since it was almost noon, I convinced myself that drinking wine was perfectly normal. I logged on to do some work. I couldn't stop my racing thoughts and the emotions that made my insides shake intensely. Nothing distracted me. Two days earlier, I had accomplished running my first medical education seminar with my new company. I should have felt accomplished, but I didn't care. I ordered another glass of wine after quickly finishing the first.

I stared at the glass of wine. I noticed an odd feeling—more of a realization. Something shifted within me. *What was I doing? Why did I order more wine?* I asked myself. I ordered it out of habit. Drink to fill time. Drink to feel numb. Drink to sleep. Drink because it tastes good. Drink because I'm bored. *But I don't want to be like them*, I thought.

I always said that I had a healthy relationship with alcohol. But the odds are definitely stacked against me. Alcoholism infected my family on both sides, and both of my parents struggled with addictions of various kinds. I began drinking alcohol with my mother at a very young age.

When my mother went out on dates after divorcing my father, she would come home really late, or not at all. She spent many nights and mornings vomiting in the toilet after drinking too much. She said that she knew she needed to "cut down on drinking" when she could handle up to ten shots in one night and not feel sick. She drove far distances after drinking, sometimes with me in the car, which scared me a lot. One time, she saw the fear in my face as I sat in the back seat and her drinking buddy, Mindy, sat in the front seat. My mother handed me a bottle of Rumple Minze and said, "Here, Laura. Give it a try. You might like it!"

I took a sip, and it tasted like very strong, rancid toothpaste.

"It's gross, Mommy!" I said, with my face scrunched up and my lips pursed together.

"You didn't have enough. Drink some more!" she demanded and giggled at the same time.

I took a big gulp. My mouth felt tingly, and within a few minutes my arms and legs felt warm and heavy. I looked around. The world moved slower than it should have. I raised my hand and stared at it. Mindy and my mother laughed at me.

"You feel good, don't you?" she asked, and she took a big gulp out of the bottle.

I giggled and said, "Yeah, Mommy. I feel good." I didn't feel like I could control my hand, or my arm, or myself. I took a deep breath and sunk into the seat.

"Oh shit, Min. I think she took too much," I heard my mother say.

What did she mean? Was I okay? Was I going to die? I thought while I laughed nervously.

"She'll be okay in a couple of hours." I heard Mindy

say in response. This was the first time I drank with my mother. I was seven.

A few weeks later, my mother took me out to dinner with the girls. My mother, Mindy, and two other women ordered margaritas. My mother took my straw, put it in her drink, and allowed me to share. "See, you're one of the girls!" she exclaimed, and everyone laughed.

My mother took me with her to bars and restaurants where she knew the bartender. I was allowed to sit next to her on the tall barstools, and I'd have to strain to see over the edge of the bar. She shared her drinks with me each time. I began to enjoy the numb feeling that her drinks created. She seemed to enjoy my company when I drank with her. We would giggle and make fun of other people.

About a month after my mother and David broke up, my mother and I jumped in the car and drove to a bar along Route 7 in Danbury. "What's Triangles, Mommy? Why are we here?" I asked.

"Triangles is a gay bar. I heard that David's with a man now. Right after me, he got into a relationship with a man," my mother explained.

I was nine, so I didn't understand. "What does that mean, Mommy?"

"Nothing, Laura. Can you help me write down the license plate numbers of these cars?" she asked.

"Um, sure," I replied, as she handed me a notebook and a pencil.

"AG 341." She listed letters and numbers. "Did you get that?"

"Yup," I said. We bonded over this process.

She continued broadcasting letters and numbers as we drove very slowly through the parking lot. She took swigs from her silver bottle and handed it to me every few minutes to drink as well.

"Mommy, why are we doing this?" I asked, feeling my words slur.

"Because if I have a list of these cars' license plate numbers, I'll never date another gay man again," she explained.

"What is gay, Mommy?"

"Gay is when a man wants to be with a man and not a woman. Or, when a woman wants to be with a woman and not a man." Her words slurred, and I didn't understand. But I was too foggy to ask for clarification.

"Do you want to go sit in the grass over there?" she asked, as I wrote down the last license plate number. My handwriting looked messy, and I thought this would upset her.

"I'm sorry. I wrote so sloppy," I said as I erased the last letter and tried writing it again.

She giggled and said, "That's okay, Laura. It's good enough. Thanks for your help."

I smiled and felt proud that she appreciated my help.

We sat on the grassy hill that was situated between the gay bar named Triangles and a remote-controlled car racetrack. A large group of people gathered around the track with remotes in their hands. The track was lit up with bright florescent lights as cars zoomed around it. It burned my eyes to look in that direction, as the lights were a striking contrast from the darkness of the grassy hill we were now laying on. My mother commented about the loudness of the car engines. I giggled and said, "It sounds like each car is saying the word 'me,' like they're telling the world who's gonna to win the race."

We then both started yelling "meeeeee" at the top of our lungs and laughing together. It was a great night.

Most nights were tense, and she stopped coming home more and more. I sought comfort in playing piano on the keyboard that had David bought me years earlier. But my mother couldn't stand the sound of my practicing. She bought me headphones to plug into the keyboard, but she couldn't tolerate the "pounding on the keys," as she put it, either. I tried sports, and I would kick the soccer ball against the wall in the parking lot outside or shoot basketballs into the hoop that was attached to the dilapidated garage at the back of our building that belonged to a landscaping company. I never mastered dribbling, since the gravel driveway caused the basketball to bounce unpredictably, but I did become a good three-point shooter. It didn't matter. I changed schools too often to try out for a team.

I searched for comfort in food and ate Subway sandwiches almost every day. This became more problematic when I noticed that my mother stopped grocery shopping. I relied on the free food that I got from my social worker, Roseanne. But canned food was not healthy. And it stopped comforting me after years and years of eating the same things. I gained about twenty pounds in less than two years.

My mother always stored a gallon-sized jug of vodka in the freezer for times when she came home. But she stopped coming home. She cleaned out her closet and dresser, and moved her things to Pete's house when I was fourteen. I sipped the cold vodka when I missed my mother or felt sad and alone, and I would listen to her old records. I'd lay on the living room floor and stare at the old writing desk my mother had found at a yard sale; it now neatly stored her other liquor bottles. I drank little bits of each bottle until I felt numb or passed out on the floor. When I randomly found them in the fridge, I brought wine coolers to school. I'd empty out a can of raspberry flavored iced tea Snapple and refill it with a berry-flavored wine cooler. I'd drink during my English class after lunch. I caught myself wanting alcohol more and more. I was fifteen.

I'd clench my jaw as hard as I could while sitting in class, hoping a teacher would notice and ask me what was bothering me. If they asked, though, I wouldn't know what to say. I couldn't tell on my mother. I would go home after school and drink before and after work. It relaxed my jaw, loosened my backpains, stopped the disgusting feeling in my stomach, and sometimes helped me sleep.

At age sixteen, I invited some friends over for my birthday. These friends knew the truth about my mother moving out and felt bad for me, but they also loved coming to my apartment because they knew they could drink my mother's alcohol. Or, they'd bring their own, and they knew no adult would be around to stop them or call their parents. About six of us were playing music and hanging out near the landscaping company's garage in back of the building. We must have had the music on too loud, because the cops showed up. As they pulled up, we threw several beer cans into the woods. The main officer asked who lived there, and I raised my hand. I shifted my legs nervously, and he asked, "Where are your parents?"

"I have no idea, sir. My father's been out of my life for a long time, and my mother doesn't live here anymore." I had been drinking too much to think about what I was saying. "I live here alone. Why do you care?" I asked.

"Why do you keep moving around?" he asked, ignoring my comments about my parents.

"I have to pee, sir. I'm sorry."

"What did you all throw into the woods?" he asked us all.

"Just some beer cans," Matt said.

"Go find them and bring them all to me," he commanded, as he emptied out the cans that he could see sitting on the makeshift bench we had been sitting on.

"All of them?" a friend asked.

"Yes," he said.

The guys all got up and started looking through the bushes, and the cop walked toward me again. "What do you mean, you live alone?" he asked.

"My mother hasn't lived here in a while," I replied, as I danced around trying not to pee my pants. "Do you mind if I go inside and use the bathroom really quick? I'll be right back."

"Go ahead," he grunted.

I ran upstairs, used the bathroom as quickly as a I could, rubbed some water on my face, and raced back down to the back of the building. As I made my way toward the bench and basketball hoop, everyone was standing around talking.

"Is anyone driving tonight?" the cop asked.

"No, sir," Matt said, as everyone else shook their heads no.

"They're all staying here with me, sir," I said.

The cop shined his flashlight on the cars in the parking lot and asked who drove which car.

"I know this car," he said, as he kept the light focused on Matt's Honda. "Weren't you guys driving in the field next to the high school a few weeks ago?"

"Yes, sir. That was us. We slid off the road and hit a sign." I repeated the lie that we had told the police after we intentionally drove in the muddy field to slide around and make funny tire tracks in the grass. It was a traditional prank. We knew the police drove by the high school often, and our car was wedged on top of a sign. We decided to call for help and say we were in an accident. We kept our stories straight, so they had no choice but to believe us. The officers called a tow truck for us.

"Don't drive anywhere. Not pretty common that I see the same kids twice in such a short period of time," he lectured.

"We're sorry, officer. We'll turn the music off and go inside," Matt said.

"No one drives anywhere tonight," he said again, as he

noted each of their descriptions and plate numbers of each car. The cops left.

We all looked at each other, and everyone laughed except me.

"What's up, Laura?" someone asked.

"Nothing. I'm just tired," I replied. What bothered me was that I had revealed my secret that my mother had left me to the cop. It didn't seem like he cared, but that didn't stop me from worrying about getting my mother in trouble.

Nothing ever happened.

By the time I turned eighteen, Matt and I had been dating for almost three years. We planned to go to the same college, to live together, and get married one day. Once I knew someone cared about me unconditionally, I drank very little. We occasionally did the stupid, teenage party thing, but I stopped drinking every day. I believe I broke the pattern just in time.

But I remember times in my life when I drank too much: after my divorce from Matt, when I first started dating for the first time in my mid-twenties, and when I met a new group of friends. Sometimes I drank every day for weeks in a row. Sometimes I drove when I shouldn't have. Each time I recognized this pattern forming, I'd stop for a while.

I took quizzes online to determine if I had a problem. I had never blacked out. I had never had a DUI, luckily. I had never missed work or school due to a hangover. I could stop when I wanted to, and I had done so several times over the years. Like when I lived on a tight budget,

I stopped buying alcohol to save money with ease.

I worked hard all my life to rebel against the unhealthy habits of my parents. I worked out every day. I ate healthy. I never smoked. I never let fear stop me from pursuing my dreams. I set lofty goals and worked hard to achieve them. I didn't make excuses. I didn't let my past define me. I didn't reflect about things and people who had hurt me. I constantly sought out the good in people. I constantly found the positive and the humor in every single moment. Even the worst times offered something positive to focus on. When I lost my job, it meant I needed a break and a new beginning. When I got sick, I treated it as a second chance at life. When I had an hour to spare, I found something productive to do. I pushed. I pushed hard. I never slowed down.

But alcohol was in undefinable battle. While I knew I wasn't an alcoholic, I hated alcohol. When someone lost control because of drinking too much, it triggered fear, anger, and grief. When I drank too much or lost control, I felt regret and shame for days afterwards.

All of the trauma from my past related to alcohol and drunk people losing control, and becoming hateful and dangerous. Alcohol equaled this unnecessary thing, this object, this nothing. I felt angry, resentful, and furious at the glass of wine that sat on the off-white table in the Newark airport restaurant.

I didn't drink the second glass of wine. As I stood up to walk over to my gate, the waiter yelled out, "Was there something wrong with your wine, ma'am?"

"No, it's fine. I'm just in a hurry," I said.

I had to wait three more hours until my flight. I sat near a window and tried to do some work. The warmth of the laptop against my jeans relaxed my legs. I closed my eyes and tried to calm down the shaking inside me. Nothing distracted me from my thoughts about that shitty glass of wine, and the shitty people who chose alcohol over everything and everyone else, especially me.

I opened a new Word document and started to make a list of ways to take better care of myself. I committed to stop drinking alcohol for at least a month, maybe forever. Once I stopped drinking for a while, I could then decide if alcohol had any place in my life at all. I would find more passion in my life. Anytime I felt stagnant, I would find something new to try. Instead of always trying to please others and make them happy, I decided to find more happiness for myself. I would put up with less negativity, and focus on positivity, strength, and humor. I needed to go back to Al-Anon meetings and go more often. Since I was traveling so much for my new job, I hadn't been to a meeting in two weeks. I planned to make it a priority to go to meetings at least twice per week. I would have to go to work late on those days. But my healing needed to be my first priority, even above work. From small to large, I listed healthy things to do for myself.

I looked at my list. It had turned more into a bunch of paragraphs instead of an organized bulleted list, but I didn't care. I enjoyed getting out my thoughts. I smiled proudly, and the shaking simmered. Over the previous couple of days, I faced the people who had hurt me so deeply. I cared for my father in his time of need, and I also let go of him forever. I could focus on taking care of myself now. I decided that the experience of the past couple of months was a sign for me to refocus on my health, so I could continue to represent that shining example of a thriving survivor of abuse living a healthy life. Maybe I'd buy a motorcycle, like I had always wanted. Maybe I'd write a book, like I had dreamt about. I felt lighter, like a soul escaping a dark shadow that was trying to envelope my body and mind. I decided to continue writing, with no particular goal in mind.

I remembered a particularly moving day in my life, and I started to write. I decided to fill the next few hours by writing about the following story...

During my last quarter of graduate school for Education and Counseling, our professor of Current Trends in Social-Emotional Counseling assigned my cohort to do a forty-five- to sixty-minute presentation on a social issue that our students faced. We needed to include data on the prevalence of the issue, the effects, the signs and symptoms that could alert us to the problem, interventions to use to make a difference, and a case study. I chose physical abuse and neglect. My presentation had forty-eight slides. I discussed the data of how many children are physically abused and neglected in the United States, how under-reported the problem really is, the list of effects on each abused child's life, the signs to look for in our students, interventions to try, when to report suspected abuse to Child Protective Services, and a very detailed case study.

When I got to the case study portion of my presentation, the initial slide showed a picture of a young woman in a motorboat. She reached one arm behind her to control the direction of the motor while gliding along a beautiful lake. Her brown hair blew in the wind, and her other hand covered her face. Her name was Elle, and she was in the tenth grade at the time the picture was taken. I explained the details of her abuse, neglect, and abandonment. "As a child she endured being punched, choked, kicked, molested, ridiculed, dismissed, verbally abused, emotionally abused, and left on her own at age fourteen. The worst of the beatings took place between ages eight and ten, resulting in a serious back and neck injury that would last a lifetime. In school, she sometimes limped in the hallway or struggled with her backpack. When asked, she would say that her back hurt. She also had a lot of headaches; some stemmed from severe migraines, which she was diagnosed with at a very young age; some stemmed from the neck pain that radiated throughout her skull."

I continued my case. "Elle earned As and Bs, despite changing schools many times. And she attended one of the most challenging, highest regarded public high schools on the Eastern Seaboard. She seemed quiet and shy, but got along with students in all groups and cliques at school. She wore baggy, old clothes that sharply contrasted to the brand-named clothing her peers wore. She clearly had less money than the other students, yet they respected her. She was a healthy weight and displayed no physical signs of abuse. Her hair and clothes hid the bruises from the punches to the sides of her head, and the kicks to her back and buttocks."

As I continued advancing the slides, I continued telling Elle's story. "She sometimes missed school due to migraines that would last for days and sometimes weeks. She completed her make-up assignments as soon as possible and scored very well on quizzes and tests. She explained to her teachers that she would look up answers to sample problems in the back of the textbooks and teach herself how to do math and science by working backwards. She memorized things she read, and she read for hours at a time. She was an excellent writer and had exceptional grammar. Several of her absences were unexcused because her parents were gone, and some of her teachers responded by reducing her grade slightly or assigning extra work. Elle didn't complain."

In grad school over the previous eighteen months, we all learned about the red flags to look for to spot an abused, or otherwise suffering, child. Elle's case didn't show any signs, other than the unexcused absences, that would have concerned teachers or school counselors. Her grades were consistently high, she did well socially, and she behaved respectfully at all times. Elle's abuse was completely missed. No one noticed, and no interventions were ever attempted. She graduated and moved on to college, carrying her secrets with her.

I then took questions from my audience. Some asked questions about the data I had included in my talk. Some asked about the interventions that my research showed to work best when trying to help abused and neglected children. But the majority of the questions were about Elle. "Was she getting help outside of school?" someone asked.

"Yes, through a free social worker who gave her donated food to live on. She would go there and play cards, but she never talked about her feelings. She started seeing the social worker at age twelve. This person did her best to convince Elle that her abusive childhood was not her fault. When Elle heard these words, she would sometimes vomit. She had learned that having feelings, emotions, or needs was dangerous. And in her home, she was constantly told that all of the turmoil was her fault. She was in a constant state of trying to control the uncontrollable—the emotions and behaviors of alcoholics." I provided a long, detailed answer.

I took this opportunity to repeat a data point within the earlier part of my presentation: "Remember, several of the studies showed, in one way or another, that if one adult, any adult, can convince an abused child that it is not their fault, specifically while they are around the age of puberty, they usually go on to lead relatively healthy lives. This one intervention statistically impacted abused children's lives the most. That helped me decide to work with middle school-aged children in my career. I want to be that one adult—that one person that can help at the right time," I explained.

Several people nodded in response.

Another person asked, "Did Elle take part in school activities?"

"No, she worked thirty-two hours a week as a

pharmacy manager to have money to live on," I replied. "She would have worked more, but that was the maximum hours allowed during the school months for a child younger than eighteen."

"Did she show any signs of anger or depression?" was another question.

I answered, "She usually ate lunch with her teachers, but there were no signs of any problems."

"What do you know about how's she's doing now?" someone else asked.

"She's an adult now. She has a degree, a good job, great friends, and she's quite athletic," I answered. The questions were becoming more and more specific, and I knew all the answers. Sharing Elle's story in this way was raw, real, honest, and an effective display of how resilient a child can be.

One of my friends in class asked, "How do you know so much about Elle? Is she a relative of yours or something?"

I smirked, hesitated a moment, and looked over at my professor, who nodded slightly. The audience thought I had finished my slides, but I held back the last one because I wanted an honest and unbiased conversation about my presentation before revealing the final image. I could also decide if the revelation would benefit the group or not, based on their questions. I clicked the slide advancer.

The last slide mirrored the first picture of the young woman in the boat, except her face was exposed. The girl had brown hair, and I dyed my hair blond. But her smiling face was markedly familiar. I stood silently in front of eighteen people, as each of them realized that the young woman in the picture was me. The silence in the room caused me to immediately regret my decision to be this exposed.

Weeks earlier I had asked my professor for permission to use my story as the case study in my presentation, and she warned me that this might happen; they may be unsure of how to respond and I might feel too vulnerable to continue my studies with this group of people after this presentation. *Maybe this was a mistake*, I thought to myself. I froze. Time stopped.

Then a few people in the back stood up and started to clap. The rest of the room followed, and I trembled with emotion and shock. I giggled nervously and felt my face heat up. I scurried to my desk and tried to act normal. I felt tears of happiness form in my eyes. I remember thinking that every single abused child should get to have that feeling in their life. The feeling of pride for overcoming such undeserved obstacles deserved a standing ovation. The feeling of acceptance and love, instead of judgment, is something that every survivor of abuse should experience. It would change the world.

I did my best to hide how emotional I felt inside. Slowly, my presentation evaluations started being passed to my desk. I completely forgot to collect them before sitting back down. It took me some time to start reviewing the responses. According to the surveys, not only was my data informative and my interventions thoughtfully developed and helpful, but my case study was powerful, informative, and eye-opening as to how hard our jobs as school counselors would be. I had successfully made my point.

I finished typing my story. I wanted to share that story with every abused child in the world. I wished they could feel what I felt in that moment, when people understood that I not only survived abuse and abandonment, but I was thriving, excelling at life, and choosing to go on to help other children. Writing it down reconnected me to that feeling of joy. I had successfully replaced my negative feelings with positive ones as I sat in the airport waiting to go home.

I looked at the clock. It was almost time to board the plane. I got up and stood in line.

34
once an alcoholic

Less than twenty-four hours after he was discharged, Ted got drunk. I talked to him on the phone for just over two minutes, but I recognized the slurring words and disjointed thoughts. I wanted the conversation to end quickly, so I told him I would call him in a few days. I hung up and felt no emotion. I felt no obligation to help or ask him about his drinking. I felt strong enough to let go.

I didn't drink any alcohol for over two months, and it was very easy to do. I loved how I felt waking up with a clear head, having no guilt about a stupid fight with Mike the night before when we were both drinking, and feeling light on my feet. I felt healthier and happier. I'd never order alcohol out of habit, boredom, sadness, or a sense of social obligation ever again.

Ted and I returned to our weekly calls of small talk: the weather, work, my hobbies, his family. While I kept my promise to Maria to stay in touch and not walk away, I no longer felt connected to Ted. My heart had had enough.

"Hi, Dad. How are you feeling today?" I asked every time I called him.

"I feel stronger every day. I think I'm going back to work tomorrow!" he exclaimed.

"That's great, Dad! Have you seen the cardiologist? How are the meds going?" I asked.

"I feel great. I'm almost back to my old self. But my voice isn't right." He still sounded feminine and raspy. "What is that from?" he asked.

"Dad, that's from the ventilator. The tubes that were down your throat. You probably have scar tissue. It should get better with time," I explained for the hundredth time.

I never asked him about drinking. His memory came and went. He became confused when we talked at times.

"How's Maria?" I asked during every conversation. I worried about Maria. She stopped returning my calls and text messages as soon as Ted went home.

"Maria's great!" my dad said, happily. Maria and I had never talked before Ted got sick, so maybe that's just how she wanted things to remain. Or, maybe Ted wouldn't allow her to stay in touch with me. I didn't push.

"How are the kids?" I asked all the time.

"Everyone is great, Laura. All better. All back to normal," he said each time.

"That's great, Dad. Are you able to get up and down the stairs?"

"I still use the chair sometimes. Allana sometimes

rides in it with me. She laughs and laughs," he explained, while giggling a little. His laugh sounded feminine, too.

I laughed, easily able to picture his young granddaughter riding up the stairs on a chair with Ted.

"Sounds like everything is going well, Dad. I'm happy to hear it."

"Me, too. I was scared when I was in the hospital for that operation." He still didn't understand or didn't want to admit what had happened.

"I bet you were, Dad. I was scared, too." I said the words, but I felt nothing. I wondered if he could tell.

I dreaded Father's Day, and June was around the corner. I struggled to choose a Father's Day gift or card. All of the "you taught me so much," "I love you dad," "I remember when...," "thanks for being a great dad," "you're my hero" cards made me nauseous. I walked through the local department store, trying to decide what to get him. I knew he was having trouble sleeping, so I picked up some chamomile tea to help him relax at night. I remembered that he loved Reese's peanut butter cups, so I picked up a bag of miniature ones. And then I went to the dreaded card aisle. I searched the humor cards, but none of them were appropriate for an alcoholic liar who had said he'd wished he had killed me when he abused me as a young child. I felt tears form in my eyes. I felt people staring at me. I felt ridiculous. I swallowed hard and re-focused on my task. I pressed my fingernail into my fleshy fingertip. *Find a stupid card and get out of here. You have to mail this thing today, or it won't get there in time*, I thought.

I looked through the cards, and then a tear fell out of my eye socket and hit my cheek. I never let tears fall. Shocked, I hurried away from the stupid cards. I scrambled to hide my face and find another aisle as fast as I could. I ended up in the cereal aisle, surrounded by kids with their parents. I made a bad choice. I took several deep breaths, as I pretended to read the labels on several cereal boxes.

I tried again. "I can do this. I do it every fucking year," I said aloud, quietly. I gripped my cart handle and pushed it hard. *Go fast and get it over with*, I thought.

I saw a card that had a jackass with large googly eyes on the front. It said, "Happy Father's Day!" When you opened it, it said, "From Your Smart-Ass Kid." *Good enough*, I thought. I grabbed the dumb thing and left the store.

I packaged up the gift and got it ready to mail. I put it on the table near the door and decided to work out before heading to the post office. Just as I was finishing my workout, Maria called. My heart sank. "Hi, Maria. Are you okay?"

"Hi, Laura. You know, he hasn't been doing good at all. He hasn't been going to the doctors. He has been lying. To everyone. To his doctor. To me. To his boss. He was supposed to have colonoscopy because he had blood in his stool for about six months. He never go. I found him in bathroom passed out. Blood all over him. He's in ICU, because he lost so much blood." She explained everything so quickly.

"Oh wow. Oh my gosh. Wow. Are you okay?"

"His heart rate is low again. His oxygen is low. He's not okay. He never go to doctor. He doesn't take medication. He forgets. Or he lies. His alcoholic dementia. I try to help him, and he yells, and he's mean. I pack my bags so many times to leave. But I can't leave." She sounded so upset, so defeated, so hurt. I worried he was hitting her.

"Do you have somewhere you can go?" I asked her.

"You don't have to worry. It's not your responsibility," she replied.

"I know that. Do you have somewhere you can go?" I asked her, firmly.

"Yes, I can go with my kids. But I can't leave now. He's back in the hospital. It's bad. He's bleeding bad," she cried softly.

"You can do whatever you need to do to be safe. I know how mean he can be, and then he feels bad. I know what he's like. It's why my mom left him. It's why I left him. It's okay to leave him."

"I understand. Not now. He's at St. Joe's. Do you want the number? He's in ICU. You can call and talk to Dr. Groves," she said.

"Sure. Thank you for calling, Maria," I responded. I could tell she didn't want to talk anymore.

"When you call, you set up password so you can get information this time. I can get information from you or when I go there in person. It will be easier than last time," she explained, acknowledging how hard it was for me to get information the last time he was in the hospital.

"Okay, I will do that. Should I call tonight, or do you think I should wait until morning?" I asked. I dreaded having to call and check on my father every day again. I didn't care anymore. And the guilt in my heart weighed me down.

"They won't know anything tonight He's sedated and they're doing a colonoscopy first thing in the morning. You can call then. The doctor will be in at eight o'clock," she answered.

"Okay, I will call in the morning," I said.

I looked over at the Father's Day package. I still needed to mail it. *But would he get it in time? Was he going to die before Saturday? Were the chocolates okay for him to eat? Should I have bought him a nicer card?* I stopped second-guessing myself, got in the car, and went to the fucking post office. I stood in the long line like an emotionless robot, holding onto the little package.

When my alarm went off at 5 a.m., Pacific time, I called the hospital. I wanted to know when they were doing the procedure, so I could get an idea of when they would have results. I thought it would be a quick conversation. And I knew that if he did have cancer, it would be advanced at this point.

"Hi, I'm trying to get ahold of Dr. Groves. He's taking care of my father, Ted," I said to the person who answered the phone.

"What's Ted's last name?"

I answered, and continued, "Ted's supposed to have a colonoscopy this morning. I just wanted to know if they have started the procedure yet."

"They're preparing now. I'll get the doctor for you."

"Thank you," I said.

"Hi. This is Dr. Groves. May I help you?" I was shocked that I had gotten ahold of the doctor so quickly.

"Hi. My name is Laura. I'm Ted's daughter. I just wanted to know how he's doing and when you plan to do the colonoscopy. Are you starting soon?" I asked.

"I'm sorry. I can't give you any information. It's not that I don't believe you. It's just against HIPPA regulations. Unless you know the password," the doctor said rudely. His tone made me angry fast.

"Since I'm on the phone and I'm far away, I'm not required to prove who I am. I know how HIPPA works. Also, there is no password on the account. I'm supposed to set one up!" I reflected his rude tone back to him. "Can you give me any information?"

"Well, do you even know why he's here?" His rude tone continued.

"Well, no. I know he was bleeding. And he's in ICU."

"So, you do know why he's here!" he yelled.

"Look. My father is an alcoholic. He lies. He's unpredictable. We have an estranged relationship. His wife doesn't speak English well. She and I spoke last night for about a minute. I've been through this for six months with him. I'm three thousand miles away and about to give up on all of it. I know he was bleeding. I know he's missed several doctor appointments. I also know he's been lying to everyone. So, to be honest, I'd like to hear, from a doctor, how he's *actually* doing. What is *actually* going on. Why is he bleeding? How long? How much? When is he having a colonoscopy? What other tests are you doing? When will you get those results? How is his heart? How is his oxygen? Is he able to take his medications? If you can't help me, maybe someone else can." I let it all out. I took a deep breath. As I breathed in, I felt stronger than I had in months. As the air left my lungs, I felt nothing for my father.

In a much calmer tone, Dr. Groves explained, "Your father lost a lot of blood. He had two blood transfusions overnight. We don't know why yet. I am prepping for a colonoscopy and an endoscopy in a few minutes. I won't know all of the results right away. I'll know if I see anything physical right away, but lab results may take a few days. His heart rate is currently high, but that's to be expected because we had to discontinue all of his medication due to the bleeding. We are monitoring him very closely. His oxygen is low, but he is stable. I can call you when I'm done with the tests."

"Thank you, Dr. Groves. That would be fantastic. Thank you for the information," I said. I had calmed down. "Also, when he wakes up, he can be unpredictable, angry, and violent, so watch your back."

"I can handle it," he said, sounding cocky.

"I'm just letting you know," I snarked.

"Thank you."

I did some research on the computer at work that day. I looked up alcoholism and intestines. Apparently, colon and stomach cancer rates were high for alcoholics. If it wasn't cancer, the intestinal wall can become very thin from alcohol abuse, and it was common for blood vessels to rupture and bleed when this occurred. Either way, he must have been suffering. He must have been in pain.

Alcoholism doesn't just take out your liver. It takes your heart, your stomach, your intestines, your throat, your lungs, your life. I read more and more about how alcoholics die. Alcohol is the third leading cause of death in the United States. However, if an alcoholic dies from another cause that is directly or indirectly linked to the addiction, the alcohol is not listed as the cause. If it was linked in all of those cases, alcoholism would then be listed as the number one cause of death. One-third of alcoholics die from accidents or suicide. The rest die from cardiovascular disease, cirrhosis, gastrointestinal or lung cancer, pneumonia, and other medical causes.

I also spent some time reading about the psychological suffering at the end of life for alcoholics. Near death, most people go through stages of acceptance of their death. They will usually feel anger, regret, and guilt before accepting that their life is ending. However, for an alcoholic, these emotions are remarkably strong. They will usually feel extraordinary regret and guilt over the pain they have caused others or the money they have spent on alcohol. They likely will feel exceptional anger toward themselves for not being able to overcome their addiction. This may be outwardly directed at others, which leads to additional suffering for all involved.

I caught myself preparing for my father's death. I wanted to understand how I was going to feel before I felt it. Losing a parent is always difficult. Losing an abusive, alcoholic parent is complicated. I wanted him to stop hurting himself and his family. I didn't want him to suffer in any of the ways I read about. I didn't see any chance that he could live a healthy, long life anymore. So, I just wanted there to be a way to minimize the hurt for all involved. I wanted the story to be over.

"Laura, have you talked to the doctor?" Marie's text message lit up on my phone.

"No, not yet. I will call when I get out of this meeting," I responded. "Is there a password on the account?" In my hasty call with Dr. Groves, I forgot to set one up.

"Buffalo," her text message replied.

I called the hospital again. As the phone rang, I stared into space blankly. A woman answered.

"Hi. I'm trying to get a hold of Dr. Groves to get an update on my father's condition. The password is buffalo," I mumbled.

"Please hold and I will transfer you to the ICU." I couldn't stand being transferred all around the hospital, listening to the horrible hold music, so I started to pace around the halls of my office area.

"ICU. How may I help you?" another voice on another line asked.

"Hi, I'm Ted's daughter, and I'm trying to get an update on his condition and his test results. Is Dr. Groves available?" I asked.

"Dr. Groves is unavailable, but I can transfer you to his nurse. Please hold." I listened to more hold music.

"ICU. This is Sarah."

"Hi, Sarah. I'm Ted's daughter. I'm trying to get an

update on his condition. Do you have any results from his colonoscopy?" I asked.

"Let me check his file. Please hold," she said. I took a deep breath. I had lost count of the number of times I had been on hold with a hospital or rehab center, waiting for an update about this man whom I didn't even know.

"There were no lesions," Sarah said.

"So, no cancer? That's good news."

"Yes."

"Were there any polyps? Anything else? Where's the bleeding coming from?" I asked more questions.

"The doctor will have to call you. The doctor is changing to Dr. Norway. She will be in at 4 p.m. Can you call back then?" Sarah asked.

"Um. Yes. I can do that," I said. I figured that was all the information I could get at the moment. I texted Maria and shared what I knew.

After several more rounds of phone tag, I finally spoke to Dr. Norway. She explained that they removed several polyps, and cauterized a broken blood vessel, which was likely the source of his bleeding. She said he would likely have more bleeding in the future.

"Is there anything he can do to prevent that?" I asked her.

"A high-fiber diet. That's about it," she said. "His intestines are not healthy."

"I understand," I responded. My father ate fried food, a lot of red meat, and virtually no vegetables. I didn't think there was much hope of this changing, and I immediately thought of the chocolate that I had sent him.

I felt guilty for sending him something so unhealthy.

"Does he need to stay in ICU?" I asked.

"We put him back on his medication, so his blood pressure and heart rate should stabilize soon. His hemoglobin is still low, so we plan to do another transfusion tonight. We did another one earlier today. He should be able to go to a regular room by morning. Do you know if he is forgetting things?"

"I know that he has been since he was in the hospital last, yes. But he also lies," I said, probably sounding impatient.

"He lies, or he forgets?" she asked, sounding a little judgmental.

"No, he's lied all his life. I thought he was sober for twelve years. Clearly, he wasn't. He lies about a lot of things. The forgetful stuff has been pretty recent. Maria would know more since I'm so far away."

"Okay, I understand," she said, sounding less critical.

"How long was he bleeding? Has the bleeding stopped?" I asked.

"We're not sure how long it was going on. He said it's been on and off for a while. He said he wasn't bleeding when he was at Waterbury Hospital, and they confirmed that. It seems to have stopped right now. We're going to keep watching him."

"I know he's going to be worried about work. Do you think he will be there for a while?" I asked. The truth is I wasn't sure if my dad was working like he said he was, or if he was lying to his family and me. With his mental and physical challenges, it didn't seem possible. But I wanted an answer to the question anyway.

"Possibly, yes. At least a few days. I know he's worried about that. We just don't know enough yet. So, I advised him to wait to call his boss until he knows more," she explained.

"That sounds good. Is he able to talk? Can I talk to him?"

"Yes, he's awake now. He's been very calm since the procedure. Would you like me to transfer you to his room?" she asked.

"That'd be great. Thank you, Dr. Norway."

"Hello?" His voice sounded quiet and raspy again.

"Hi, Dad. It's Laura. How are you?" I asked.

"Laura. Why didn't you call my cell phone?"

"Oh, I didn't know you had it with you. Can I call you on that while you're there?"

"Yes. And why were you talking to my doctor?" He sounded very angry.

"I didn't know you were awake. I was just trying to find out how you were doing," I explained.

"From now on, you call *me* to find out how I'm doing," he demanded.

"Okay, Dad. Don't get mad. I had to talk to your doctors a lot for the past few months. It was the only way for me to know how you were. And I thought you were sleeping. I just wanted to get your test results."

"Well, I don't have cancer. I was really scared that I did."

"I was scared, too, Dad. How are you feeling now?" I asked.

"I'm really tired, but I feel okay."

"Why don't you get some rest. I'll call you tomorrow morning."

"Okay, Laura. I love you."

"Love you, too," I said, and I hung up the phone.

The next morning, my father and his nurse both informed me that his heart rate was elevated and his hemoglobin was still low. He needed a new heart medication and another blood transfusion. While he was stable enough to be moved to a regular room, he would be in the hospital for several days. My father worried about returning to work. He worked on a contractual basis, and he could push off his jobs to the following week without telling anyone that he was back in the hospital. And he wanted to keep it that way.

"I hope to go back to work on Monday," he said.

"That's possible, Dad. Just focus on resting. It's only Wednesday. If you keep improving and you get enough rest, it could happen," I encouraged.

Mike told me that night that he didn't think my father would leave the hospital. I wasn't so sure. Ted seemed determined to get out of there, even if it was to just die at home.

"I won't come back to the hospital, no matter what happens," Ted said the next day. "They can't make me."

"Dad, they're just doing their best to take care of you. Maria is so worried about you."

"I guess."

I couldn't tell if his alcoholic dementia had taken over, if his lies were continuing, or if he just didn't want me to worry even though it was pretty obvious the end was near, but my father's behavior became quite erratic. They discharged my father on Sunday of that week.

"I'm driving to work. It's so nice out!" he said, sounding elated, manic, and high the next day.

"You're driving? You just left the hospital yesterday? You just had a blood transfusion a day ago. You probably should be resting, Dad," I said.

"But I feel great! I slept great! The doctor gave me a prescription of pills. Feels good to finally sleep."

"Where are you going?" I asked.

"To work! Job in Stafford Springs. Like a two-hour drive."

"Dad, be careful driving. You might get really tired all of a sudden," I said.

"I'm fine. I feel fantastic. Best I've ever felt...in all my life!" he said.

"You sound good, Dad. I'm at work, so I can't really chat. Let's talk later, when you get home from work, okay?" I wanted him to focus on driving. He sounded really out of it. I worried he might get into a car accident. Should I call someone to give some kind of warning? Do I call 911? I didn't even know what road he was on. I sat in a chair in a common area near my desk, with my head in my hands. *What if he got into in a wreck and killed someone?* I couldn't stop thinking such a horrible thought. I coworker walked by and asked if I was doing all right. I simply said, "No."

Another similar conversation occurred a few days later. "Dad, how are you doing?" I asked.

"Hello? Who is this?"

"It's Laura, Dad. Are you feeling better?"

"Laura, it can't be. You sound different. Oh wait. I have my speakerphone on, and it was too loud near my ear. Now it sounds like you. I'm great! Better than ever! How are you? Hey, how's the weather? How's your blood pressure?"

"It's raining today, so I took the car and not my new motorcycle. I have been taking my blood pressure regularly," I answered. At a routine doctor's appointment several months earlier, my blood pressure read dangerously high. My doctor instructed me to monitor it at home several times per day.

"It's the silent killer, you know. Hey Allana, say hi to Laura! Come here! Come here, Allana!" Ted yelled for his granddaughter to come say hello to me on the phone. She must have been running away. I heard a lot of movement on the other end. "Allana, I said, come here!" he barked.

"It's okay, Dad. She's shy. How are you feeling?" I asked.

"I'm great, but I got bad news today." My heart sunk. I thought maybe his cardiologist told him some bad news.

"What's the bad news?" I asked.

"I have cataracts. They must not be too bad, because I don't have to go back to the eye doctor for two months," he said.

"Cataracts. Oh. That's not too bad. Have you been to the cardiologist?"

"Oh, no. My heart is fine. Stronger than ever!" he

exclaimed. He had advanced congestive heart failure and had been on and off a ventilator for months recently, but somehow, he thought he was now perfectly healthy.

"Dad, I think you're supposed to follow up with the cardiologist."

"Nah, I'm great! That's what they told me. They said I'm all healed. Good to go!" He sounded like he was over the moon or strung out. If he slurred his words, I'd know he was drunk, but he spoke clearly, quickly, manic.

"Dad, I'm worried about your heart and your lungs," I said.

"I'm great, Laura. You don't have to worry about me! You want to say 'hi' to your sister?" he asked.

She's not my sister. We've met once. And I'm sure she didn't want to say anything to me.

"Dad, I really have to go. Traffic is getting bad, and I should get off the phone." I used this excuse to get off the phone with my parents all the time.

"Oh, okay. Hey, how's the weather out there?" he asked loudly.

"It's stormy, Dad. Thunderstorms and rain. I'll call you tomorrow." I hung up.

I continued to reach out to Maria to check in, to see if she was safe, to make sure Ted wasn't hurting her. But she never responded.

A particularly strange conversation with my father began when he asked me if he had told me about the helicopters. "Helicopters? No, Dad. What about helicopters?" I asked.

"Last Tuesday, helicopters were trying to land on my

car! I couldn't believe it. I was driving on the highway, and I look up and see a helicopter, maybe two, about fifty feet above me," he exclaimed.

"Were they traffic helicopters?" I asked him.

"That's what I thought at first. But then they tried to land on my car. They got closer and closer and I slowed down." He paused. My brain hurt from the confusion. He continued, "they were trying to look into my car, I guess, and see what I was doing."

"Was it a drone, Dad?" I asked.

"What's a drone? No, it was a helicopter. Then my alarm went off in my car telling me that I was about to hit something. The car in front of me was stopping, because they were looking at the helicopter, too!"

"That's crazy, Dad. Did you report it to anyone?" I asked. I didn't believe him, but I humored him. I learned that questioning him about anything only made him angry.

"No, I didn't know who to call. I might call the news or the newspaper to tell them about it. It's quite the story!"

"Yes, it is quite the story, Dad!" I then told him that I was almost home from work, and that I had to go work out before cooking dinner. "I have a busy night ahead of me," I said.

"Okay, love you, Laura!"

"Love you, too." I hung up the phone, and I continued to drive home. I knew that he had suffered some brain damage from what he had been through. I knew he had some form of alcoholic dementia. But I wasn't expecting such outlandish stories. I wondered how long he could go on like this.

My father worried more about getting his teeth and cataracts fixed than he did about his failing heart, lesions on his lungs, and bleeding intestines. Months went by with little change in his health and our relationship simmered. The emotions and bond no longer existed.

35
grandpa ed

"Laura, your grandfather is not doing well," my mother said on the phone one day.

"I know that. He's had nine heart attacks," I snarked. We had all heard that my grandfather, Ed, was near death many times over the previous ten years.

"They are pretty sure this is it. I'm trying to figure out when to fly down there." She explained that several of my aunts and uncles were flying there to say goodbye, including my Aunt Connie.

Connie and I hadn't been as close since my father got sick. As I struggled to understand his condition and his prognosis and wrestle with my reaction to learning of his lies and the return of his violent behavior, I reached out to Connie countless times. I texted and called daily for weeks. Then I contacted her weekly before giving up on seeking her support. I had been able to count on her before, and she was always able to count on me. When her mother-in-law died, I listened and checked in with her constantly. When she had miscarriages, I dropped everything and stayed with her. After I learned of the rumors she spread through the "family" about my relationships with Mike and Ted, I shut down. One skill I mastered in response to so much pain and loss is shutting down and becoming emotionless.

"Keep me posted, Mom. Maybe I'll try to get down there, too. But I'm not sure that I'm welcome," I said.

Most of my family members and I didn't agree politically, and the recent election of Donald Trump sent a chilling divide between my aunts, uncles, and grandparents. Some stopped communicating; others posted hostile, threatening posts on social media pages. One of my aunts called me a "liberal bitch" and a "liberal whore" on my Facebook page. We had seen each other only a few times during my lifetime, so I felt no loss when I completely let her go.

"It's probably best that you stay away from those people," my mother blurted out.

"Okay." I paused, and then said, "I guess I should get back to work. I'll talk to you later."

I called Connie a few days later, and she actually answered. She planned to go to Texas for two weeks to help her mother. All of Ed's nine children spent time with him during his final days. The same people who judged me for spending time with my father when he was near death and criticized me for forgiving him for abusing me instead of offering a kind word or an iota of support were now in the same position. They leaned on each other and faced their abusive father's death.

I stayed in touch with my mother and Connie until my grandfather died very slowly in his home. Connie shared details about his weeks of suffering before he died. My mother broke down on the phone with me a few times. "It is so hard to see him like that. And I'm not sure how to feel," she said.

"It's complicated because he wasn't a good dad," I replied.

"Exactly. That's exactly it. And some of the others are so sad. I haven't cried about it. I don't know how to feel," she muttered.

"You can feel however you want to feel. And there is no right or wrong way to feel. Just keep breathing in and out, and take it one moment at time. That's what I did when I sat with Dad for those days when I thought he stopped breathing, or when he pissed on the floor, or when he shit everywhere. One moment at a time." I couldn't help but relate the two situations. And I repeated the helpful words that Mike told me during that time, hoping they would help her as well.

"You're right. Some of my sisters said I was wrong for not being sad," she explained.

"That's bullshit, Mom. No one has any right to dictate how you should feel, judge you for feeling the way you do, or look down on you in any way. You are there to help Grandma. Everyone is doing the best they can. They're probably just angry that he's dying and their taking it out on you."

"Yeah, you're probably right," she said.

After a moment of silence, I heard her voice quiver before she said, "And you went through this last year, and no one was there for you. You were alone in that room with him, and he was dying." She started to cry.

I took a deep breath. Suddenly I felt the full force of the anger, loneliness, fear, and sadness of watching my father die. "Mom, I'm doing okay. And somehow my dad is still alive. We don't know how. But I said goodbye, and I'm doing okay now. You need to focus on helping Grandma right now. Don't worry about me," I reassured her.

Connie called me after Ed died. She shared the details of how hard it was for her to watch her father suffer. I became angry and resentful inside. I didn't want to feel that way, but I couldn't bury my emotions. I was being asked to support the people who ignored, judged, and criticized me when I sat by my father as he laid close to death. I held my breath. I didn't say a word.

"Laura, are you okay?" Connie asked.

"Yes, I'm okay. It's just that it's upsetting. I was excluded from being there, from getting my closure, and I can't help but think back to when I was dealing with my father last year, alone. No one cared. No one called me back; no one was there for me. You say that I don't know how hard it was, but I do. He's still alive right now, but it's been a hard year, and I said goodbye last February. I was alone," I opened up.

"I didn't mean to upset you," she replied.

"You didn't. I've been upset for months. I'll get over it. I know it's hard for everyone. I'm also dealing with more crap from my dad. The bullshit just won't stop," I said, and then I briefly explained the latest story. I knew my aunt's patience for me speaking about myself was nearly nonexistent, so I kept the story short.

A few days earlier, my father called me to ask for a favor. Since he never called me, I thought something horrible had happened. "I'm not sure I should tell you what happened," he said.

"Of course, you can, Dad. What's going on?" I asked.

He then said that his stepdaughter's new eleven-month-old baby boy was found bleeding from his mouth and nose a week earlier. Janice and her husband rushed him to the emergency room, and the doctors concluded that his injuries were from abuse. The parents denied all of the allegations. Connecticut's Department of Children and Families removed all three of their children from their home. The oldest moved to his biological father's house, and the two youngest moved in with Ted and Maria.

"Oh wow, Dad. How is the baby doing?" I asked.

"He was released, and he's here now. He seems to be doing fine. But we won't know the long-term damage for a time, if there is any."

"I understand. What do you need from me?" I couldn't imagine how I could possibly help.

"I need you to be a reference for me, so that the two babies can stay here," he said.

My jaw dropped. This person, who abused me, lied to me, and hurt me wanted me to be a reference for him to the state.

"What exactly does that mean, Dad?" I asked, cautiously.

"I'll email you the form. It's just a bunch of questions. You can be as vague as you want, say as little as you can. Will you do it?" he asked, desperately.

"What are the questions like?" I asked. I couldn't think of a way to get out of this situation.

He listed some of the questions. "What is the candidate's discipline style? How does the candidate respond to stress? Have you seen the candidate abuse alcohol or use illegal drugs? Would you describe the candidate as stable?" He went on and on.

I thought to myself, *I really had only one question to answer if I agreed to help. Were the babies safer with him, a now frail old man, and his wife, who adored her grandchildren, or would they be safer with strangers?* I needed time to think.

"When do you need it by?" I asked.

"I need it tonight. They have a meeting in the morning," he answered.

"Tonight? It's Sunday. Um." I hesitated as long as I could. "I guess I can fill it out and email it back to you," I said. I felt myself go numb.

"That would be great, Laura. I'll send it over now," he said.

"Okay, Dad."

"Thank you."

"You're welcome," I said, and I hung up the phone. My mind raced. How was I going to answer questions about my father as a parent? I hoped the questions weren't too specific, and that I could wiggle my way out of the answers creatively without lying.

The form included four pages of very direct questions. I answered them by describing my father's actions in the most recent years, through phone calls. I could only attest to what I had heard on the phone, because I lived three thousand miles away.

To answer the question "What is the prospective foster parent's disciplinary style?" I said, "When I talk to him on the phone, I hear him redirect his grandchildren very effectively." I did not lie.

To answer the question, "Have you seen evidence of drug or alcohol use?" I said, "I have not seen my father drink in a very long time." I did not lie.

"How does the prospective foster parent respond to stress?" I responded by saying, "When I talk to my father, and he seems stressed out, we talk about it. And that seems to help," which was also true.

I made my way through the four pages of questions and felt good about my decision to help his family stay together. After I emailed the document back to my father, I felt sick to my stomach. The familiar disgust and lower back pain returned.

Connie said, "How dare he put you in that position? I can't even imagine. Are you sure you did the right thing?"

"I have no idea," I replied. "But I didn't have a ton of time to think about it, and I did the best I could in the moment."

"That's just awful," she said.

"Yeah, it's been a shitty year all around, I guess," I said.

After I hung up with Connie, I turned my phone off for several days. I had nothing left to give to anyone. I focused on work, working out, spending time with Mike, and taking care of my home.

A few weeks later, a conversation with my father took a drastic turn. He sounded angrier than usual.

"What's going on, Dad? You sound frustrated," I said.

"I am. I don't know what to do with Maria. I don't think she even likes me. Does she talk to you?"

"No, she and I haven't spoken since you were in the hospital the last time. I texted her a few times, but she's never responded," I replied.

"Oh, I thought she talked to you. What was she like when I was in the hospital? Did she even care?" he asked.

"Of course, Dad. She was very worried about you. We both were. We talked to your doctors every single day and updated each other on how you were doing as much as possible. She was very scared when you were on the ventilator," I explained.

"I remember dying," he said from out of nowhere.

"What do you mean?" I asked.

"In the hospital, I died. I liked it," he said.

"What was it like?" I asked, ignoring the second part of his statement.

"I was in a bright room, and there were a lot of doors. I felt really light, and I had no pain at all. I guess it was purgatory, or whatever," he explained.

"Wow, do you think you might have been dreaming?" I asked.

"I could have been. I don't know. It could have just

been the drugs. But was Maria nice to me when you were there? She's not nice to me anymore. I think she hates me now. But she has every right to hate me. And so do you. And so does your mother. I have been a really bad person my whole life. I don't deserve to live anymore. And it felt nice to die anyway."

"Dad, Maria was very nice to you when I was there. Why do you think she hates you?" I asked.

"She only talks in Portuguese, so I never know what's going on. I don't know what's happening with the case with the state and the kids. I don't know anything. And when I ask, she just says that I don't need to know."

"She doesn't tell you about the case or the kids? Why not?" I asked.

"Because she doesn't care if I'm involved. She hates me. She should hate me. I've been so mean to her."

"Dad, when you were in the hospital, you were really sick and really stressed. No one acts like themselves when they are that stressed or scared." I tried to comfort him.

"No, I've never been nice to her, and now she can get her revenge. I wasn't nice to you, either. I remember the things I did to you. I touched you. I choked you." He paused for a second.

"Dad, I'm fine," I abruptly interrupted him. I didn't want him to continue. I didn't want him to go into detail. I didn't want him to apologize. I felt nothing anymore, and it wouldn't change anything anyway.

"Well, I've had an okay life, but I was not a good man," he said.

"Dad, it sounds like things are just really stressful right now. Maybe you need to get some rest," I suggested.

"Rest? That's all I do. I can't get a job. Everyone hates me. And I deserve it. I just can't keep going like this."

Ted lost his job two weeks after DCF approved him and Maria as foster parents for their two young grandchildren. Maria had to stop working in order to care for the children.

"I thought you had a lead on that job that you took the assessments for." I tried to change the subject.

"Oh, that one? I didn't get it. But the company did say that another client might need my help."

"Well, that's good. When do you expect to talk to them again?" I asked.

"I have no idea. It doesn't matter," he said.

"I think it matters. I think you'll feel a lot better once you're working again," I said.

"Yeah, maybe you're right. It's so frustrating not to be working, and Maria hates me," he said.

"I don't think she hates you. She's just probably frustrated with everything."

"Yeah, I guess," he said.

"Well, Dad. I'm just about home, so I really should go. I have to work out, clean house a bit, and cook dinner. Busy night ahead. Can I talk to you in a few days?" I asked.

"Okay, stay in touch," he replied.

"Okay. Love you."

"Love you, too, Laura."

I hung up the phone and felt numb as I drove my car down the highway. I recognized that my focus was not on my driving, and that I needed to be extra careful on the rest of my commute. I told Mike what my father and I had discussed, and I went to bed early. I did not sleep, because I remembered being choked and touched inappropriately by my father. I tried to read, to watch television on my Kindle, and to think about anything else.

The next day, I had plans to see Connie and a girlfriend. I tried to include Connie in my social plans from time to time, since it seemed like she never had any of her own. On the way to my girls' night, I called my father to check on him.

"Hey, Dad. How are you doing today?" I asked after he answered the phone.

"I'm okay. How are you?" he replied. His voice still sounded angry.

"You seemed very frustrated yesterday, so I wanted to check on you. You doing better today?"

"I'm exactly the same. I can't do this anymore." He sounded completely defeated.

"Oh, I'm sorry. I was hoping after a good night's rest that you'd feel a little better," I said.

"I didn't sleep. I'm so sorry for the things I did to you." He said it. I had no reaction, no emotion, and no clue how to respond.

"Dad, I'm doing well. Don't worry. What are you up to today? Where's Maria?" I asked.

"I don't do anything. I don't know where Maria is. She might be at work. She's the only one who can work, but she has to take care of the kids too, since I can't do anything," he explained.

"Are you by yourself?" I asked.

"Yeah, but it's what I deserve."

"What do you guys usually do for dinner on Saturday nights?" I asked.

"Nothing. I don't know. What are you doing?" he asked me.

"I'm heading to a girlfriend's house to hang out. I haven't seen her in months," I said.

"Oh, that sounds nice. Are you almost there?" he asked.

I took the opportunity for an out and said, "Yeah, I'm a few minutes away. I just wanted to make sure that you were okay."

"I'm not. I won't ever be," he said. As he said this, I parked in front of my friend's house, and Connie drove up right behind me. I pointed to my phone at my ear to let her know that I'd be in when I was finished with my conversation.

"Ok, Dad. Well, I better go. I'm sorry you're having a bad day. Can I call you next week?" I asked. I had had enough of the pity party.

"Yeah, that sounds good. Bye, Laura."

"Bye, Dad." I hung up the phone. I sat in the car for a few minutes, because I didn't want to be in a bad mood in front of Connie and my friend.

As I sat down at the kitchen island, the three of us laid out a variety of healthy snacks. Connie talked about her horses, her job, and her daughter for about an hour. I had heard all the updates a few days earlier. I listened, but I didn't engage much in the conversation. She then talked about her father's death, and we all discussed this for a while. Then, I brought up the conversations I had with my father over the past two days. As soon as I began talking, Connie picked up her cell phone and started reading her emails. She completely disengaged as I spoke about my father. I quickly changed the topic, because I wanted to stop feeling so insignificant and unimportant.

As the conversation began to shift again, Connie's cell phone rang, and she took the call in the hallway. My friend walked around the kitchen island, sat down next to me, and asked for more details about the recent phone calls with my father. It felt nice to be heard and supported. The night ended, and Connie and I drove our separate ways. I decided to stop trying to talk to her about my life. Her lack of interest over the past two years was rude, disrespectful, and hurtful.

For months I wrestled with the idea of visiting my mother. I wanted to see how we got along without the stress of my father's breakdowns or her getting sick. I scheduled a four-day visit and hoped for the best.

While I was there, my mother talked to me about her father's death.

"I haven't cried about my dad," my mother said. "And it keeps leaking out in weird times."

"Of courses it's going to come up when something bothers you, and probably when you least expect it, mom. You have to find a time to let it out."

"He tried to talk to me when I saw him last October,

you know," she said.

"Who? Grandpa?" I asked.

"Yes, I brought him water while he was working on the tractor. Out of nowhere, he brought up how bad of a dad he was to me, and he started saying things like he was going to apologize. I stopped him because I didn't want to hear it. I'm not sure if that was the right thing to do," she shared.

"I don't think it's a matter of right and wrong. It wouldn't matter at this point if he apologized, right?"

"That's what I thought. I just told him that I'm fine, and I walked away," she said. "He knew he was dying. I think he got a really bad diagnosis from the doctor and didn't tell anyone. I think it was lung cancer." She took another puff of her cigarette.

"Really? You think so? I remember he stopped letting Grandma go into the doctor's office with him," I said, remembering the rumors that I heard back then.

"Yeah, he knew he was dying, and he was trying to tell me, or make it right or something. And my sisters were so mad at me for not crying."

"They have no right to judge you for feeling however you feel whenever you feel it. That's unfair, and it pisses me off," I said.

"They do judge everyone."

"Yeah, I know. The difference between you and me is you have something to lose by not talking to them anymore. I don't have anything to lose, since we have no relationship whatsoever. Having them in my life, or reaching out to them, has only ever caused me pain. But for you, you have history, memories. That's why I get so mad when they make you feel bad for just being you during a hard time. You took care of Grandma after Grandpa died. You cleaned the house, and went through all of his things. No one else would have done that," I said, hoping to help.

"Yeah, I had to leave when everyone was yelling at me all the time," she said.

"You did the best you could to help. But you really have to find the right time and way to let out how you feel about your dad. Otherwise, it will all come out when you don't want it to or in ways you don't want it to," I advised.

"Yeah, my doctor wants me to see a counselor. But I don't want to rehash all the crap from my childhood," she said. She puffed hard on her cigarette.

"You don't have to. There are so many therapies. There are so many types of counselors now. If your doctor refers one, just look up their webpage. You can get a sense of their strategy to make sure they won't just want to know all of the details about your childhood. If you don't like their approach, ask for another name," I suggested.

"That's a good idea," she said.

"Trust me, connecting to all the horrible memories isn't effective for a lot of people. You don't have to do it that way. I didn't, and I never counseled my kids like that in the schools," I said.

"I worry about you, too," she said.

"Dad had a very similar conversation with me last

weekend," I said.

"What do you mean?" she asked.

"He talked about dying in the hospital, and said that he wants to die, and that he's a bad man. He said his wife hates him and he deserves it, because he's hurt her, and you, and me. He started to tell me all the bad things he remembers doing to me. I got out of the conversation the first time, but he apologized the next time I talked to him."

"He was horrible to you. He never held you, he never fed you, he was furious and yelled when you cried." She tried to continue, but I stopped her.

"Ma, I don't want to get into listing things. I'm just saying this because I'm wondering if he knows he's going to die soon," I said.

"You might be right. I worry about you, and how you're going to feel," she said.

"I feel nothing. My grief started last year when I said goodbye to him in the hospital. I know I'll feel things later, but I am numb right now," I said.

"Yeah, I know what you mean."

36
moving on

Ted's health continues to decline and his stress level continues to rise as the household has become more chaotic. The young children still keep everyone up at night, the financial troubles have increased, and I doubt he will ever get back on his feet in his career. The tension has contributed to his nearly constant delusions and hallucinations about various conspiracies against him. I speak to him every couple of weeks, but I will never visit him again.

I had not anticipated my father living this long after spending so much time on life support over the past year and a half. And I have braced myself for the news of his death. I will not attend the funeral. Instead, I will take my bereavement time from work and do exactly what I want to do, exactly when I want to do it. On the day of his funeral, I imagine myself finding a quiet moment to envision the service. I can picture his family sobbing, or possibly feeling relief that his suffering is finally over. Perhaps they will feel just like I do: confused and conflicted. I don't imagine that I will ever learn the truth about how he treats them. If he has been abusive toward them too, we might be feeling the same way in this very moment.

His friends will judge me for letting him down, and they will grieve for their loss. My father will not be there to know if I attend his funeral or not. He will have known, as he knows now, that despite the lies, abuse, mistreatment, drinking, drug use, temper tantrums, and trauma, I love him. Each time I asked him a question to get him to open his eyes in the hospital room, each time I made him cough three times to get the cemented fluid out of his lungs, each time I call to ask how he was, and each time we talked about the weather, he knew I loved him.

And that is going to have to be enough.

Surrounded by my closest friends, I will drink a large Coke with three shots of vodka in remembrance of my dad on the night of his funeral. I will make each of my friends drink one too, and they will cringe. I can picture us laughing as we sip my father's drink of choice. No tears will fall. I will do my best to smile, happy for the good conversations Ted and I had during the brief façade of a father-daughter relationship we had for the few years when I thought he had stopped drinking and doing drugs. He lied, but he lied *for* me. He did the only thing he knew to keep me in his life. As dishonest as it was, it was a gift. Without the lies, I wouldn't have those happy memories. That brief connection would have never occurred.

I will continue to hear from Maria only when my father is back in the hospital. When he is home, she will not be allowed to speak to me. This pattern will continue until he dies.

My mother and I still talk weekly. I focus on her positive qualities, and work hard to enhance those characteristics within myself. I have been asked if I ever told her how I felt about everything. In some ways, I have. But when I see or hear the pain that it causes her, I withhold the details. I understand where she is coming from. She took on the responsibility of trying to protect all of her younger siblings when she was a child herself— an impossible feat. She never found a therapist who could help her in the ways she needed. She did the best she could, and I will always honor her. She taught me to be strong and resilient.

Resilience does not mean bouncing back to exactly where you were before, or pretending that the shitty stuff wasn't shitty. Admitting something was hard does not mean you are weak. My brain has protected me by blocking a lot of memories from my youth. But triggers hide everywhere. When one of these reminders jolts me backwards to a place of anger, fear, resentment, and loneliness, I fight my way out by allowing myself a quiet moment to heal the little girl who was denied so much.

When the song "I Wanna Dance with Somebody" by Whitney Houston comes on the radio, I change it as quickly as I can, and I breathe slowly and quietly to myself for a while. That song played lightly on the stereo the morning Manny beat me for making noise before school by looking up information in his encyclopedia. He struck my head, side, stomach, and back multiple times; it was the worst beating that I remember, because I somehow stayed conscious. My bruises never fully healed, because more beatings followed. But that one stays with me to this day.

When I smell sweet, musty cologne, like the brand my father wore, I cringe, sweat, and gag. I reconnect to the feeling of disgust and strange pains in my lower back. I give myself a little time to take deep breaths or meditate, and I let it go.

I sometimes find myself feeling like I lost this enormous support group—a family. But I never really had one. And things people innocently say about their own families trigger this sense of loss. I respond by taking a deep breath quietly, and I think to myself, *You're doing great, Laura. Just keep going.*

I dread Christmas every single year, even though I always appreciate the company of the people I choose to be with during that time. My body stays tight, and my voice hardens during the holidays; I either eat too much or hardly anything at all, and I search for alcohol every day until New Year's Day. Ironically, I don't celebrate New Year's Eve. It's the first chance for me to finally relax after months of tension and pressure.

I have found many positive outcomes from my experiences as well. Because I moved around so much, I have no problem making new friends. I also read people very quickly. I can look a person in the eye and immediately know if they are trustworthy and safe, or if I should avoid them. I give every person who passes that test the benefit of the doubt, and I search for the positive in everything they do. But once I am betrayed or hurt, I say "goodbye" without looking back. The ability to shut down so easily becomes a gift, because I feel no remorse and can move on easily.

If I want to make a change in my life, I do so quickly, decisively, and with very little effort. If fear is the only reason not to do something, I always do it. I find humor in every situation. I'm the friend you call when something horrible has happened, because I can always find a way to make you laugh.

Surviving implies breathing in and out and making it through. Thriving means living an exceptional life despite obstacles. Every person gets to define their own success. And that definition can morph and change over time. For me, I am succeeding, exceeding expectations, and beating the odds when I am smiling, laughing, focusing on happiness and positivity, and finding the healthiest way to handle any situation. Usually the transition from surviving to thriving is not an epic, fantastical, finite event. It's an accumulation of many experiences over time that test you and push you past your breaking point. On the other side of those moments, you have a choice. You can live in the pain and the past, wallow, whine, cry, and victimize yourself. Or, you can toughen yourself up, hitch up your big-girl pants, do anything it takes to get the help you need, work hard on yourself every single day, and find the positive, the lesson, and even the humor in all of it.

I learned from Dr. V. that in order to heal, you do not need to share every horror story with another person or therapist; that reconnects you to negative energy. You can do more than put a Band-Aid on every "bad" that has happened to you. You can change yourself to your very core. If you strengthen the deepest parts of yourself, you remain open to good, vulnerable to bad, but strong enough to handle it all. I call that victory.

But sometimes success is seen in smaller moments. I celebrate riding my motorcycle to work each day, staying acutely aware of how dangerous motorcycle riding is, but not letting fear dissuade me. I embrace hard work and the sense of accomplishment from each and every day at work. I appreciate the moments when I look around and truly appreciate the friends that I have chosen to be my family. I value the times when I have the courage to be really honest with someone I love, knowing that this makes me extremely vulnerable. But I'm strong enough to take the risk anyway. I am proud of finding a balance between the extreme and the monotonous. When I get through a day without thinking about the hole that's in my heart that cannot be filled, I acknowledge it. And I realize that it doesn't need to be filled in order for my strength to win.

Telling your story is honest. It doesn't mean you're over it, that you think you're better than anyone, or that others don't have worse (or better) stories. It just means that you have the right to stand up and say, "This happened to me and it mattered." If every survivor of abuse could receive a standing ovation after telling their story, a great deal of healing in the world would be achieved. I used to fight the presumption that your childhood defines who you are. I fought it so hard that I went to extremes to prove everyone wrong. Of course, my past has affected me, but it does not decide what I do in response to those effects.

I still look over my shoulder. I still do not like unpredictable, loud noises. I still get very, very nervous if someone yells in anger. I still don't like things wrapped around my throat. I still hate the sound of loud high heels hitting a hard floor. I still get very angry when I throw out food that I let go to waste, thinking of the times when I was so hungry. When I'm sick or struggling to sleep in the middle of the night, I'll still watch old episodes of *The Golden Girls*, just like I did when I lived with my grandmother. I still worry that the people I love the most will walk away without notice. I still would rather spend Christmas on a beach or in the mountains alone than with someone else's family.

On a bad day, the words *family*, *father*, *mother*, and *childhood* make me want to cower in a corner and cry. When listening to others talk about their childhood, I am immediately triggered and broken on the inside. But I don't let them know. I smile, relate, ask questions, and listen intently to their stories. I choose this response because I care deeply for others. I want to hear about their lives. On the inside, I find a nice thought and use it to comfort myself and move on, knowing the harshest parts of me will subside eventually, and no one needs to be the wiser. In my darkest moments, I cradle myself, swing forward and backward or side to side, and whisper quietly, "you're nothing," "you're not worth it," "you mean so little to the people who mean so much to you." But I wake up the next morning, and I try again. I see every interaction as an opportunity to prove the negative bullshit wrong. Sometimes I win, and sometimes I'm betrayed. But the trying part is the victory. Anyone can fold. Anyone can be a victim. I choose to start each day fresh, even if the night before was a nightmare.

I still buy my clothes at thrift stores, and I do not enjoy buying things for myself. I still love to buy presents for others and make people laugh and smile. I still lift weights or exercise every day and keep my body strong and fit, so that I can walk confidently and not be seen as a target. I no longer have any back or neck pain; the physical reminders of my trauma are gone. I still picture my boxer stance in times when I need to be extra-strong.

And I am still a light sleeper.